David Bowie and the Moving Image

David Bowie and the Moving Image

A Standing Cinema

Katherine Reed

BLOOMSBURY ACADEMIC
NEW YORK • LONDON • OXFORD • NEW DELHI • SYDNEY

BLOOMSBURY ACADEMIC
Bloomsbury Publishing Inc, 1385 Broadway, New York, NY 10018, USA
Bloomsbury Publishing Plc, 50 Bedford Square, London, WC1B 3DP, UK
Bloomsbury Publishing Ireland, 29 Earlsfort Terrace, Dublin 2, D02 AY28, Ireland

BLOOMSBURY, BLOOMSBURY ACADEMIC and the Diana logo
are trademarks of Bloomsbury Publishing Plc

First published in the United States of America 2023
This paperback edition published 2025

Copyright © Katherine Reed, 2023

For legal purposes the Acknowledgments on pp. 224–225 constitute
an extension of this copyright page.

Cover design: Louise Dugdale
Cover image © StudioCanal Films Ltd/Mary Evans Picture Library

All rights reserved. No part of this publication may be: i) reproduced or transmitted in any form, electronic or mechanical, including photocopying, recording or by means of any information storage or retrieval system without prior permission in writing from the publishers; or ii) used or reproduced in any way for the training, development or operation of artificial intelligence (AI) technologies, including generative AI technologies. The rights holders expressly reserve this publication from the text and data mining exception as per Article 4(3) of the Digital Single Market Directive (EU) 2019/790.

Bloomsbury Publishing Inc does not have any control over, or responsibility for, any third-party websites referred to or in this book. All internet addresses given in this book were correct at the time of going to press. The author and publisher regret any inconvenience caused if addresses have changed or sites have ceased to exist, but can accept no responsibility for any such changes.

Library of Congress Cataloging-in-Publication Data
Names: Reed, Katherine M. (Musicologist) author.
Title: David Bowie and the moving image : A Standing Cinema / Katherine Reed.
Description: [1st.] | New York : Bloomsbury Academic, 2023. |
Includes bibliographical references and index. |
Summary: "An analysis of David Bowie's decades-long use of the
moving image, from music video, to advertising appearances,
to planned film projects"– Provided by publisher.
Identifiers: LCCN 2022019609 (print) | LCCN 2022019610 (ebook) | ISBN 9781501371257 (hardback) | ISBN 9781501371400 (paperback) | ISBN 9781501371264 (epub) | ISBN 9781501371271(pdf) | ISBN 9781501371288
Subjects: LCSH: Bowie, David–Criticism and interpretation. | Musicians in motion pictures. | Rock music–History and criticism. | Motion pictures–History. | Music videos–History and criticism.
Classification: LCC ML420.B754 R44 2023 (print) | LCC ML420.B754 (ebook) | DDC 782.42166092–dc23/eng/20220506
LC record available at https://lccn.loc.gov/2022019609
LC ebook record available at https://lccn.loc.gov/2022019610

ISBN: HB: 978-1-5013-7125-7
PB: 978-1-5013-7140-0
ePDF: 978-1-5013-7127-1
eBook: 978-1-5013-7126-4

Typeset by Integra Software Services Pvt. Ltd.

For product safety related questions contact productsafety@bloomsbury.com.

To find out more about our authors and books visit www.bloomsbury.com
and sign up for our newsletters.

For Bill Reed,
the Kook who believed in me

Contents

List of Figures   viii
List of Tables   ix

1   Introduction   1

Part 1   Bowie as Auteur

2   Semiotics and the Creation of "David Bowie"   19
3   Cracked Actor: The Music Video and Bowie as Moving Image   43
4   Screen Dreams: Theatrical Staging, Film, and *Diamond Dogs*   71

Part 2   Bowie as Sign

5   Hollywood Highs: Acting Roles and Bowie's Star Image   113
6   Mass Motivation: Advertising, Audience, and the Bowie Star Image   143
7   Who Can I Be Now?: Fannish Creation and Depictions of Bowie on Film   169
8   Conclusion: Living On   203

Bibliography   211
Acknowledgments   224
Index   226

Figures

4.1 Stills from *The 1980 Floor Show* (1973)	81
4.2 Stills from *Cracked Actor* (1975, dir. Yentob)	81
4.3 Still from *Metropolis* (1927, dir. Lang)	105
4.4 Still from *The Cabinet of Dr. Caligari* (1920, dir. Wiene)	108
5.1 Still from *Into the Night* (1985, dir. Landis)	121
5.2 Still from *The Hunger* (1983, dir. Scott)	126
5.3 Still from *The Hunger* (1983, dir. Scott)	129
5.4 Still from *The Hunger* (1983, dir. Scott)	130
5.5 Still from *Labyrinth* (1986, dir. Henson)	133
6.1 Still from Vittel ad (2003)	159
6.2 Ball scene from *Labyrinth* (1986, dir. Henson) versus "L'Invitation Au Voyage" (2013)	164
7.1 Museme 1: piano rhythm, mm. 1–4 (author's transcription)	183
7.2 Still from *Velvet Goldmine* (1998, dir. Haynes)	192
7.3 Still from *Velvet Goldmine* (1998, dir. Haynes)	195
7.4 Still from *Velvet Goldmine* (1998, dir. Haynes)	200

Tables

4.1 Formal structure of "1984/Dodo": *Diamond Dogs* versus
1980 Floor Show   79

5.1 Comparison of Acting Roles versus Filmic and Musical Star Images,
1983 and 1986   140

1

Introduction

The central image of David Bowie's "Life on Mars?" could have been ripped from his own experience: a child (with their "mousy hair") sits "hooked to the silver screen," reliving fantastical scenes played out on film. This palpable thrall of the moving image pops up again and again in Bowie's lyrics. This is hardly surprising as, throughout his life, Bowie was similarly transfixed by the power of film. He is perhaps best known among younger generations for his turn on the silver screen as Jareth, the goblin king of Jim Henson's *Labyrinth* (1986), and his music videos enjoy similar status across age demographics. His visual presence is almost as strong as his aural legacy. Today, this use of the moving image is practically required of a pop star. For a pop or rock musician coming of age in the late 1960s, though, a strong multimedia presence was not necessarily an integral part of a public persona. Of course, the Beatles, the Monkees, and the Rolling Stones had made film appearances and short promotional videos. Elvis had a burgeoning film career, spearheaded by his management and linked to his musical output. For many other contemporaneous artists, film remained a separate domain. In his career, spanning more than five decades, David Bowie would change all that.

Bowie's music came to be intrinsically connected to the moving image. As early as 1969, Bowie and manager Kenneth Pitt were committed to the idea of a multimedia sort of stardom. The pair conceptualized the compilation film *Love You till Tuesday*, named for a song from Bowie's eponymous 1967 album. The film is composed of short vignettes: Bowie in Edwardian costume to croon "Rubber Band," an early space age fantasy version of "Space Oddity," and the mime showcase "The Mask." The project shows, in microcosm, an understanding of the power of Bowie's particular brand of stardom. His voice and compositions are of central importance, but so too is the way that his audience understands and relates to them. That understanding can be more carefully controlled through a multisensory expression, crafted through movement and its framing on film. Bowie would carry that approach through his groundbreaking music videos, as well as his screen acting performances and use of film and video in concert.

Beyond his own appearances, though, film was important for him as a spectator and an artist. In the years before his worldwide superstardom, we have accounts of his voracious film-watching appetite, encompassing new releases as well as arthouse revivals.[1] In communicating with other artists, he frequently turned to cinematic touchstones as a *lingua franca*. Stage designers Mark Ravitz and Jules Fisher both point to Bowie's erudite understanding of visual art as a lynchpin of their collaborations.[2] That appreciation for the moving image showed up in Bowie's own work. 1972 concerts began with Ludwig van Beethoven's "Ode to Joy" from Symphony No. 9, a nod to Stanley Kubrick's 1971 film *A Clockwork Orange*.[3] 1974 concerts took place on a set influenced by the visual language of German Expressionist classic *Metropolis* (1927, dir. Lang).[4] 1976 concerts opened with the surrealist classic *Un chien andalou* (1929, dir. Buñuel and Dalí). In so many ways, from his first film role in *The Image* (1969, dir. Armstrong) to the final music video released before his death, "Lazarus," Bowie's musical output has long been intrinsically linked to images.

Given this relationship to film, it is surprising that Bowie's audiovisual work remains underexplored. More narrowly focused studies address the artist's individual music videos or film roles. However, none provide a comprehensive view of the two-way street that was Bowie's work with film, theorizing the way he engaged with the medium in all its forms throughout his long career. Indeed, the biographical note that accompanies one of his film-adjacent works (the script for the musical *Lazarus*) describes Bowie's career as experimenting "with boundaries of musical genres and *the potential of live performance and multimedia as applied to music*"[5] (emphasis added). That potential was central to the unique works Bowie created, and to the way we can understand them. Analyzing Bowie's music videos, planned film projects, acting roles, and depiction in films, *David Bowie*

---

[1] See, for example, Kevin Cann, *Any Day Now: The London Years 1947–1974* (London: Adelita, 2011). Cann recounts Bowie's daily activities, many of which feature films such as *Metropolis*, *Cabaret*, and *A Clockwork Orange*.
[2] Mark Ravitz in conversation with the author, October 18, 2019.
[3] Ken Scrudato, "David Bowie: Life on Earth," in *Bowie on Bowie: Interviews and Encounters with David Bowie*, ed. Sean Egan (Chicago: Chicago Review Press, 2015), 367.
[4] Mark Ravitz in conversation with the author, October 18, 2019.
[5] David Bowie and Enda Walsh, *Lazarus: The Complete Book and Lyrics* (London: Nick Hern Books, 2016), 8.

and the Moving Image: A Standing Cinema enters the debate about Bowie's artistic legacy, addressing Bowie as musician, actor, and auteur.

This book, then, asks you to focus on Bowie's marriage of music and image as a preeminent example of what Michel Chion dubbed "added value."[6] Sound and vision work hand in hand throughout Bowie's output, but they do so in a transformative way. The images are not ancillary to the music, but are frequently co-conceived with them. As Nicolas Pegg notes, "his [Bowie's] best music is often organically and inextricably linked to his painting, his writing, his stage presentations and his trailblazing video work."[7] Bowie's own "Ashes to Ashes," for example, is in some ways incomplete without its David Mallet co-directed video. The images and music complete and amplify each other in their combination. Such an approach is not unique in music history, of course. Its application in the sphere of popular music, though, was not broadly accepted at the start of Bowie's career. *David Bowie and the Moving Image: A Standing Cinema* shines a light on Bowie's engagement with film, a perspective that deepens our understanding of Bowie's work as a whole. His use of the moving image is not a mere addition to his musical work, but a key aspect of David Bowie as artist.

Gesamtkunstwerk and Bowie's Moving Image

From a musicological perspective, it is tempting to label Bowie's approach to his work as a kind of *gesamtkunstwerk*, Richard Wagner's conception of a total artwork.[8] Though he never worked in Wagner's favored form (opera), Bowie skirted around its edges, yearning throughout his career to create a staged musical work. Like Wagner, Bowie recognized that, when all the arts are brought together in the service of single aim, their powers are amplified in ways beyond what poetry, music, costume, and film could accomplish separately. In fact, we might see in Bowie an aspect of Wagner's "actor of the future, who would be dancer, musician, and poet in one."[9] Shelton Waldrep recognizes the same sort of impulse, labeling Bowie's output as a "different version of the total

---

[6] Michel Chion, *Audio-Vision: Sound on Screen*, edited and translated by Claudia Gorbman (New York: Columbia University Press, 1994), 5.
[7] Nicolas Pegg, *The Complete David Bowie* Revised and Updated Edition (London: Titan Books, 2016), 9.
[8] Barry Millington, "Gesamtkunstwerk," *Grove Music Online* Accessed January 17, 2020.
[9] Millington, "Gesamtkunstwerk."

artwork," one concerned with crossing "boundaries of art and reality, inside and outside, subject and object."[10] In an almost operatic way, the facets of each of Bowie's multimedia works are crafted so as to be intrinsically indebted to each other. As in Wagner's "artwork of the future," Bowie's works drew together gifted collaborators from a variety of artistic disciplines.

In addressing Bowie's multimedia works, then, the comparison to Wagner's *gesamtkunstwerk* seems an apt one. Bowie certainly professed to approach his work as a unified artistic expression that encompassed many art forms. Many of his projects incorporate music, narrative, and often staging. In his still-unreleased *Ernie Johnson*, for example, Bowie created what Peter Doggett and David Buckley each describe as a rock opera.[11] This "opera" exists as a brief thirty-five minutes of four-track recording, dating from 1968.[12] Though there are apparently stage directions (according to Doggett), *Ernie Johnson* does not appear to have been particularly tightly plotted: it involves a young man who, intending suicide, plans a party before his death and shops for a tie for the occasion. Though the story is loose, this nascent rock opera shows the unification of music, story, and image that Bowie would pursue throughout his career. *Ernie Johnson* points to throughlines present in his published works, including death and its marking or observance, as Leah Kardos notes.[13] Many of his albums were unified by almost operatic storylines, including *The Rise and Fall of Ziggy Stardust and the Spiders from Mars* (1972), *Diamond Dogs* (1974), and *1. Outside* (1995). While each of these albums has attendant music videos, none of them are accompanied by extensive visual representation. Of his extant, completed works, *Lazarus* seems to be the closest to such a *gesamtkunstwerk*.

One of Bowie's last major projects, the musical *Lazarus*, premiered in New York mere months before his death. The musical, in development at the same time as his final album, features music from *Hunky Dory* (1971) through *Blackstar* (2016). *Lazarus* centers around Thomas Jerome Newton, the titular *Man Who Fell to Earth* portrayed by Bowie in the 1976 film. In that film, Newton attempted to return to his home planet, but was thwarted. *Lazarus* imagines a present-day Newton, isolated in a New York City high rise and yearning to return to his family and his home. In the play's loose narrative, Newton and those around

---

[10] Shelton Waldrep, *Future Nostalgia: Performing David Bowie* (New York: Bloomsbury, 2015), 27.
[11] Peter Doggett, "David Bowie's Lost Rock Opera," *Record Collector*, June 1995, 92.
[12] David Buckley, *Strange Fascination: The Definitive Story* (London: Virgin Books, 2005), 48.
[13] Leah Kardos, *Blackstar Theory: The Late Works of David Bowie* (New York: Bloomsbury Academic, 2021), 69.

him struggle with alienation, identity, freedom, and ultimately death—all key themes within Bowie's broader oeuvre. The show blends spoken dialogue, sung performance, and light/image projection in a surreal, immersive experience. Leah Kardos's *Blackstar Theory* presents a thorough and compelling analysis of the work, its genesis, and its connections to the rest of Bowie's output.[14] In many ways, it marks the culmination of a number of important Bowie themes, techniques, and lifelong fascinations.

I do not devote a chapter to the examination of *Lazarus* for a few reasons, chief among them the process of its conception. In each of Bowie's audiovisual creations analyzed in this book, the visuals and music are conceived as a unified expression. Music videos are shot around the time of the songs' recording and release and, in many cases, the themes and images of these videos or planned films are in keeping with the visual style and content of that era of Bowie's output. This unified expression aligns with the sort of musical theater ambitions Bowie has described in interviews: he desired to turn tours into musical versions of the albums they promoted, populating those shows with the characters and images of their albums' world. *Lazarus*, however, presents a different approach. It is more closely aligned with the jukebox musical, though Bowie and his collaborators protested that label. As a concept, the jukebox musical finds its roots in the mid-twentieth-century film showcases, but James Perone situates its birth more recently.[15] *Mamma Mia!* and *Movin' Out*, based on the work of ABBA and Billy Joel, respectively, are turn-of-the-twenty-first-century examples of the popular format. These musicals draw together songs not originally conceived as part of a broader narrative and create from these songs a decade-spanning throughline in an artist's oeuvre. *Lazarus* does something similar, but is unique in its integration of music and plot.[16]

The integration of the music into *Lazarus*'s world separates it from the typical jukebox musical. In something like *Mamma Mia!*, for example, the songs of the band ABBA direct the action of the musical and appear in both the shared diegesis of the characters and in their individual, internal worlds as expressions of their experience. Some of the women in the show are presented as a girl group, Donna and the Dynamos. The play does not, however, make

---

[14] Kardos, *Blackstar Theory*, 67–130.
[15] James Perone, *Listen to Pop! Exploring a Musical Genre* (Santa Barbara, CA: ABC-CLIO, 2018), 202.
[16] Bowie and his collaborators seem intent on separating *Lazarus* from the traditional jukebox musical. Walsh, van Hove, and Henry Hey have all spoken on this point. See, for example, Kardos, *Blackstar Theory*, 125.

explicit reference to the songs' origins as ABBA hits. In *Lazarus*, Bowie's music, career, and person are both present *and* absent. In the manner of *Mamma Mia!* and other jukebox musicals, many of the songs are presented as the natural outpouring of characters' emotions and seem to be authored by those characters. It is notable, however, that Bowie's physical albums appear onstage in *Lazarus*; at one point, the character Thomas Jerome Newton picks up Bowie's *The Next Day*, puts the record on the turntable, and sings "Where Are We Now?". The musical arrangement is very similar to the album version, as Michael C. Hall rewrites Bowie's vocals in a faithful interpretation.

This moment, while isolated, points to the most fascinating aspect of *Lazarus*. Like many of Bowie's other multimedia works and appearances, it does not exist on its own, independent of Bowie and his larger star image. *Lazarus* paradoxically seems to directly invoke Bowie's existing star image while also retroactively rewriting it. While Hall embodies the play's main character, Bowie is present in albums on stage, in the specter of original depiction of Newton, and in a projected image that closes the production. Here, as always, David Bowie shows a keen awareness of the inextricable linkage of his star image, his music, and his literal image. It is striking that he chose to play with this most powerful aspect of his persona in this final work.

Lazarus is clearly elegiac, not simply because it shows the final chapter of Newton's life and journey. The show was written and produced in the final year of Bowie's life and represents the achievement of a career goal: Bowie had long wished to pass on the characters he created to others, to be embodied and reborn as are characters on the stage. In this rebirth of Thomas Jerome Newton, *Lazarus* shows just that. The show also unites disparate eras of Bowie's career through the songs chosen for the show. This process seems to have been collaborative, with Walsh, Bowie, and Bowie's longtime righthand woman Coco Schwab present throughout the hashing out of plot, musical details, and more. Director Ivo van Hove helped bring the musical to life on the stage, his distinctive style shaping many of the visual choices.

This musical, then, represents a joining of many of the threads this study seeks to explore. The show works in a narrative form, something Bowie brought to many of his albums. Here, that narrative is built from songs spanning five decades. Beyond this, Bowie's continued work to include projection in stage shows finds greater integration here than in his own tours. (The Glass Spider, Sound + Vision, Earthling, and other tours all incorporated some moving image projection, though in later shows that took the more common form of representing the artist in real time for greater visibility in all parts of the large arenas he played.) In *Lazarus*, projection expands the world of the show, providing entrance points for characters, setting, and connections to the past.

Interestingly, Bowie frequently expressed an interest in the marriage of music and drama through musical theater. In a 2002 interview with Terry Gross, Bowie listed the composition of a stage musical as one of his original goals as an artist.[17] Though Gross sounds incredulous, the seeds of such multimedia dramatic expression are evident throughout Bowie's oeuvre. With the completion of *Lazarus* in 2015, he finally realized this ambition. However, planning documents from earlier endeavors show that this mode of expression had long captivated Bowie. By delving more deeply into these unrealized works, we gain a clearer image of his working process and the importance of a multivalent mode of expression within those works.

Beyond the multimedia conception of single works, though, we must wrestle with the role of the moving image in the crafting of David Bowie and his career. Like each of his recorded works, "David Bowie" is a creation and an integral part of the *gesamtkunstwerk* of Bowie's oeuvre. The man himself, christened David Robert Jones, created David Bowie as a musical avatar, serving for some fifty years as the public image of Jones' work. Just as in the careful crafting of music videos and concert performances, Bowie also understood the importance of the moving image in communicating his public character to his audience. He used costuming, movement, interviews, photographs, and more to craft each iteration of "David Bowie" for his audience, to communicate his changes and evolutions in the clearest way possible. The moving image—whether music video, filmed interview, acting role, or commercial advertising appearance—served as a direct conduit for that communication. It is clear in Bowie's embrace of such media that he understood their power.

Bowie and the Visual Arts

It is perhaps of little surprise that the moving image would become so central to Bowie's musical output. From a young age, the visual arts were one of his passions. His studies at Bromley Technical School in suburban London included

---

[17] Terry Gross, "David Bowie on the Ziggy Stardust Years: 'We were creating the 21st century in 1971,'" *NPR*. https://www.npr.org/2016/01/11/462653510/david-bowie-on-the-ziggy-stardust-years-we-were-creating-the-21st-century-in-197 Accessed March 20, 2019.

the visual arts; in fact, fellow musician Peter Frampton's father Owen served as young Bowie's instructor. From there, he pursued yet more artistic activity. On leaving school, Bowie found work in an advertising agency, apparently through the auspices of Owen Frampton. His time at the Nevin D. Hirst agency of Bond Street was short-lived, but influential. There, he worked as a "junior visualizer," linking advertising message to image.[18] Clearly, the process stuck with him. In interviews decades later, he pointed to his time in advertising as the main driver of his practice of storyboarding his film and video ideas. Armed with this expanded expression of his visual language, Bowie would create his own music videos a few short years later.

Even before those music videos, Bowie's conception of live musical performance was always carefully crafted with an eye toward the visual via costumes, set, and more; evidence of that importance predates his own solo endeavors. As Bowie stated, "it didn't occur to me that you were supposed to only stay in one of them [the arts]. So for me it was quite appropriate that if I'm doing music, then I should also actually design some scenery for the stage and probably the costumes, and I'll do some paintings while I'm at it."[19] Designs for the stage and costumes for various early bands still exist in his archive. For the group the Konrads, Bowie was designing stage sets by 1962 and costumes by 1963. Kon-rad member David Hadfield remembers Bowie drawing ad campaigns for the group (never realized in print, it seems).[20] His emphasis on the visual was so centrally important that he preserved these drawings; they remain in his personal archive today, some six decades later. Also evident in these early drawings (and others from his time at Bromley Technical) are some of the visual preoccupations that appear again and again in his work. Drawings from 1958–63 feature Egyptian-inspired, sphinx-like figures, much like the costuming Bowie would use in a photo shoot originally intended to promote *Hunky Dory* (1971). Of course, sci-fi imagery features prominently, too. Even in this era, Bowie established the visual encyclopedia that defined his style throughout his long career.

Despite these early efforts to command and shape every aural and visual aspect of his work, collaboration was a central feature of Bowie's art. From an early age,

---

[18] Robert Dimery, "'By the age of 14, he was already a cult figure': How David Bowie's Formative Years Shaped His Art," *GQ UK*, February 5, 2021, https://www.gq-magazine.co.uk/culture/article/david-bowie-childhood Accessed March 17, 2021.
[19] Quoted in Pegg, *The Complete David Bowie*, 9.
[20] Victoria Broackes, "Putting Out Fire with Gasoline: Designing David Bowie," in *David Bowie Is Inside*, ed. Victoria Broackes and Geoffrey Marsh (London: Victoria and Albert, 2013), 117.

he worked with friends like George Underwood to develop a distinctive visual style. Underwood, who also gave Bowie his mismatched pupils in a schoolboy brawl, designed the back cover of the Phillips release of *Space Oddity*. Later in the 1960s, the Beckenham Arts Lab proved vital to Bowie's development. Working in the community with an artistic collaborative, Bowie explored new forms of expression as he moved closer to the style that would win him the attention of the British public at large. Victoria Broackes has written at length about the myriad collaborative threads that define Bowie's visual style (too numerous to follow here).[21] Lisa Perrott highlights collaborative relationships in Bowie's music video output. Despite this study's focus on Bowie and his own audiovisual language, it is clear that that language owes much to Bowie's artistic relationships, as well as to his consumption of others' artistic works.

Bowie as Cinephile

Collaborators from Mark Ravitz to Jules Fisher to Laurie Anderson speak of Bowie's voracious appetite for art: he read, he viewed, he listened broadly. An avid reader and intellectual magpie, Bowie incorporated poetic allusions to everything from Ballard to Burgess to Burroughs. As John O'Connell's *Bowie's Bookshelf* shows, he was well read and diverse in his literary interests.[22] The same holds true of Bowie's cinematic pursuits. In interview after interview, he makes reference to the filmic worlds that inspired his own visions. Celebrating auteurs like Wim Wenders and Stanley Kubrick, Bowie understood and appreciated the power of cinema. His viewing appetite can be seen as an important piece in the puzzle of his musical and visual style.

In a July 1975 fan club newsletter, this aspect of Bowie's artistic consumption comes to the fore. Writing during his time in Los Angeles, the newsletter author describes Bowie's exploration of the home video format, stating, "David is such a videotape enthusiast that his acquaintances around town have taken to calling him 'Video Dave.'"[23] Not only was Bowie an avid movie theater attendee, but he also accessed the burgeoning video format in its very early years. The fact that this propensity was important enough to disseminate to his fan base seems

---

[21] Broackes, "Putting Out Fire," 117–61.
[22] John O'Connell, *Bowie's Bookshelf: The Hundred Books That Changed David Bowie's Life* (New York: Gallery Books, 2019).
[23] David Bowie Fan Club, Newsletter, July 11, 1975, Jeff Gold Collection ARC-0037 Box AF3, Folder 18, Rock and Roll Hall of Fame Library and Archives, Cleveland, Ohio.

significant: Bowie as video/film fan is an important part of how we were to see and understand him during this and subsequent periods. John Lennon is said to have used that nickname for Bowie during their work together on "Fame," too: it is clear that Bowie's embrace of the video format was enthusiastic and proselytizing in its avidity.

More than a superficial love or enjoyment of films, though, I see Bowie's engagement with the medium as true cinephilia. He was certainly a knowledgeable film lover, but his appreciation of film expanded well beyond trivia or familiarity with obscure titles. Rather, we might understand his engagement with the form as cinephilic—a form of filmic love. In Christian Keathley's definition, an important aspect of cinephilia is the ability of the cinephile to project themselves *into* the world of the film, and indeed to in some way participate in its construction and meaning-making.[24] This strain of cinephilia is made manifest in many of Bowie's non-visual works: he seems to expand upon and explore filmic moments even when he is not recreating them on screen or stage. We could take, for but one example, his use of Beethoven's "Ode to Joy" from the Ninth Symphony as his introduction music on the Ziggy Stardust tour. Coupled with his costuming choices, this music expands upon his experience of *A Clockwork Orange* in ways that are not meant to directly recreate the film, but rather step inside and expand its world. Such engagement with film is not entirely divorced from more contemporary fan practices, such as fan fiction and vidding. In those practices, fans engage with their chosen film objects not by simply recreating, but expanding and, in some ways, taking creative control of the films' world.

In the most successful fan creation, this labor helps the original work to gain depth and greater resonance for a group of fans. We might see the Harry Potter fandom as a prime example of this approach. Through sites like Pottermore and practices like wizard rock, Harry Potter fandom has succeeded in deepening the books' lore and, in some ways, wresting control of it. In a move not dissimilar to Potter fans, Bowie is expanding the filmic worlds he loved in order to make them overlap with and participate in his own world. It is not surprising that Bowie's own works have inspired the same sort of response. Indeed, Bowie's creations as cinephile are almost constructed in order to inspire their own expanded cinephilia.

---

[24] Christian Keathley, *Cinephilia and History, or the Wind in the Trees* (Bloomington: Indiana University Press, 2006), 26.

This impulse animates many aspects of Bowie's work and reveals the depth of his engagement with the cinematic arts: more than mere inspiration, they serve as objects of cinephilic fascination that take part in Bowie's new creations.

Specific films served as important touchstones for Bowie throughout his life. *A Clockwork Orange* influenced his costume design and musical choices during the Ziggy era; Kubrick's *2001: A Space Odyssey* was similarly, obviously, present in his work. Groundbreaking early cinema held an important place for him, too. RCA press releases for *"Heroes"* make reference to Bowie's love of "the German Expressionists of the early 20th century … particularly the film director Georg Wilhelm Pabst," perhaps most famous for his *Pandora's Box* (1929), starring Louise Brooks.[25] Bowie's engagement with the Expressionists is most frequently discussed with respect to the cover image of *"Heroes"*: loosely inspired by Erich Heckel's work, both this album cover and Iggy Pop's *The Idiot* point to the centrality of Expressionism in Bowie's artistic language of the time.[26] Beyond the inspiration provided by Heckel and the paintings of Weimar Germany, the stark lighting and grotesque figures of Pabst's Expressionist films informed Bowie's stage design for the Isolar (*Station to Station*) tour. Expressionist films like *Pandora's Box*, *The Cabinet of Dr. Caligari* (1920, dir. Wiene), and *Metropolis* (1927, dir. Lang) made up the fabric of Bowie's film engagement and film work. Kevin Cann's chronology of Bowie's life in London documents the screenings he attended; repertory theater showings of Lang and Pabst number among them.[27] Even in an era when classic silent cinema was more difficult to view, Bowie consistently sought it out and expanded his cinematic knowledge.

While his *Diamond Dogs* visual language and narrative are clearly shaped by Lang's masterwork, Bowie's engagement with it went deeper. In the 1980s, while working with producer Giorgio Moroder on "Cat People (Putting Out Fire)," Moroder mentioned his intention to secure the rights to *Metropolis* and re-score it himself. According to Moroder, Bowie was taken aback: "he was really surprised and disappointed: he told me he wanted to do the same thing."[28] In

---

[25] RCA Press Release, 1977, Jeff Gold Collection ARC-0037 Box AF1, Folder 17, Rock and Roll Hall of Fame Library and Archives, Cleveland, Ohio.
[26] Pop's *The Idiot*, produced by Bowie, is sometimes referred to as an unofficial part of Bowie's Berlin Trilogy. The visual connection merely strengthens this affinity.
[27] Kevin Cann, *Any Day Now: The London Years, 1947–1974* (London: Adelita, 2011).
[28] Annette Insdorff, "A Silent Classic Gets Some 80's Music," *New York Times*, August 15, 1984, https://www.nytimes.com/1984/08/05/movies/a-silent-classic-gets-some-80-s-music.html Accessed March 15, 2021.

fact, Bowie never scored a film, though there was talk of his doing so for *The Man Who Fell to Earth* (1976, dir. Roeg), in which he starred. It is striking that *Metropolis* remained so important to him—important enough that he entered a bidding war against Moroder once he learned of his plans. In the end, Bowie accomplished little more than driving up the cost for Moroder's project, but the incident is instructive. Cinema, and the link between music and the moving image, remained central to Bowie's artistic practice and conception of himself as an artist.

In this same time period, Bowie gave numerous interviews about his desire to direct film.[29] This in and of itself is not surprising: "what I really want to do is direct" has become a cliché for a reason. For Bowie, though, it seems to have been not only a sincere wish, but also the culmination of much of his earlier multimedia work. He served as director for some of his *Let's Dance*-era music videos and, throughout the press coverage from that era, repeatedly mentioned his desire to move behind the camera. This was also a period of increased screen acting for Bowie, in films like *The Hunger* (1983, dir. Scott), *Merry Christmas Mr. Lawrence* (1983, dir. Ôshima), and more. Bowie speaks of his excitement about many of these projects, but also hints that he would see directing as more fulfilling work. As late as 1991, Bowie spoke of a project in the works, on which he would serve as director and perhaps screenwriter.[30] This unnamed project joins the ranks of a long line of promised Bowie films, up to a reimagined *Ziggy Stardust* film, hinted at in a *GQ* interview in 2000. There, Bowie mentions that he himself will not appear, not even as Ziggy's father (spiritual or otherwise).[31] Like so many tantalizing film possibilities before it, 2000's *Ziggy* never made it to production or release. Still, it shows the continuing fascination Bowie held with directing a film based on his own musical works. More than that, it points to the inherently multimedia nature of those albums, in Bowie's own conception. That he would see a Ziggy film as not only possible but important, even three decades after the album's release, shows how central the moving image was to Bowie's conception of his art.

---

[29] See, for example, *Bowie 83* promotional material, Jeff Gold Collection ARC-0037 Box AF3, Folder 18, Rock and Roll Hall of Fame Library and Archives, Cleveland, Ohio.

[30] Robin Eggar, "Tin Machine II Interview," in *Bowie on Bowie: Interviews and Encounters with David Bowie*, ed. Sean Egan (Chicago: Chicago Review Press, 2015), 199–200.

[31] Dylan Jones, "Bowie: Most Stylish Man," in *Bowie on Bowie: Interviews and Encounters with David Bowie*, ed. Sean Egan (Chicago: Chicago Review Press, 2015), 353.

Organization

To understand the role of the moving image in Bowie's work, it is important to focus on each facet in turn. This study, then, will concentrate on each aspect in (comparative) isolation before stepping back to assess the power and legacy of their combined whole in sharper focus. Bowie's engagement with the moving image is not present solely in his own works, though. For this reason, I separate this study into two large sections: Bowie as auteur and Bowie as sign. First, I examine the way that Bowie embraced and explored the power of the moving image in his own work. His cinephilia and interest in visual art primed him for such a multimedia approach, but his interest in cultural theory and meaning making truly deepened and expanded that use. The next chapter addresses these influences and charts an analytical approach to Bowie's relationship to the moving image, both as author and as potent sign in his own right, before approaching specific works as case studies. The second section of this book deals with the use of Bowie *as sign* or star image. Given his care in crafting and controlling his own star image through his music, interviews, and visuals, it is especially instructive to analyze how that star image is put to use by others. In this section, I explore his film roles, advertising appearances, and depictions of Bowie on screen. These areas illuminate not only how Bowie saw and wished to present himself, but also how the general public viewed him. Finally, his importance for fans comes into focus as we examine his ever-evolving persona and its audiovisual presentation. As Nick Stevenson has argued, "Bowie offered not simply the opportunity to put ordinary reality on hold for a short while, but the possibility of imagining a creative future *for myself*"[32] (emphasis added). Ultimately, Bowie's engagement with the moving image is fascinating not only for what it shows us about rock stars and the creation of a star image, but also for its template for engagement with reality in our own lives. This final section of *David Bowie and the Moving Image: A Standing Cinema* shows Bowie's methodology expanded beyond Bowie himself and, in that, shows its true and lasting impact.

Music video is probably the clearest and best-known example of Bowie's multimedia endeavors. Beginning with the 1967 *Love You till Tuesday*, he crafted a variety of shorts, ranging from straightforward musical performances

---

[32] Nick Stevenson, "David Bowie Now and Then: Questions of Fandom and Late Style," in *David Bowie: Critical Perspectives*, ed. Eoin Devereux, Aileen Dillane, and Martin Power (New York: Routledge, 2015), 286.

to more extended narratives built around songs. Chapter 3 will focus on these projects, analyzing three examples from different stages of Bowie's career. With "Life on Mars?", "Ashes to Ashes," and "Where Are We Now?", I examine the development of Bowie's audiovisual style, with particular focus on the development of an idiosyncratic approach to the filmed subject. Anecdotally, directors like Julien Temple have listed Bowie among the most involved artists they have worked with.[33] Archival material supports this assessment, showing Bowie's strong visual conception of all aspects of his work, from costuming to set design to visual framing. This chapter ends with a brief examination of the "Love is Lost" video. A project undertaken by Bowie without the support and constriction of a traditional music video production, "Love is Lost" shows the auteuristic impulse present throughout Bowie's career.

Chapter 4 investigates a related aspect of Bowie's career that is rarely mentioned: his planned film projects. These projects are often overlooked for the simple reason that they never existed in a finished form. In 1974 and 1975, Bowie conceptualized feature film projects based on his musical works. Through archival materials held by the David Bowie Archive and the Rock and Roll Hall of Fame Library and Archive, I reconstruct the film project based on 1974's *Diamond Dogs*. This project's many iterations give insight into Bowie's overall conception of the work. I examine first the *Midnight Special* episode *1980 Floor Show*, recorded in London in 1973, which Bowie envisioned as a cabaret show that featured new songs destined for inclusion on *Diamond Dogs*. From there, this chapter charts the evolution of imagery from the TV special to the album and eventually the "TheaTour" in support of that album. New interviews with collaborators Mark Ravitz (set design) and Jules Fisher (production design) paint a clearer picture of this tour, from which almost no film footage survives. Finally, I consider the extensive film planning materials from *Diamond Dogs* as the culmination of this yearlong project: how had Bowie's visual style and influences carried through to this final iteration of the story told by the album?

The second section of this study, Bowie as sign, deals with the presentation and permutation of Bowie in the work of others. In interviews, photos, and public appearances, Bowie crafted a distinct and evolving public persona. His feature films roles, the focus of Chapter 5, are an important component in the use and alteration of what Richard Dyer would call the artist's star image. In this

---

[33] Charles Shaar Murray, "Sermon from the Savoy," in *Bowie on Bowie: Interviews and Encounters with David Bowie*, ed. Sean Egan (Chicago: Chicago Review Press, 2015), 171.

first chapter of the "Bowie as Sign" section, I consider Bowie's public persona through the lens of film roles at career inflection points: 1983's *The Hunger* (dir. Tony Scott), and 1986's *Labyrinth* (dir. Jim Henson). Bowie's persona was in a moment of transition; these film roles served to complicate and unmoor that star image. The characters Bowie played offer distinct tensions with his contemporaneous public appearances. Examining these tensions, this chapter reveals a targeted strategy for the creation of a fluid and recognizable star image for David Bowie through his film roles.

At the same time that Bowie starred in films, he also lent his music and face to advertising campaigns. Much like his cinema appearances, these strategic commercial choices show a nuanced understanding of the public's perception of Bowie. Drawing examples from the 1980s, 2000s, and 2010s, Chapter 6 examines Bowie's public image through its use in commercials. As short form statements of brand and consumer identity, commercials are ideal distillations of contemporary understandings of a star's image. I use these commercial spots to read not only Bowie's star image, but also his relationship to fans' own self-image. In appealing to potential consumers through the figure of David Bowie, corporations like PepsiCo and Louis Vuitton bank on the idea that consumers will see, in Bowie, aspects of themselves that they wish to amplify.

Chapter 7 deals with specific filmic uses of that Bowie star image through musical and visual reuse. In countless films from the 1970s onward, filmmakers have capitalized on Bowie's social capital. This chapter concentrates on one main example of reuse—Todd Haynes' 1998 film *Velvet Goldmine*—contrasting it with the fannish creation of *Flight of the Conchord*'s "Bowie" episode. A clear example of both fandom and filmic relationships to Bowie, *Velvet Goldmine* dramatizes the importance of Bowie's musical and visual worlds for those who consume them. Through close semiotic analysis of the film and fan creations inspired by it, I argue that Bowie's own mode of creation has been filtered into fans' personal creations, providing an example by which fans can continue in his artistic footsteps. Within the film, fan characters show how powerful Bowie's mode of creation can be in self-determination. In the construction of the film, we can see an application of this very approach. This analysis of *Velvet Goldmine* brings us full circle: just as Bowie's use of the moving image helped him to define himself for the public, so too have Bowie's shaping of sound and vision allowed his fans reach a similar self-definition through their use.

Finally, I conclude by taking stock of the current state of Bowie audiovisual legacy, both via official releases and through his influence on others. At the time of his death in January 2016, Bowie had begun to implement several large-scale legacy-building projects. Among these were reissue box sets, each covering about five years of Bowie's career; documentary films *Five Years* and *The Last Five Years*; and the *David Bowie Is* exhibition, mounted with the Victoria and Albert Museum in 2013. Each of these large projects featured unseen materials from the David Bowie Archive, a privately held archive of the artist's materials from throughout his long career. This careful release of materials (many of them audiovisual) shows yet another way in which Bowie saw the moving image as central to his public persona and his work. Beyond this constructed afterlife, we might see Bowie continuing on through the work of others, whether professionally produced visual albums or fanmade unofficial creations. In so many ways, the work of Bowie lives on through his fans and through their understanding of him. This study explores the ways Bowie's use of the moving image enlivened and empowered his works and, with them, the creations and lives of his audiences.

Part One

Bowie as Auteur

2

Semiotics and the Creation of "David Bowie"

"I was starting to build Ziggy, he was starting to come together, and I was naturally falling into the role; and it was using one's own resources, *and you sort of pick up on bits of your own life when you're putting a role together. Bang! It was suddenly there on the table. It was a simple as that.*"
—David Bowie on the creation of Ziggy Stardust (emphasis added)[1]

Speaking with journalist Michael Watts in 1978, David Bowie (in the quote above) sought to clarify and contextualize his most headline-grabbing interview of the decade: the 1972 piece in which he, in character as Ziggy Stardust, told Watts he was gay. He tried to make clear that the original interview, much like the songs on *The Rise and Fall of Ziggy Stardust and the Spiders from Mars*, is an extension and expression of the role of Ziggy, not necessarily true of Bowie himself. Bowie's language here is instructive. He refers to Ziggy as a role, and carefully separates himself as a person from that role. Though some aspects of Ziggy's presentation and personality come from Bowie's life and experience, the artist takes pains to make clear that any statements made in the 1972 interview were made in the voice of Ziggy, not the voice of his creator. This *modus operandi*—creating a character to act as his public persona—is one that Bowie resurrected throughout his career. One need only think of the appearance and public pronouncements of Aladdin Sane and the Thin White Duke to understand the diversity of characters inhabited by Bowie. In order to create lived-in, believable characters, Bowie used every means at his disposal: music, speaking and singing voice, gesture, costume, interviews, and (importantly for this study) audiovisual art. This medium, comprising music videos, Bowie's planned feature films, acting roles, advertisements, and depictions of Bowie on screen, is one of the most powerful expressions of these embodied personae. The

---

[1] Michael Watts, "Confessions of an Elitist," in *Bowie on Bowie: Interviews and Encounters with David Bowie*, ed. Sean Egan (Chicago: Chicago Review Press, 2015), 79.

various unique possibilities of film and video allowed Bowie to shape the public's understanding of his music and characters in ways that would not be possible without it. Indeed, the moving image allowed him to create David Bowie.

Bowie used the moving image to create striking, memorable moments, but also to create himself. Through the careful manipulation of cultural markers on screen, he was able to craft a detailed, nuanced understanding of the character David Bowie and each of his masks. The raw material for this construction came from the world around him: the voices of Anthony Newley and Marc Bolan, the images of Greta Garbo and Marlene Dietrich, and the filmic language of Stanley Kubrick and Fritz Lang all contributed to the audiovisual realization of David Bowie and each of his distinct characters. Of course, with such a distinction between creator, public presentation of self, and presentation of distinct, ever-changing characters comes some confusion. When is Bowie speaking in the voice of his character, and when is he speaking in his own voice? Is "David Bowie" not just another role for David Jones? Such questions have been posed and explored by many able researchers; Shelton Waldrep's *The Aesthetics of Self-Invention* provides one such analysis, while Philip Auslander addresses this approach in the context of Bowie's on-stage performances.[2] My purpose here is not to retread this debate. Instead, I hope to enliven it by addressing other, sometimes overlooked aspects of this mode of self-construction. Specifically, this study focuses on Bowie's manipulation of the moving image as an important tool in creating and marketing a public face for himself and his music. An early adopter of the music video form and an avid consumer of audiovisual media, Bowie understood the power of the moving image. Indeed, we may approach his work of self-creation as we might the work of an auteur film director.

Following the French film theorists of *Cahiers du Cinéma*, I use auteur here to refer to the sort of director whose control and style are evident throughout their works. Introduced in the 1950s, this auteur theory holds that such directors may be seen as the authors of their films.[3] Of course, as film is a highly collaborative

---

[2] Shelton Waldrep, *The Aesthetics of Self-Invention: Oscar Wilde to David Bowie* (Minneapolis: University of Minnesota Press, 2004), 105–40; Philip Auslander, *Performing Glam Rock: Gender and Theatricality in Popular Music* (Ann Arbor: University of Michigan Press, 2006), 106–49.

[3] See, for example, François Truffaut, "A Certain Tendency of the French Cinema," in *Movies and Methods*, ed. Bill Nichols (Berkeley: University of California Press, 1976), 224–37. Of course, this Truffaut article, originally published in January 1954, is but one part of a nuanced and varied debate about the value of auteur theory. See, for example, André Bazin, "On the *politique des auteurs*," in *Cahiers du Cinéma: The 1950s: Realism, Hollywood, New Wave*, ed. Jim Hillier (London: BFI, 1985), 248–59.

art form, there are many aspects of film production that could not possibly be controlled by a single person. However, the *Cahiers* critics held that these directors' styles so permeated their works that the single author designation was warranted and useful: it can allow insights into the nuances of that director's output that might not be as readily apparent without such framing. Similarly, I acknowledge that the creation of a public persona is multifaceted and collaborative. In the shaping of one's look alone, a makeup artist, costume designer, hair stylist, and movement coach may all work in collaboration with the artist. Bowie certainly had many such collaborators, from Pierre Laroche to Freddie Burretti to Kansai Yamamoto to Suzi Ronson (to speak only of the Ziggy era). Far from trying to erase their contributions, I instead seek to better understand the unifying factor behind their work: the conscious manipulation of David Bowie's star image.

It is unsurprising that the *Cahiers* theorists identified Classic Hollywood directors (among them Hitchcock and Hawkes) as such auteurs. With stylistic signatures and often domineering approaches, these directors not only crafted strong individual styles, but also helped to establish the visual grammar that came to dominate feature films. Bowie's lyrical and visual references betray him as a cinephile deeply familiar with this era and style of filmmaking. Like these directors, Bowie exerted excessive control over his own image, limiting which photographers were allowed to shoot his live shows and how the public was allowed to see him. Given these restrictions, he was able to present the same sort of unified style evident in the work of auteur directors. In his use of the moving image, Bowie exerted Hitchcock or Kubrick levels of control.

In addressing Bowie's control over his musical star image, I have purposefully elided a few points. First, that his record company and management also exerted a great deal of control over his star image. (In fact, his record company press releases are among the clearest sources to chart the evolution of Bowie's public persona.[4]) More than this, though, I have avoided a discussion of the way that Bowie's potent star image was used by others. In crafting an evolving, outré image for himself on stage and in interviews, Bowie was creating a tool for his own use. However, once that image existed in the world, it was coopted and used by others, often through some of the same audiovisual mechanisms employed by Bowie himself.

---

[4] See, for example, RCA biography of David Bowie, November 1974, Jeff Gold Collection ARC-0037 Box AF3, Folder 53, Rock and Roll Hall of Fame Library and Archives, Cleveland, Ohio.

I divide this study into two broad sections. The first focuses on Bowie's strategies in creating his own star image through the use of the moving image. Building on the *Cahier du Cinema* critics' auteur theory and Richard Dyer's analyses of star image, I examine the auteurist strategies at play in Bowie's multimedia creation (and recreation) of self in the public eye. The second section of this study deals with the use of Bowie's persona by others in advertising, film roles, and depictions on film. The carefully crafted, multivalent constellation of cultural signs that is "David Bowie" has been used by others because of its complexity and overdetermination. This use and consumption of the figure of Bowie has fascinating connections to Bowie's own working procedures, causing P. David Marshall to label such use "constructive consumption."[5] In order to fully understand how that use functioned, however, we must delve more deeply into Bowie as auteur. Examining his construction of self through music, moving image, and more, this chapter provides a semiotic framework for analysis. Subsequent chapters will use these semiotic tools to examine connective threads in Bowie's music, videos, and planned films. With these threads established, constructive consumption of Bowie (by fans and the media) becomes yet clearer.

Bowie's Masks: Developing Personae

From the very beginning of his music career, David Bowie adopted different mantles, meant to align with the tenor of his work at any given time. The idea of the pop star as actor was not new; as Simon Frith writes, "a pop star is like a film star, taking on many parts."[6] Those parts were important for the pop star's music and relationship to their audience. Only a year before Bowie's biggest break (with the release of "Space Oddity" in 1969), Ellen Willis wrote in *The New Yorker* of the importance of "attractive packaging" in creating a new rock star.[7] Analyzing the rise of such rock luminaries as the Beatles, the Rolling Stones, and Bob Dylan, Willis sought to pinpoint what allowed them to rise above the rest and why, exactly, the focus on "packaging" was changing in the late 1960s. Willis bemoans the takeover of rock by a sort of elitism, one that would ignore the

---

[5] P. David Marshall, "Productive Consumption: Agency, Appropriation, and Value in the Creative Consuming of David Bowie," *Continuum* 31, no. 4 (2017): 564–73.

[6] Simon Frith, *Performing Rites: On the Value of Popular Music* (Cambridge: Harvard University Press, 1996), 199.

[7] Ellen Willis, "Records: Rock, Etc," *The New Yorker,* July 6, 1968: 56.

trappings of celebrity for an almost formalist focus on the music itself. Luckily, this clinical approach to rock did not develop in quite the way Willis foresaw. Instead, an almost academic approach merged with the appreciation of celebrity, persona, and iconicity in the form of David Bowie.

Many commentators see Bowie as breaking the mold of a rock star by abandoning the authenticity that genre formerly prized. Shelton Waldrep argues that Bowie is, in many ways, the spiritual follower of popular cultural figures such as Oscar Wilde, Truman Capote, and Andy Warhol: he, like them, fashioned a self out of performance in all public areas of his life.[8] Like these earlier innovators, Bowie's construction centers around his main artistic outlet (in this case, music) but is not limited by it. In the same way Wilde constructed his public persona, so too did Bowie. He referred to himself as "the actor" on the sleeve of 1971's *Hunky Dory* for good reason. He embodied his roles in all aspects of his career. However, Bowie had many more media at his disposal than did Wilde or his contemporaries. His use of the moving image is in service of the "self-invention" Waldrep identifies; the moving image amplifies, fleshes out, and sometimes questions Bowie's personae. Waldrep sees the visual as so important to Bowie's work that he argues for the artist's music as a sort of reverse-engineered outgrowth. He writes that "in an effort to make his music seem visual, Bowie attempted to find corollaries and analogues in sound for these visual and performative aspects he was able to demonstrate live onstage or on video or film."[9] While I agree that the audiovisual is central to Bowie's construction of self, his musical style and compositional approach are not simply an attempt to recapture that aspect. Instead, we might hear Bowie's music as always already theatrical in nature. It is not trying to express the visual, but is rather conceived as a part of an artistic whole in which the visual is also entwined. Early songs like "Rubber Band" or "Please Mr. Gravedigger" (both from his eponymous Deram debut record) posit a character and era within their music—not in an attempt to recapture that theatrical moment, but because of an intrinsic linking of storytelling, character, visualization, and music in Bowie's work. The vocal personae of each of these songs is a central part of the musical text—something like "Please Mr. Gravedigger" becomes much less powerful and more confusing without its vocal timbre—and also implies a strong attendant visualization. Both the musical and the visual are already a part of each other. In this, Bowie seems to follow the *gesamtkunstwerk* ideal.

---

[8] Waldrep, *The Aesthetics of Self-Invention*, 106.
[9] Ibid., 114.

Beyond artistic expression, though, this total artwork served to establish Bowie as a public figure, an artist, and a celebrity. Waldrep also sees this celebrity marketing as an outgrowth of Wilde and his innovations. Director Todd Haynes seems to agree, as his *Velvet Goldmine* (analyzed in Chapter 7) creates a rock star who is recognizably Bowie by way of Wilde, quoted both in visual styling and words. We might see in Bowie, then, a continuation of various artistic provocateurs for whom personal celebrity acts as an important part of their artistic work. Waldrep links Capote and Warhol as other prime examples in this mode. For none (with the possible exception of Warhol) was the moving image more important than for Bowie. He was able to use film and video as related outgrowths of his primary artistic work, his music. In doing so, he explored existing modes of celebrity and helped to create a different type.

Through the lens of Willis's contemporaneous writing, we can approach Bowie as an entirely new sort of rock star. His relationship to celebrity differed from his contemporaries' in important ways. Following Su Holmes, though, I resist the idea of a late twentieth-century sea change in celebrity culture.[10] Though Bowie adeptly maneuvered the construction of his own fame through some six decades, his understanding of celebrity was, at its core, informed by the kind of traditional star image construction discussed by Richard Dyer in his seminal study *Stars*. It is tempting to label Bowie as *sui generis*, especially considering the many accounts of his impact on popular music iconography in the early 1970s. However, this impact was created in rather traditional ways, with an understanding of the crafting of celebrity that flourished in Classic Hollywood. In particular, Bowie's approach reveals an understanding of the relationship of individualism and identification to the creation of a star. While Bowie honed outsider personae throughout his career, that othered status resonated with fans who saw themselves similarly. The move is a canny one, and one that echoes the branding choices of various movie stars, among them Marlon Brando and Montgomery Clift.[11] In fact, Bowie's early manager Tony DeFries refers to him as a "James Dean or Marlon Brando-type star" in an unpublished Steve Turner piece from 1974.[12] Like these actors, Bowie was marketed as an original, a star

---

[10] Su Holmes, "'Starring … Dyer?': Re-Visiting Star Studies and Contemporary Celebrity Culture," *Westminster Papers in Communication and Culture* 2, no. 2 (2005): 6–21.

[11] Richard Dyer, *Stars* (London: BFI, 1979), 60.

[12] Steve Turner, "How to Become a Cult Figure in Only Two Years: The Making of David Bowie," in *The Sound and the Fury: Rock's Back Pages Reader*, ed. Barney Hoskyns (London: Bloomsbury, 2003), 17–26.

unlike his peers. While I am not suggesting that Bowie's approach to celebrity arose from the kind of academic study that Dyer undertakes, it seems clear that Bowie's close attention to film and its governing systems informed his star strategy.

Describing himself and his contemporaries as the "small, pompous, arty ones" seeking to change rock in the early 1970s, Bowie showed a clear self-awareness about his approach to stardom.[13] Namechecking semioticians and cultural theorists like George Steiner, he has, in interviews spanning his career, shed light on the approach that informed his spectacularly successful creation of himself as a star. Treating fame and public image as a construction, Bowie left the seams of his constructed personae visible—an interesting choice in a field that so prized authenticity. He spoke of the way he created a character, pointing, for example, to Ziggy's connection to himself while also differentiating the character's statements and traits from his own lived experience. The two Michael Watts interviews referenced in this chapter's opening shine a spotlight on this disjunction between character and self. Though Bowie may have had other reasons for his disavowal of Ziggy's sexuality, it remains clear that a strong understanding of the roleplaying involved in star images drove his approach.

Bowie took this part-playing to heart, making it central to his approach to music. Among his most famous characters or roles are Ziggy Stardust, the titular alien of Bowie's smash album—a glam rock alien god come to "let all the children boogie"—and the Thin White Duke of the mid-1970s—a drugged out, nihilist European aristocrat, dancing as the world falls down. Each of these persona changes seems a bit like method acting, as Bowie inhabited the characters both on and off stage. In fact, in a 2002 Terry Gross interview, the artist acknowledges Ziggy as an all-consuming role, and one which he would have liked to have given life beyond his own incarnation. Ideally, he "would love to have handed it on to somebody else ... put the wig on and send him out to do the gigs, you know."[14] Though this hand-off never came to fruition, Bowie's comment shows an innate understanding of the power of the persona: rather than gaining his potency from a closeness to the "authentic" David Bowie, Ziggy drew recognition and definition from a few clear iconic costume choices and mannerisms. This understanding permeated Bowie's performance of

---

[13] Terry Gross, "David Bowie on the Ziggy Stardust Years: 'We were creating the 21st century in 1971,'" *NPR*, https://www.npr.org/2016/01/11/462653510/david-bowie-on-the-ziggy-stardust-years-we-were-creating-the-21st-century-in-197 Accessed March 20, 2019.

[14] Gross, "David Bowie on the Ziggy Stardust Years."

character, whether he was overtly playing a named alter ego, or simply defining the public's star image of David Bowie.

Despite Bowie's comments to Gross, his characters never became like parts in a play: they were never inhabited by anyone else. Ziggy's mantel did not fall to another rocker, nor did the Thin White Duke. Rather, these characters became more like those of a film, inextricably linked to one performer. As Andrew Klevan writes, following Stanley Cavell, "on film, characters have no existence apart from the particular human beings on screen, and no life apart from the particular performers who incarnate them."[15] Though Bowie did bring his characters to life on stage, they were only ever his to inhabit (unlike the *dramatis personae* of a stage play), and his portrayals of them on film and in recorded song remain the most vital and vivid records we have. Though both stage and screen play a role in Bowie's acting, it is in film and video that he links his physicality most clearly to his musical art, blending the grain of his voice with the movement of his body.

Publicly, Bowie's appearance and interviews aligned with each musical persona shift. Everything from wardrobe to professed influences would be altered to match the latest iteration of the Bowie character, showing clearly in Bowie's pronouncements throughout the 1970s. In the *Diamond Dogs* era, his most frequently cited influences included the Beat poets and George Orwell.[16] Christopher Isherwood would replace them in only two years. As Ziggy Stardust, he espoused a bisexuality that he would hedge in later interviews.[17] Most notably, Bowie landed in hot water over the controversial pronouncements of his Thin White Duke character. Playing the disaffected Weimar-era aristocrat in 1976, Bowie told interviewers that he could have been the Adolf Hitler figure he thought England needed.[18] Most transformations did not include such troubling political shifts, but did necessitate changes of wardrobe, physical appearance (in makeup and hair), and mannerisms.

With each change came new, clear icons (in the semiotic sense) of the current persona: a shock of red hair, an eyepatch, a stark black and white wardrobe.

---

[15] Andrew Klevan, *Film Performance: From Achievement to Appreciation* (London: Wallflower Press, 2005), 4.
[16] Craig Copetas, "Beat Godfather Meets Glitter MainMan: William Burroughs Interviews David Bowie," *Rolling Stone*, February 28, 1974, https://www.rollingstone.com/music/music-news/beat-godfather-meets-glitter-mainman-william-burroughs-interviews-david-bowie-92508/ Accessed March 17, 2019.
[17] Michael Watts, "Oh You Pretty Thing," *Melody Maker*, January 22, 1972, 19.
[18] Crowe, "David Bowie: Ground Control to Davy Jones."

Working with specific photographers at the beginning of his career (and strictly controlling access and published images), Bowie and his management were able to craft a very specific and clear public image. In 1974, Steve Turner wrote of the "making of David Bowie" into a "cult figure;" his choice of words was apt.[19] Bowie had indeed been *made*, crafted into a specific image that was quite separate from his earlier public appearances (the shaggy pseudo-hippie of "Space Oddity"). Manager Tony DeFries set careful limits on still and moving images of Bowie in concert, outlawing all but MainMan-authorized photos. Mick Rock's photographs, in particular, have indelibly imprinted a consistent image of the Ziggy Stardust era. In these photographs, Bowie is seen in costume, with hair and makeup styled. He is shown at a remove—not laughing with fans and bandmates, but an aloof rock god in the mode of Ziggy himself. As Turner wrote, "No photographer was going to catch our David with his frail humanity exposed."[20] Authenticity and humanity were not the purview of this rock god. Rather, the artifice was clear and embraced, and all the more powerful for it.

This alignment of character and person was consistent throughout Bowie's career. When the final Ziggy Stardust show ended at London's Hammersmith Odeon in July 1973, Bowie told the audience it was the "last show we'll ever do." In D. A. Pennebaker's concert film of that night, the audience's shock at the pronouncement is palpable—though Bowie only meant that this was the last appearance for the Ziggy character.[21] For the audience, this performance of a character had become real: David Jones, David Bowie, and Ziggy Stardust all elided. Such clear crafting of style and persona would continue for years in the performer's public life. In his personal appearance and stage dress, Bowie carefully constructed each persona with a clear look, meant to immediately evoke that character and the sound of their world and work.

While control of still images whetted the public's appetite for more of this mysterious, changeable Bowie, video was a main tool in the service of image craft. Bowie dabbled in promotional videos from the late 1960s onward. It is his collaborations with photographer Mick Rock, though, that solidified the idea of moving images as central to Bowie's persona, and that produced looks and moments that would follow him throughout his career. The "Life on Mars?"

---

[19] Steve Turner "How to Become a Cult Figure in Only Two Years," 17–26.
[20] Ibid., 20.
[21] *Ziggy Stardust and the Spiders from Mars: the Motion Picture*, directed by D. A. Pennebaker (1979; London: EMI Films, 2003).

video is perhaps the clearest example. (I address this video in greater detail in Chapter 3.) Shot in 1973 to promote a song from 1971's *Hunky Dory*, the video features Bowie alone on a completely white backdrop. Clad in a Freddie Burretti suit, the performer's shock of red hair and dramatic makeup stand out starkly. Rock's decision to wash out the color of the video helps to intensify the impression of Bowie's constituent parts: a red crop, eyes with uneven pupils, and a trim, powder blue figure dominate the short film. The look would become so iconic that, even in the 2000s, magazine spreads of Tilda Swinton and Kate Moss would mimic it. The clear honing of image shown in these early videos provides the lexicon from which Bowie, his management, and advertisers would draw for years to come. He used the pop cultural materials around him in new and exciting ways, crafting the alien from the familiar.

Bowie's Semiotics: "A Singing Warhol"

In a 2013 roundtable, Sir Christopher Frayling discussed Bowie's groundbreaking approach to art and public presentation in the 1970s. He points to the way that Bowie engaged with different questions than were permeating the academic zeitgeist: less concerned with class (although that certainly turns up in Bowie's work), Frayling saw him as questioning gender, persona, and meaning. In his words, "Bowie was completely different, he was standing aside from all that and creating all these roles and being very detached, like a Pop artist manipulating all these signs. A singing Warhol."[22] Such a comparison would have pleased a young Bowie, for whom Warhol was something of an artistic hero. He was influenced by a London production of Warhol's *Pork*, along with the artist's other work. His fascination with Warhol and his coterie continued: Bowie sought out Warhol collaborators Leee Black Childers, Cherry Vanilla, and Tony Zanetta, all of whom worked with Bowie in the early 1970s. On Bowie's first American trip, he reached out to Warhol himself for a meeting (though apparently, the admiration was not entirely mutual). Nevertheless, the Warhol comparison is apt. Much like the legendary Pop artist, Bowie's work was drawn from popular culture, semiotically rich, and frequently denigrated as derivative. Again like Warhol, the image—particularly the moving image—was central to Bowie's creations,

---

[22] "David Bowie Then … David Bowie Now," in *David Bowie Is Inside*, ed. Victoria Broackes and Geoffrey Marsh (London: V&A Publishing, 2013), 284.

even though he was best known as a musician. As Frayling states, we find Bowie "manipulating all these signs" in complex ways. In my analysis of his works in later chapters, I will rely on a semiotic framework to make sense of the meaning of these varied and interconnected uses of the moving image in Bowie's work.

My semiotic analyses are indebted to two main thinkers: Charles Sanders Peirce and Umberto Eco. Peirce's writing forms the basis of much twentieth- and twenty-first-century semiotic work. In particular, his triadic formulations outlining the way that signs relate to their meaning and interpreter are of central importance to many semioticians who followed. Given this, I will refer to Peirce's triads throughout my study, as they form a sort of *lingua franca* for semiotic analysis.[23] In the first instance, Peirce identifies three types of signs: icon, index, and symbol. Each describes the way a sign relates to its meaning, in increasing levels of abstraction. Beyond Peirce, Umberto Eco's work has direct bearing on my approach to Bowie and his semiotic play. In particular, Eco's concepts of unlimited semiosis, the importance of the encyclopedia, and the role of the ideal reader (or viewer, or listener) inform my semiotic understanding of Bowie's work.

"Unlimited semiosis," in Eco's formulation, is not unlimited at all. The name refers to the idea that a sign and its meanings could proliferate in perpetuity, leading to more and more obscure and distant (though related) meanings. Peirce similarly explored what he called infinite semiosis, concentrating on the problem that any sign in his formulation must have an interpretant and, having one, could not represent the end of a chain of meaning. In a logical sense, this is clear and correct. In practice, though, meaning is constrained by the system it exists within and the codes by which it is structured. In order for effective communication to exist, all semiosis cannot be infinite. It can, however, be complex and contingent upon a shared understanding between the sign's creator and its interpreter. There exist many possible meanings for any given sign, but those meanings are constrained by what Eco calls the codes that govern communication between people. In semiosis, then, the receiver or interpreter of a sign is important for their recognition of the sign as part of a familiar system of meaning; a sign in total isolation would not be as effective, since the meaning is socially constructed. The "unlimited" aspect comes into play when we address

---

[23] Some theorists I cite, including Roland Barthes, are more influenced by Ferdinand de Saussure's theory of signs. This does not present a major complication, as my invocation of Barthes does not directly touch upon the semiotic. However, it is important to note the centrality of Saussure to other thinkers.

signs that give rise to a series of different meanings. Paolo Desogus uses the example of a red traffic light to explore this idea: not only does it tell us to stop, but it also, in practice, communicates the various steps of that process, as well as how to react when that light changes. In Desogus's words, "the content of signs is interrelated with other contents the whole of which can give rise to a semiosic stream that involved the entire system of knowledge, which Eco calls encyclopedia."[24] This shared system of knowledge is central to the efficacy of semiosis and to the way that social groups understand one another.

In applying a semiotic framework to popular song, I follow the work of theorists like Kofi Agawu and Philip Tagg. Drawing on Tagg's terminology, I identify musemes—units of musical meaning that connect individual works to their systems of meaning. Other Tagg neologisms like interobjective comparison material (IOCMs) also help clarify my analysis, in this case providing a label for the other musical works to which we might compare the work at hand, and in which we might find common musemes. Tagg's extensive analysis of ABBA's "Fernando" provides a sterling example of the efficacy of a semiotic approach to popular music: within it, Tagg is able to make clear countless layers of meaning through close analysis.[25] Though not every analysis in this study will explicitly invoke Tagg's semiotic language, all are influenced by his approach and seek to incorporate a similar level of analytical nuance.

Similarly, Agawu's seminal approach to nineteenth-century song also provides a starting point for understanding Bowie's semiotic play in the audiovisual medium. Though Agawu focuses on a very different corpus of songs, he nonetheless points to the interplay of semiotic registers within a single work. For him, these nineteenth-century *lieder* create meaning on the level of their poetry, their music, and in the combination of both on the level of song.[26] Though each can be analyzed separately, it is together that they are heard and understood. Following this formulation, we might add yet another layer with the incorporation of the visual: not only song, but image-song is at play in these works. Of course, as Agawu emphasizes, these registers should not be considered as entirely separate; we experience them simultaneously,

---

[24] Paolo Desogus, "The Encyclopedia in Umberto Eco's Semiotics," *Semiotica: Journal of the International Association for Semiotic Studies* 194 (2012): 504.

[25] Philip Tagg, *Fernando the Flute: Analysis of Musical Meaning in an ABBA Mega-hit* (Liverpool: University of Liverpool Institute of Popular Music, 1991).

[26] Kofi Agawu, "Theory and Practice in the Analysis of the Nineteenth-Century 'Lied,'" *Music Analysis* 11, no. 1 (March 1992): 3–36.

as a complete expression.[27] For this reason, any analysis of Bowie's use of the moving image must, of necessity, also analyze his music. I would argue that the inverse should be true, too: to take stock of Bowie's work without acknowledging his incorporation of the moving image is to discount an important facet of his compositions and communication.

As Eco writes, semiosis, or the process of meaning-making and transmission, "explains itself by itself."[28] We can understand semiosis by the very things that make it up. In order to better trace the process of semiosis in Bowie's work, we can take, for example, Bowie's *The Next Day* album—both the music on the album and the physical album itself, with its cover image. This stark image shows the *"Heroes"* album cover obscured by a white square, overlain with the text "The Next Day" and "David Bowie." There are, of course, countless ways to interpret this cover. As Eco writes, the message (here album cover) is to a certain extent an open form, one with a matrix of suggested interpretations but no one concrete "correct" one. Eco finds that "the basic denotation of a sign-vehicle can be understood just as the sender intended it to be but different connotations can be attributed to it simply because the addressee follows another path on the compositional tree to which the sender referred."[29] There are many connotational possibilities in any given artwork, but the shared cultural understanding of the creator and audience forms the codes that help govern interpretation.

If we are to take Eco's approach, this album image's meaning is governed by the encyclopedia of which it is a part. That is, it is shaped by the system of meaning that it taps into. That system includes knowledge of *"Heroes"* and the era it represents (Bowie's Berlin period). It may include the Expressionist art that inspired the *"Heroes"* cover pose, or the spiral of associations with the song "Heroes"—among Bowie's most famous, most covered, and most licensed songs. All this and more is brought to bear in this new cover, as it both implies and obscures Bowie's face, seeming to negate some of the meaning associated with it. When we bring all these disparate associations to *The Next Day's* cover, it becomes a complex, polysemic expression. As such, it became one of the most discussed aspects of the album itself, illustrating the power of the shared encyclopedia Bowie has created in his decade-spanning career. In fact, designer

---

[27] Quoted in David Brackett, *Interpreting Popular Music* (Berkeley: University of California Press, 2000), 30.
[28] Umberto Eco, *A Theory of Semiotics* (Bloomington: Indiana University Press, 1976), 71.
[29] Eco, *Theory of Semiotics*, 139.

Jonathan Barnbrook stated that working with Bowie on *The Next Day* and *Blackstar* "showed him the value of there being symbols everyone can use, share, and be a part of."[30]

Of course, the above interpretation concentrates only on the visual and not on the aural content of the album. Once the interpreter of the album cover has heard the music linked to it, their interpretation will become part of an encyclopedia that contains their knowledge of Bowie and his work, both broadly and as pertains to this album in specific. The songs on the album serve to reinforce both the references to Bowie's past and the idea of a rewriting or reinvigoration. "Where Are We Now?" in particular has lyrical links to the Berlin period referenced by the album's cover. (This song and video are analyzed at greater length in Chapter 3.) The album itself is produced by longtime Bowie friend and collaborator Tony Visconti, drawing in associations ranging from *The Man Who Sold the World* to *Blackstar*. The ghosts of Bowie's past are present throughout.

Beyond this, we can find timbral and stylistic musemes that can be read as a sonic version of the same sort of nostalgic remaking seen on *The Next Day's* cover. We might take "Dirty Boys" as an example. The second track on the album, it hearkens back to earlier songs in its dirge-like saxophone groove. Throughout, Bowie plays two vocal roles. The first, in the verse, is processed and husky. The second, in the prechorus and chorus, is cleaner, much closer to the listener within the soundbox, and occupies a higher part of his vocal range. These two features—its saxophone soundscape and vocal part-playing—link "Dirty Boys" fairly directly to a number of antecedents, most notably the sinister centerpiece of Bowie's *Diamond Dogs* album, "Sweet Thing"/"Candidate." The performances on this song only serve to heighten the connection. Guitarist Earl Slick is featured on "Dirty Boys"; Slick's first appearance on a Bowie release came with 1974's *David Live*, which features a scathing guitar solo on "Sweet Thing"/"Candidate." The style and timbre of his guitar collaborators have frequently marked the stylistic shifts in Bowie's career, so Slick's presence on this and two more *The Next Day* tracks is evocative. As Slick's guitar and Steve Elson's saxophone intertwine at the end of "Dirty Boys," one hears musematic echoes of *David Live's* "Sweet Thing" apocalyptic apotheosis. For the ideal listener (to borrow and bastardize Eco's "ideal reader"), "Dirty Boys" is a rich

---

[30] Leah Kardos, *Blackstar Theory: The Late Works of David Bowie* (New York: Bloomsbury Academic, 2021), 207.

text, one that plays upon their shared musical encyclopedia in precisely the ways they have come to expect from Bowie.

Much like the cover image itself, the album's music wears its references and evocations proudly and clearly. Indeed, Leah Kardos's description of the album as "carefully assembled layers of signification" is particularly apt.[31] In his review, *Pitchfork's* Ryan Dombal describes the album in recognition of this allusive style: "Musically, *The Next Day* isn't radical or dreary, as it bounces around from style to style, casually suggesting past greatness while rarely matching it."[32] Dombal points to some of the stylistic features mentioned above, as well as production decisions like the processing of the drums at the opening of "Love Is Lost" as stylistic nods to the past. These musical choices, in conjunction with the album's visuals and lyrics, form a layered sign complex that relies on the shared encyclopedia and codes of Bowie's listeners in order to be fully understood.[33] While, as Dombal implies, *The Next Day* is unlikely to be posthumously hailed as another *Low* or *Aladdin Sane*, it is certainly an adept example of the sort of semiotic play that defines those albums and the majority of Bowie's musical and audiovisual output. It serves as an emblematic text for the sort of cultural consumption Bowie modeled for his audience, and which they in turn have modeled in their use of him and his star image.

Bowie's Persona and "Productive Consumption"

Central to the second section of this study is the way in which the carefully constructed star image of David Bowie was consumed and translated by others. Just as the moving image was critical to Bowie's creation of self, it was also of paramount importance in the way that audiences understood and consumed him. This applies not only to the way that corporations would use the Bowie image in their advertising, but also in the way that audiences consumed and engaged with that advertising, Bowie's acting career, and depictions of Bowie onscreen.

---

[31] Kardos, *Blackstar Theory*, 35.
[32] Ryan Dombal, "David Bowie: The Next Day," *Pitchfork*, March 11, 2013, https://pitchfork.com/reviews/albums/17855-david-bowie-the-next-day/ Accessed March 19, 2021.
[33] In fact, full understanding may not be possible through an engaged listen to *The Next Day* alone. In addition to the album's music videos, many of these songs also found new life in Bowie's *Lazarus*, deepening and complicating their meanings. As with many of the works discussed here, *The Next Day*'s web of signification becomes more tangled as it exists and evolves in the world and in Bowie's oeuvre.

The artist had a semblance of control in his musical output: he wrote his music, performed it, chose his own styling, and reached out to specific collaborators in crafting his music video style. In the broader media landscape, though, the final presentation of Bowie was out of his control, as was the audience's consumption of him and his output. The final chapters of this study address the ways that Bowie's conscious construction of self and use of audiovisual media correlate to his audience's consumption and use of him as a product. Judith Peraino points to Bowie's *Pin Ups* as a prime example of this consumption. Both visually modeled upon and overtly invoking through its title a midcentury fashion and fan magazine gaze, the album "invites listeners to think of these songs not just as covers but also as visual objects," a close linkage of the musical and visual that many authors and I identify throughout his career.[34] More importantly, though, Peraino frames this moment as indicative of Bowie "in the role of consumer and fan as much as creator or interpreter."[35] Bowie's borrowing is a frequent feature of both critiques and praise of his style, but Peraino homes in on an important aspect of that borrowing: it is fannish, and it provides for his audience a mode of engagement with his own work.

My use of similar language to describe Bowie's creative output and his audience's creative consumption is intentional. Following the work of Dick Hebdige on subcultural creation (glam rock included), Henry Jenkins on fan communities, and P. David Marshall on creative consumption in Bowie fandom, the unifying factor in the myriad audiovisual presentations and consumptions of Bowie is a similarity in method.[36] By openly constructing himself as a sign built from various pop cultural parts, Bowie presented a blueprint of sorts. Fan accounts support such a reading, frequently citing the freedom they found in Bowie's example, freedom that allowed them to live as themselves within a shared cultural milieu. Marshall highlights the complex interrelationship of the artist, their work, the audience, and modes of distribution and consumption:

> The complexity of musical consumption with all the elements of performing identity embedded into the ambient meaning of the music along with all the very diverse ways that people 'use' the music in their own settings for their

---

[34] Judith Peraino, "Plumbing the Surface of Sound and Vision: David Bowie, Andy Warhol, and the Art of Posing," *Qui Parle* 21, no. 1 (Fall/Winter 2012): 153.

[35] Peraino, "Plumbing the Surface," 153.

[36] See, for example, Dick Hebdige, *Subculture: The Meaning of Style* (New York: Routledge, 1979); and Henry Jenkins, *Fans, Bloggers, and Gamers: Exploring Participatory Culture* (New York: New York University Press, 2006).

own purposes and ends makes it very difficult to identify where the productive element of consumption ends. A child in 1975 choosing to dress as Bowie/Ziggy Stardust for Halloween is as much a part of the productive consumption of Bowie as the musical fan who owns all of Bowie's records and attends each of his concerts. Each extends and manipulates the clustered and impacted nature of the popular music cultural commodity and appropriates it for their own purposes and directions.[37]

All forms of consumption of an artist's work are in some way creative (here, taken to mean both the act of creating something new and the act of transforming or creating value). In the case of Bowie, that creativity is cultivated in a unique way, linked to the processes of creation in the artist's work.

Bowie is not unique in his overt construction of self, but his use of the moving image has helped to draw the audience ever closer into conversation with his methods. We might see in Bowie's construction an explicitly fannish mode of creation. Lisa Perrott describes the hauntological tendency of Bowie's self-creation: he consistently recalls the voices and work of other artists within his own creations. Like other scholars, she highlights, for example, the influence of Anthony Newley on Bowie's nascent style in the 1960s. Perrott describes *The Rise and Fall of Ziggy Stardust and the Spiders* from Mars as "an album that functions much like a spiritual medium, tapping into the vast haunting grounds of rock and roll, *avant-garde* aesthetics, kabuki theater, and cabaret performance."[38] Such an analysis highlights the borrowing that is central to Bowie's creative process; this is a process that he also taught to his audience. Bowie famously referred to himself as a human photostat machine, an oft-quoted comment that points to the importance of others' work in his own creations.[39] As Perrott shows, though, the translation of the past into new, original works is not mere mimicry. In the final chapters of this study, I consider the ways that Bowie and his audiovisual presence have been used and interpreted by others. Highlighting this aspect brings Bowie's use of the moving image full circle: not only did he explore different, multimedia modes of meaning-making, but he also taught

---

[37] P. David Marshall, "Productive Consumption: Agency, Appropriation, and Value in the Creative Consuming of David Bowie," *Continuum* 31, no. 4 (2017): 567.

[38] Lisa Perrott, "Time Is Out of Joint: The Transmedial Hauntology of David Bowie," in *David Bowie and Transmedia Stardom*, ed. Ana Cristina Mendes and Lisa Perrott (New York: Routledge, 2020), 123.

[39] See, for example, Steve Turner, "The Rise and Rise of David Bowie," *Beat Instrumental* August 1972. http://www.5years.com/RRDB.HTM Accessed March 17, 2021.

that approach to others. In fact, in some works created by fans, we find a direct application of Bowie's mode of operation.

How, then, does the moving image fit into this complex semiotic approach? *The Next Day* cover showed a hauntological approach to his own encyclopedia of still imagery. Beyond this, we can certainly find within Bowie's music a similar combinatory tendency: "Starman" borrows from its chorus-opening leap from "Somewhere Over the Rainbow" and its prechorus ostinato from "You Keep Me Hangin' On," while "Strangers When We Meet" picks up a bass line from "Gimme Some Lovin'" (not to mention the many *self*-referential borrowings we find in his work). These musical signs serve many purposes, pointing the listener to a variety of different performers, contexts, and styles, all of which deepen our engagement with Bowie's songwriting while revealing his own fannish tendencies. On a less obvious level, Bowie borrows and plays with familiar musical elements all the time. He apes the singing style of Newley, the music hall influences present in the Kinks and the Beatles, and even some of Led Zeppelin's rock style (all in recordings before 1971!). The work of Leah Kardos and of Chris O'Leary both show this very clearly.[40] Among fans, both academic and general, there is great interest in not only the *what* of Bowie's work, but also the *how* (i.e., the construction of his works). How did Bowie make and remake his own style through the manipulation of common cultural signs in music, or what Tagg calls musemes? Musical analysis of Bowie's songs can make this clear; with it, we discover threads of influence and reference that expand the meaning of familiar songs. We have been taught to delve deeply into Bowie's projects and are rewarded with labyrinthine references and connections.

The addition of the moving image, then, is an extension or completion of the working procedure that already existed in Bowie's music and still imagery. Here, too, we see his tendency to borrow and carefully craft a shared lexicon of signs within his fan community. For Bowie, the moving image was not ancillary, but central to his work. Yes, his music *could* exist in isolation, but with the addition of music videos (a staple from his earliest days) and other filmed projects, it became more complete and powerful, a modern day *gesamtkunstwerk*. His works' encyclopedias became more baroque, more complex as he built an audiovisual world, one that encompassed not only his music but also his public-facing self.

---

[40] See Leah Kardos, "Bowie Musicology: Mapping Bowie's Sound and Music Language across the Catalogue," *Continuum* 31, no. 4 (2017): 552–63; and Chris O'Leary, *Ashes to Ashes: The Songs of David Bowie 1976–2012* (London: Repeater Books, 2019).

As Frayling notes, such an approach was frustrating for 1970s cultural observers. In an era that prized authentic expression in rock, Bowie sought instead to express himself through a web of references. This procedure was evident in his earliest works, including his first music videos.

Case Study: *Love You till Tuesday*

In 1969, young David Bowie struggled to break through to a broader audience. He had released one solo album, with another due that year, but had not yet found wide popularity. His manager Kenneth Pitt decided to make a promotional video for Bowie, on the advice of German television producer Gunther Schneider.[41] The project became the twenty-eight-minute *Love You till Tuesday*, a compilation of sorts that featured music from Bowie's debut album (released by Deram in 1967) along with "Space Oddity," which would appear on his second album, *David Bowie* or *Space Oddity* (depending on the market). An audiovisual document of a performer immediately before he became a well-known star, *Love You till Tuesday* is a fascinating curio. Within it, we can see some of the latent stylistic tendencies that would mark Bowie's later work. However, in this iteration, the seams are visible. That is to say, the process by which David Jones became "David Bowie" is all the clearer in this moment before the transformation was complete. As such, it provides an excellent case study for the way the moving image would become integral to Bowie's persona and public image.

Love You till Tuesday did not become a touchstone in Bowie's public image for one simple reason: it was not widely released in 1969. Rather, the film was shelved for some fifteen years before receiving a UK videocassette release.[42] The film, then, is not interesting for its role in the collective memory or visual lexicon of Bowie fans. Instead, it shows us the way Bowie's idiosyncratic use of the moving image developed. Notably, this short film seems to have had more of a budget than some of Bowie's later, more famous music videos. There are costumes, sets, some outdoor shooting, and even a few extras. In comparison, the videos for "John, I'm Only Dancing" and "Life On Mars?" seem primitive.

---

[41] "David Bowie—Love You till Tuesday (short film, 1969)," *DavidBowieNews.com*, December 14, 2016, https://www.davidbowienews.com/2016/12/love-you-till-tuesday-short-film-1969/ Accessed March 6, 2021.

[42] Ibid.

They show relatively little in the way of planning, narrative, or environment; much of their power comes from the strength of the performance captured and the editing of image to music. This availability of funds for *Love You till Tuesday* is telling in the final analysis: it would seem that Pitt and Bowie were able to create a detailed plan for the film with director Malcolm J. Thomson. We might approach *Love You till Tuesday* as an early example of Bowie's vision for his use of the moving image, then. It is revelatory of the sort of performance a young Bowie valued (gestural and theatrical) as well as the way he related to and used the filmic apparatus as an outgrowth of his music-theatrical work. In *Love You till Tuesday*, we can see the shift from stage to film acting or character embodiment. This shift came to be central to Bowie's conception and dissemination of his characters, as the next chapters show. Though *Love You till Tuesday* does not match later works in its visual sophistication, it is nonetheless instructive for its approach to character and its incorporation of popular culture signs and images. It shows the foundations of Bowie's burgeoning style.

Camera and the Gaze

For viewers coming to *Love You till Tuesday* after 1969, it is easy to see and feel the difference between its approach and that of later Bowie music videos. It shares some surface visual similarities, especially in its use of a stark white studio background (also visible in later videos for "Life on Mars?" and "Be My Wife"). Beyond this, though, the promotional compilation feels quite different, in large part because it uses the filmic apparatus in a different way. In "classic" Bowie videos of the 1970s, there is an upending of filmic tradition: Bowie is treated as an object of desire, on display in ways that even objects of male beauty were not in traditional Hollywood film. Here, though, the camera treats him differently. He is seen performing as he might in a concert setting, most notably in "Let Me Sleep beside You" and "Sell Me a Coat." In most cases, he avoids direct address to camera in these songs and imports the trappings of staged rock performance to this short film.[43] (That is, he plays his guitar and uses a microphone, despite the fact that he is performing to a pre-recorded track.) One notable difference comes

---

[43] The opening song, "Love You till Tuesday," is a notable exception. The film opens with Bowie singing directly to camera and ends with him playfully popping back into frame to speak directly to the audience. The treatment is notable in the context of the entire short film: Bowie's relation to the camera and the audience changes and is somewhat unstable. It suggests some of the style that will mark his later videos but does not commit to it.

at the end of the title song, when he speaks to camera. In this way, these songs are most similar to earlier promotional rock films. The Beatles recorded such promos for songs from *Help!* (1965). These also feature the group performing as though live: they hold their instruments and mime playing as the album track is heard. As in "Let Me Sleep beside You," the performance itself is not particularly surprising or exciting. It merely documents the band at the height of their popularity, performing songs that would sell around the world. The point, it seems, is to record and show off the young musicians in action, not to create a piece of video art.

Alternatively, some numbers in *Love You till Tuesday* embrace the narrative possibilities of the music video form. Bowie is cast as a traditional love interest in "When I Live My Dream." This sequence features Hermione Farthingale, member of Bowie's band Feathers and real-life love interest, as the female object of Bowie's desire. She is presented in a way that aligns with filmic tradition, allowing audience members to see themselves in her and imagine a relationship with Bowie. When Bowie sings to the "you" of the song's lyrics, the film cuts to Farthingale, reinforcing the narrative of Bowie and Farthingale as the couple depicted in the song. Throughout, Bowie remains the main character and narrator, while Farthingale is extorted, viewed, and loved from afar. She has no real agency within the short film, but is given ample screen time. She does not speak or lipsync in the video; rather, she is a female audience insert, present to embody the narrative of the song. John Berger describes the visual treatment of men and women as divided into the acting and the acted upon, respectively, and here Bowie's use of the moving image retains that distinction.[44] Unlike later videos in which Bowie will problematize this formulation, here he makes use of the common grammar of film as understood by his audience.

Allusion, Mime, and Gesture

Bowie's magpie-like use of common cultural signs is present even in this earliest music video venture. As already noted, the sound of many of the songs featured in this short film owes much to other contemporary artists, as well as to more distant British popular music history. Visually, the film uses similarly allusive moves to link Bowie to his current persona: young, hip Londoner. The second

---

[44] John Berger, *Ways of Seeing* (New York: Penguin, 1972), 46.

song's establishing shots do some of this work. Street scenes serve to ground us in the cultural milieu of the artist and to set up the theme of "Sell Me a Coat." It is notable that the sign for designer Mr. Fish is displayed prominently. Not only would this have connoted a rock star type of sartorial cool (Mr. Fish dressed, for example, Mick Jagger), but it can be retroactively read today as representative of some of Bowie's own iconic fashion. He wears a Mr. Fish dress on the British cover of *Man Who Sold the World* in a marked stylistic turn from the late-1960s mod on display in this film.

Beyond references to time and place, *Love You till Tuesday* also includes allusions to specific works and people. More importantly, though, Bowie creates in *Love You till Tuesday* the first video for "Space Oddity," a short film that is more cinematic than much of what surrounds it and is directly influenced by film. Written expressly for this *Love You till Tuesday* project, "Space Oddity" is undoubtedly the most well known of this collection's songs, even if the recording featured here is not the most famous version. Introducing the character of Major Tom, "Space Oddity" casts a long shadow over Bowie's career and songwriting. Though much of the video features Bowie (playing multiple roles) enacting the narrative of the song, there are moments that break from strict narrative. "Space Oddity" is, of course, influenced by Stanley Kubrick's *2001: A Space Odyssey*. Though a recreation of that film would have been impossible on the budget presumably available for *Love You till Tuesday*, there are still moments here that point toward *2001's* visuals and style. Its integration into a somewhat campy music video is interesting and a little jarring. It is, of course, in keeping with the mixing of genres, styles, and references that marks so much of Bowie's work more broadly.

Indeed, bodily gesture acts in *Love You till Tuesday* as a type of allusion, too. Bowie utilizes gestural mimicry to place himself in a lineage of rock stars: "Let Me Sleep beside You" features a pelvic performance that points to Elvis Presley. Though the movement here is borrowed, it points to the careful control of the body that can be seen in decades of videos and stage performance to follow. It is revealing that some famous Bowie gestures are present even in this embryonic stage. As he cries in "Rubber Band," he brings his hands to his face in a gesture that would be immortalized in Mick Rock's concert photography of the Ziggy era. His hip-thrusting rock performance in "Let Me Sleep beside You" echoes in the opening of the 1979 "Boys Keep Swinging" video.

The studied physicality of his performance throughout his career is likely an echo of his mime training. That training is explicitly showcased in *Love You till*

Tuesday, in the segment titled "The Mask (A Mime)." This is the only part of the video that is not in support of Bowie's music; it features only spoken voiceover. It is tempting to read this segment as prophetic: a man steals a mask from a junk shop that, when he puts it on, garners positive attention and leads to fame. Eventually, the mask takes over and changes its wearer. In a final performance with the mask, it gains complete control. The camera pulls back as Bowie, alone in a spotlight, writhes and attempts to tear the mimed mask from his face. "Strangled on stage, they said!," he narrates, adding, "funny, though, they didn't mention anything about a mask." Of course, in this mime performance, the mask is not present at all: it was the performer's own face all along.

It is hard not to interpret this skit as an allegory for fame and, particularly, for Bowie's relationship to it. Waldrep reads the skit as predictive of the 1970s, a decade when Bowie "seemed afraid to take it [the mask] off lest his fame fade."[45] Instead, one might see the constant switching of masks as a mechanism against this strangulation: if no single mask is allowed to take hold, Bowie cannot be controlled by it. Masks were a feature of his public persona even from this early stage, when each song in *Love You till Tuesday* found a different bodily and facial expression. Bowie's actorly approach to both fame and musical expression is on display in this early promotional video.

Conclusion

Love You till Tuesday displays the typical features of Bowie's approach to the moving image. Intertwined with the complex meaning of his music, audiovisual media served to deepen and complicate those original auditory meanings. This transmedia communication was central to Bowie's creation of self on the public stage. The early promotional film shows some of the modes of visual communication that would become central to Bowie's music video style, most especially his emerging relationship to the spectator and camera, as well as his treatment of the body as object. *Love You till Tuesday* presents these ideas in their embryonic form, setting the stage for more experimentation in a variety of moving image applications. Even at this early stage, it is obvious that Bowie and his management recognized the power of the screen for his particular brand

---

[45] Waldrep, *The Aesthetics of Self-Invention*, 110.

of rock stardom. For Bowie, dubbing himself "the Actor" even on his audio recordings, the embodiment of a character (particularly on screen) is a central aspect of many of his musical works. Analyses in the following two chapters interrogate this power, approaching it through an implicitly semiotic lens. Seeing Bowie as auteur of his own public image, these case studies locate the specific methods used in his manipulation of the moving image.

3

Cracked Actor: The Music Video and Bowie as Moving Image

We begin with a blank white screen. As the camera moves down, stark images come into focus. Shockingly red-orange hair fills the screen, followed by mismatched pupils. Finally, it becomes clear that these features make up a whole: David Bowie. The singer's 1973 "Life on Mars?" video opens with a reframing of his most identifiable features; he is refracted through the video format and becomes even more striking. This approach is typical of Bowie's music videos and helps to show exactly how important the medium was in the development of his career.

It seems obvious to state that musicians shape and manipulate their public image through the use of the music video. From the 1970s onward, this medium has been a central tool for the music industry. In the case of David Bowie, though, the music video is yet more important. In these short films, Bowie establishes a longstanding visual lexicon for himself. He also incorporates a visual language drawn from feature films before flipping the script on that filmic style, empowering the viewer, and creating a closer bond between the spectator and the subject of the video. In many ways, Bowie's videos not only helped define him in the eyes of the public, but also helped to define a music video style that would be used by many other artists.

At the beginning of Bowie's career, the music video form was not what we know today. While Bowie did shoot promotional shorts in support of his early 1970s work, such films lacked the platform and audience attention that would come in later years, with the rise of MTV in 1981 and the internet more recently. However, Bowie recognized the importance of the form and adopted it, incorporating music video as another tool in his complex creation of a public self. Speaking in 1972 of his stage performances, Bowie stated, "I'm the last person to pretend that I'm a radio. I'd rather go out and be a color television set."[1] The visual

---

[1] Quoted in "Museum of Television and Radio Screening Series: David Bowie: Sound + Vision {Package 1}," https://www.paleycenter.org/collection/item/?q=all&p=529&item=T:70895 Accessed October 4, 2021.

had always been important to Bowie, and here he seems to have conceived of his music as a hybrid audiovisual text. This is indicative of the strong multimedia turn in Bowie's work, and is all the more striking for its early appearance. (That is, for a musician in 1972 to be so overtly media-focused.) Even before a musician was virtually *required* to craft a clear, impactful multimedia presence, Bowie saw it as important and moved toward the establishment of his own visual style. That style incorporated influence from German Expressionist cinema, Andy Warhol and his superstars, Kubrick and other contemporary filmmakers, and various stage performance styles including mime and kabuki. This mélange helped to distinguish Bowie from his contemporaries; the press materials circulated by his record label highlight this.

Though his music videos are not mentioned in RCA press biographies until the very late 1970s, these publicity materials nonetheless focus on Bowie as multimedia artist. A 1974 release speaks of his *1980 Floor Show*, aired on NBC's *Midnight Special* in 1973 (and discussed in the next chapter). In the words of that release, "both the critics and the public agreed that the program was the most outrageous and successful marriage of rock theatrics and television ever conceived."[2] This focus on theatrics and new media outlets couches one of Bowie's most consistent interests: storytelling. The music video apparatus is, of course, a very useful way of expressing a story. Bowie seems to have come to serial, image-based storytelling quite early. In interviews, he credits his work at an advertising agency with planting this seed. Storyboarding, he says, or "putting your ideas down on paper in chronological order," stayed with him from that experience and "right from the beginning, [he] was storyboarding videos."[3] He kept this practice through his final videos; storyboard-style drawings for "Lazarus" were displayed in the final iterations of the *David Bowie Is* exhibition in the summer of 2018. With a solid understanding of visual art principles from his school days and the capacity to storyboard, Bowie was able to communicate his visual ideas to the directors with whom he collaborated.

Bowie's music video output spans the years from the form's emergence to the development of what Carol Vernallis calls the current "new media swirl"—a media landscape in which music videos influence film language, and vice versa. This new media swirl is also shaped by the way music videos are consumed: on

---

[2] RCA biography of David Bowie, November 1974, Jeff Gold Collection ARC-0037 Box AF3, Folder 53, Rock and Roll Hall of Fame Library and Archives, Cleveland, Ohio.
[3] "David Bowie Episode of Video Killed the Radio Star" uploaded by Richard's David Bowie Channel, February 15, 2020, https://www.youtube.com/watch?v=QY59_Dgp7EI Accessed March 13, 2021.

demand, on a variety of personal devices, and with online paratexts informing their meaning. Rather than attempting to document each stage of Bowie's music video development, I instead focus on important moments that relate to his establishment of a distinctive style and manipulation of self through the moving image. This chapter's case studies come from three eras: the birth of the music video form in "Life on Mars?" (1973), the nascent MTV aesthetic of "Ashes to Ashes" (1980), and the "new media swirl" of "Where Are We Now?" (2013). Each shows a different stage and strategy in Bowie's approach to the art form. Each also illuminates a different collaborative effort with the video directors and artists. Lisa Perrott has written at length about these collaborative videos, focusing on Bowie's interaction with the *avant garde* art world, as well as his position as a conduit, a medium expressing his own work and the work of others.[4] Rather than retread this nuanced research, I instead concentrate on the final product as text in each case, reading that text for its visual style and relationship to Bowie's complete oeuvre.

Throughout his career, David Bowie was both conscious of and consistent in his establishment of a semiotic toolbox through which he could present himself. This musical and visual encyclopedia, shared among his fans, allowed for nuanced and highly referential audiovisual texts to be created and consumed with a relatively stable common understanding or meaning. In Bowie's music videos, we see the distillation of a style that permeated all of his output, presenting an important first step toward unpacking Bowie's other works. Music video provided an ideal form for the development of this style. In "Life on Mars?", we see the establishment and refinement of the main signposts of the Ziggy Stardust persona. The video is an essential component of Bowie's early success and a key to understanding his use of the medium. "Life on Mars?" also highlights Bowie's idiosyncratic use of the filmic apparatus, an approach that differentiated him from his contemporaries. "Ashes to Ashes" and "Where Are We Now?" represent a more self-reflexive approach. Explicitly utilizing the public images of Bowie's decades-long career, these videos expect a certain multimedia competence of their viewers and create intertextual connections. They serve not only to bring each song to life in a visually arresting way, but also to draw the viewer into the complex meaning-making of David Bowie, connecting to *his* past but also to their own as spectators.

---

[4] See, for example, *Transmedia Directors: Artistry, Industry, and New Audiovisual Aesthetics*, ed. Carol Vernallis, Holly Rogers, and Lisa Perrott (New York: Bloomsbury Academic, 2020).

This chapter is not intended to be an exhaustive survey of Bowie's music video work. In highlighting these three videos, I seek to analyze representative texts as a way to understand the whole of his output. Because of this, there are some obvious and striking gaps. I do not discuss the music videos of the 1990s, including the visually arresting *1. Outside* and *Earthling* videos. Similarly, Bowie's final videos from *Blackstar* are not a focus of this chapter. I do not exclude these works because they are unimportant; rather, I focus on other videos as more emblematic of Bowie's overarching style and indicative of its development. Other analyses of these important final videos exist and, for my purposes, they are less directly applicable.

I include music videos in the "Bowie as auteur" section of this study, rather than the "Bowie as image" section. Given the traditional power dynamics within the music industry and music video production, this may seem counterintuitive. However, as Carol Vernallis and Lisa Perrott have shown in their respective studies, it is not always the case that record labels alone control music video endeavors. Perrott investigates the collaborations between Bowie and his video directors. Vernallis and Hannah Ueno, in their interviews with video directors, provide some insight into the process by which videos are made. As they state, the power dynamic within video production is a fluid one: "In truth, power and creative direction shift continually along several dimensions and exist in tension between commercial requirements and aesthetic aims."[5] Though it is now common for directors to storyboard and pitch a video concept, such planning was not typical at the birth of the medium. In fact, Bowie began his music video career with much more input and control than is the current norm for a musician. His later music videos show a continuation of this assertion of control, as is typical of many of his works.

These three case studies ("Life on Mars?", "Ashes to Ashes," and "Where Are We Now?") represent different stages in the development of the music video as a form. They present different working methods, final products, and approaches to audience engagement. Authors like Vernallis and Mathias Bonde Korsgaard have charted the form's development, arguing for different approaches to the analysis of, for example, videos from 1981 versus ones from 2010.[6] Each of the Bowie videos discussed in this chapter falls into a different era of music

---

[5] Carol Vernallis and Hannah Ueno, "Interview with Music Video Director and Auteur Floria Sigismondi," *Music, Sound, and the Moving Image* 7, no. 2 (Autumn 2013): 170.

[6] See, for example, Mathias Bonde Korsgaard, *Music Video after MTV: Audiovisual Studies, New Media, and Popular Music* (New York: Routledge, 2017).

video history: standalone, pre-MTV works; the MTV golden age; and online, streaming distribution. Andrew Goodwin, Carol Vernallis, John Richardson, and others have proposed analytical frameworks for understanding music video in its various stages of development and stylistic permutations.[7] These eras differ in technology, aesthetics, aims, audience, mode of engagement, and accessibility. To pair such videos together may seem a fool's errand, given their stark contrasts. However, all are united by Bowie's unique approach to the audiovisual and, of course, by the music itself. As Leah Kardos has shown, there is much in Bowie's songwriting and performance that suggests unity rather than division throughout his long and varied career. She identifies certain musical features as particularly Bowiean: for example, "throwing his voice like a javelin" with a leap and slow descent that typifies many of his choruses.[8] Indeed, "Life on Mars?" and "Ashes to Ashes" both show such construction. I propose a similar sort of analysis: building on the productive musicological work of Kardos and others, this chapter unites that aural analysis with a similar visual approach. The chapter seeks to chart the core features of Bowie's music video audiovisual style, across and in spite of many changes to the medium itself.

One important, groundbreaking manipulation of the filmic apparatus visible in Bowie's early music videos is their play with gaze and power. In Laura Mulvey's seminal "Visual Pleasure and Narrative Cinema," she addresses the power dynamics and psychological implications of the filmic gaze.[9] Traditionally coded as male, that gaze in Classic Hollywood film offered male spectators a voyeuristic escape and wish fulfillment. The camera's gaze and the construction of film narratives afforded them a position of power with respect to the object of the cinematic gaze. Of course, music video is an entirely different form with very different conventions. It lacked the structure and history attached to golden age Hollywood film. But Bowie, present near the very birth of music video style as we know it, borrowed and upended traditional filmic conventions in many ways, not least of which relates to the gaze. Where female characters were, by

---

[7] See, for example, Andrew Goodwin, *Dancing in the Distraction Factory: Music Television and Popular Culture* (Minneapolis: University of Minnesota Press, 1992); Carol Vernallis, *Unruly Media: YouTube, Music Video, and the New Digital Cinema* (New York: Oxford University Press, 2013); and John Richardson, *An Eye for Music: Popular Music and the Audiovisual Surreal* (New York: Oxford University Press, 2012).

[8] Leah Kardos, "Bowie Musicology: Mapping Bowie's Sound and Music Language across the Catalogue," *Continuum: Journal of Media and Cultural Studies* 31, no. 4 (2017): 556.

[9] Laura Mulvey, "Visual Pleasure and Narrative Cinema," in *Film Theory and Criticism: Introductory Readings*, ed. Leo Braudy and Marshall Cohen (New York: Oxford University Press, 1999), 833–44.

and large, the object of the gaze in what Mulvey calls "hermetically sealed" Hollywood film, Bowie would trouble that closure and its gendered dynamics. When Mulvey calls Hollywood films' narrative worlds "sealed," she means that they exist in their own, complete world, separate from our own. Audiences (particularly male audiences) are able to insert themselves into that narrative through identification with a character, but by and large, film worlds were observed from the outside without the viewed subject's overt acknowledgment of that observation. Visual pleasure was voyeuristic: one viewed, but was not viewed in return, as the interaction was not reciprocal.

In Bowie's music videos, though, there is a distinctive change in visual pleasure. Such pleasure is indeed present: it seems to be the *raison d'etre* for these short films. However, unlike the pleasurable possibilities presented in Hollywood cinema, these videos are not "hermetically sealed." When Bowie is on display, it is a conscious, open display. That is, Bowie displays himself, welcoming and acknowledging the gaze of the camera and, by extension, the audience. He stares straight to camera, seeming to obliterate the fourth wall that divides him from his audience. Unlike the objects of scopophilic pleasure in traditional narrative film, Bowie directly presents his body for the viewing pleasure of the audience. There is no fig leaf of narrative separation, nor is there, generally speaking, a female object of similar scopophilic interest.[10] Bowie flips the script inherited from narrative film and offers himself, in all his unique, androgynous, early 1970s glory, as the object of a consensual moment of viewing pleasure. This acknowledgment of the audience's viewing is sometimes extraordinarily overt. For example, in the "Jean Genie" video, we see fragmented shots of Bowie's face and body, a hallmark of his early style. Here, though, he sees us: creating a rectangle with his hands, Bowie views the camera through his own "viewfinder," clearly acknowledging and welcoming the gaze of the camera and, by extension, the audience.

To see himself as both surveyor and surveyed is part of Bowie's approach to the moving image. It is also part of the revolutionary nature of his use of audiovisual media. In the same year the early video "John, I'm Only Dancing" was filmed, John Berger released his seminal BBC series and book, *Ways of Seeing*. Berger

---

[10] The only possible female object of visual pleasure in early Bowie videos is Cyrinda Foxe in the "Jean Genie" short. She is, however, given much less screen time than Bowie and his band. Though she and Bowie appear in a single shot together, they do not interact at all. The traditional cinematic framing that Mulvey criticizes (that of the male protagonist as audience insert and the female character as object of visual pleasure to be possessed) is still upended within this video.

and his collaborators took on classical painting, advertising, "girlie magazines," and more, addressing how certain subjects are presented and seen. In his music videos, we can see Bowie troubling many of the established power dynamics of viewing that Berger and company lay bare. In the third section of Berger's study, he examines presence and depiction, differentiating between the treatment of men and women in visual media. A man, in Berger's formulation, has a presence based on "power which he exercises on others," while traditionally a woman is "manifest in her gestures, voice, opinions, expressions, clothes, chosen surroundings, taste," and more.[11] The distinction may be useful in thinking about the way Bowie chooses to present himself in promotional films. Unlike the active, act*ing* man, Bowie presents himself in the role of the "surveyed," to use Berger's formulation. He presents himself to be seen and, as Berger suggests, seems aware of that gaze in much the same way that the subjects of nude classical paintings seem to be. It is not surprising that this strategy occurs during Bowie's most ambiguous period, in terms of sexuality and gendered presentation. To challenge such engrained ways of seeing is disruptive.

This may seem to be too much importance to place on some direct eye contact and sequences that frame Bowie's body as an object of viewing pleasure. However, these stylistic choices take on outsized importance when viewed in context. The form of the music video and its conventions had not been solidified in 1972. Bowie's stylistic choices resonated throughout not only his music video career, but also the promotional shorts of those who would follow. Vernallis discusses this intimacy as an integral convention of music video's language.[12] By the time of her writing in 2004, this idea of a traversal of the boundary between audience and performer was accepted and expected. While this is, of course, not entirely due to Bowie and his choices, we can see the clear shift happening in his work. His choice to separate from a traditional filmic style and apparatus marks his early music videos as different and important. Indeed, they garner much of their power from precisely this difference. As the following case studies show, Bowie's auteuristic manipulation of the camera and its relationship to the filmic object helped to define him in the eyes of generations of audiences. This choice also helps to clarify his developing audiovisual style in a broad range of projects beyond the music video.

---

[11] John Berger, *Ways of Seeing* (New York: Penguin, 1972), 46.
[12] Carol Vernallis, *Experiencing Music Video: Aesthetics and Cultural Context* (New York: Columbia University Press, 2004), 57.

Bowie and Music Video in the 1970s

Among Bowie's first true music videos were those shot by Mick Rock in 1972. The "John, I'm Only Dancing" video is the earliest and perhaps the most undiluted Bowie vision. Rock speaks of the video shoot, sharing that Bowie called him with a problem: the song was to be released as a single and it needed promotion. Rock notes that there was no budget to speak of, and absolutely no preplanning.[13] How did the video succeed in becoming what Lester Bangs pinpoints as the "very moment the modern idea of the video was born"?[14] "You're talking about a very special performer. Maybe it wouldn't have worked with another performer," according to Rock.[15] Bowie's performance and sense of his own impact on film were central to the final product. Though he did not have a hand in the crucial editing stage, the artist did play to and for the camera in ways that are consistent throughout his later work.

For "John, I'm Only Dancing," the video's success is at least partially due to Bowie's live stagecraft. Rock shot the clip at London's Rainbow Theater, where Bowie was scheduled to perform. The stage was already set for that performance, complete with the scaffolding that would surround Bowie and his band, the Spiders from Mars. That stage set was apparently influenced by a production of *Cabaret* that Bowie had seen.[16] (In fact, that musical would be a source of inspiration for later projects, too, as seen in the next chapter.) Bowie himself drafted sketches for the set design, now preserved in his personal archive. The sketches show a close attention to detail, even specifying the look of the stair steps on stage.[17] Longtime Bowie friend and collaborator Lindsey Kemp was also present with his dancers. Bowie had worked with Kemp for years, as evidenced by *Pierrot in Turquoise (Or The Looking Glass Murders)*, broadcast on Scottish Television in 1970. Much of Bowie's gestural language is influenced by Kemp and the tradition of mime; this was the case throughout his career and is certainly true of "John, I'm Only Dancing." Thus, the total lack of preproduction cited

---

[13] "Music Video Night Presents: 'David Bowie Is' an evening with Mick Rock @ Brooklyn Museum," video, 12:22, uploaded January 5, 2019, https://vimeo.com/309676188 Accessed October 4, 2021.

[14] Quoted in Nate Chinen, "David Bowie, Master of the Music Video" *New York Times*, January 11, 2016, https://www.nytimes.com/2016/01/12/arts/music/david-bowie-master-of-the-music-video.html Accessed October 4, 2021.

[15] "Music Video Night Presents: 'David Bowie Is' an evening with Mick Rock @ Brooklyn Museum," video, 12:22, uploaded January 5, 2019, https://vimeo.com/309676188 Accessed October 4, 2021.

[16] Kevin Cann, *Any Day Now: The London Years 1947–1974* (London: Adelita, 2011), 264.

[17] See David Bowie Is augmented reality app, released 2019.

by Rock was only partially true: the video itself may have had no planning, but the *performance* certainly did. This is unsurprising, as Bowie frequently commented on the importance of the visual to his stage performance style. D. A. Pennebaker's documentary of the final Ziggy Stardust concert in 1973 shows this clearly: staging, lighting, and choreography all come together in each song like a miniature stage musical. To see "John, I'm Only Dancing" as entirely spontaneous, then, might be misleading. To see it as an accurate depiction of Bowie the performer, though, would be spot on.

Perhaps the most striking moments in "John, I'm Only Dancing" are those that clearly manipulate and acknowledge the filmic apparatus. Much of the video shows Bowie and the Spiders from Mars performing the song on the dramatic, dimly lit stage; the only interpolations are shots of Kemp and his dancers and, separately, closeups of Bowie. It is in these closeups that we can see the development of his music video language. Framed to capture his head and shoulders, these interpolations show Bowie lit from the side, enveloped by an empty black setting. With the stark lighting, his distinctive Ziggy coiffure seems to glow. Rock holds a frontal view of Bowie when he is singing in these shots, but cuts quickly to different views between lyrical lines, sometimes showing a slowly rotating Bowie in bust form. This abstraction of Bowie's face and features serves to do what much of his music video output does: it establishes the visual lexicon by which this era of Bowie's persona is known and recognized. While the remainder of the video follows the general parameters of music video from this era (namely, documenting performance with little deviation), these sections point to the way Bowie would come to use music video in his multimedia approach to rock stardom.

Interestingly, Rock is insistent upon Bowie's collaborative nature, stating, "he never asked me to alter a frame … he knew how to work with other people."[18] We might see this, especially in the "John, I'm Only Dancing" and "Life on Mars?" videos, as a reflection of the strength of Bowie's pre-performance planning and his comfort with Rock as a photographer. The two had worked together many times on still photography prior to these music videos. Rock's images of the Ziggy Stardust era are some of the best known and most instantly recognizable of Bowie's career. Much like the elaborate stage sets Bowie collaborated on for later tours, we might see these early videos as direct extensions of a planned, iterable performance. While Bowie did not ask Rock to alter any captured images, he

---

[18] "Music Video Night Presents: 'David Bowie Is' an evening with Mick Rock @ Brooklyn Museum," video, 12:22, uploaded January 5, 2019, https://vimeo.com/309676188 Accessed October 4, 2021.

did plan *what would be captured* very carefully. This is perhaps unsurprising in a performer who was so very open about the construction of his public self. These early videos, then, present a mutation of his stagecraft that points toward greater future experiments. In these videos and his early television appearances, Bowie evinced a clear understand of the camera and its gaze. His later work in storyboarding and collaboratively planning his music videos is a more complex realization of that innate, early understanding of the moving image apparatus.

"Life on Mars?" and Bowie's Visual Vocabulary

If music video was born with "John, I'm Only Dancing," we might say it came of age with "Life on Mars?". The nascent style in the "John" closeups comes to the fore in "Mars." In fact, that stylistic approach is almost the entire concept of the latter video. In this, we can see Bowie's developing understanding of his own visual strengths and the mode of communication that would bring him the broadest audience. The video's focus on Bowie's iconic features, use of direct address to create intimacy, and abstraction of its subject all point to Bowie's mature audiovisual style.

The "Life on Mars?" video, recorded in July 1973, has become one of Bowie's most recognizable. This is, at least in part, due to its economy of image: nothing is present apart from Bowie himself and a stark, white background. Bowie sings "Life on Mars?" while Rock's camera documents him at varying distances. In 1983, Bowie described the video and his early style as having a "very graphic, white, almost *Vogue* look."[19] This "*Vogue* look" does indeed copy midcentury fashion magazines in their examination of faces. It is undoubtedly a main feature of Bowie's videos: "big faces, big bits of faces, eyes, against stark white backdrops" populate "Life on Mars?" and "Jean Genie."[20] Apart from looking like a fashion magazine, this visual approach also serves to do what *Vogue* does: the style turns its human subject into a collection of parts, indeed into an object. The result, then, is an abstracted Bowie, turned into a collection of features through the camera's close scrutiny. Apart from his face and body, nothing else is shown against the video's white background. This approach shares much in common with the style

---

[19] "David Bowie Episode of Video Killed the Radio Star," uploaded by Richard's David Bowie Channel, February 15, 2020, https://www.youtube.com/watch?v=QY59_Dgp7EI Accessed March 13, 2021.
[20] Ibid.

of Busby Berkeley's film musicals, described by Lucy Fisher as being set "in the realm of pure imagery."[21] In fact, Fisher argues that in such musicals, Berkeley "generates an image of woman as 'image' itself."[22] Bowie and Rock take a similar tack in "Life on Mars?", abstracting and fetishizing Bowie's face and body.

Because so little changes within the image, Rock's editing choices become even more important in establishing the video's pace and tone. Rock treats Bowie's musical text as a framework for his visual rhythm. In the opening of "Life on Mars?", we see a fragmented image: Bowie's bright hair out of context against a white background, before the camera pans down to his mismatched pupils. The camera holds this view throughout the opening lines, not even showing Bowie's singing lips until Rock cuts to a midshot on the second stanza. This wider shot establishes the performer's image, showing Bowie's head and torso. The shot connects to the opening through its similarly limited color palette: orange, blue, and white, now shown in Bowie's attire as well as his face. Rock holds here until the pre-chorus, with the entrance of the cello line pushing both camera and song ahead into the more active and more thickly orchestrated chorus. Within this section, Rock cuts on each lyrical line to a different, closeup view of Bowie. The linkage between image and music is closer here than in "John, I'm Only Dancing": Rock speeds up his visual rhythm to match the heightening drama of the song as it reaches its first chorus and the highest literal and figurative pitch thus far. Throughout the chorus, Rock cuts repeatedly, often in the middle of lyrical lines. Mixing close and mid shots with the occasional wide view, Rock examines Bowie's performance from a number of angles. Finally, as the first chorus ends, the camera rests and captures Bowie's ecstatic sigh over the guitar riff that moves the song to its next section.

Beyond the editing, Rock's framing links closely to the musical work and its sound world. "Life on Mars?" alternates between a close, intimate sound world and much wider, more dramatic and fully orchestrated environment. It is interesting that Rock mimics the soundbox treatment at the video's opening, centering Bowie's face and keeping very close.[23] Aurally, the listener hears

---

[21] Lucy Fisher, "The Image of Woman as Image: The Optical Politics of *Dames*," *Film Quarterly* 30, no. 1 (Autumn 1976): 3.

[22] Fisher, "The Image of Woman as Image," 6.

[23] The soundbox as analytical framework comes from the work of Allan F. Moore and refers to the sonic space created by the audio mix. Production choices can create the illusion of physical proximity or distance within large or small aural spaces, all of which affect the way the listener perceives the work. See, for example, Allan F. Moore and Ruth Dockwray, "The Establishment of the Virtual Performance Space in Rock," *Twentieth-Century Music* 5, no. 2 (2008): 219–41.

Bowie's voice, centered and equally prominent alongside the piano. As the song progresses and the soundbox expands, more instruments are added and Bowie's voice recedes in prominence. In these opening verses and pre-chorus, Rock mirrors that expansion visually, giving wider shots of Bowie's body. It is all the more striking, then, when Rock cuts to extreme closeups in the chorus, picking out Bowie's features in the ways described above. This visual choice runs counter to the expanding soundbox and, in doing so, heightens the intensity of the chorus. The final chorus is shot in a similar, but even more impactful way. In addition to the closeups, Rock uses panning motion in a disorienting way, playing with the virtual space of the video. On the line "but the film is a saddening bore," Rock pans to the right, across Bowie's face at eye level. Mere moments after Bowie's face disappears to the left of the screen, it reappears on the right in a seemingly continuous pan. The illusion is one of an unreal space—or an unending phalanx of Bowies.[24] Rock keeps the audience on their toes, visually, when that panning motion changes direction at the end of the line. By playing with the audience's sense of space and position, Rock draws our focus ever more directly to the icons of this video: Bowie's fragmented features. It's a surprisingly dynamic and exciting video, for all of its limited visual content. Much of this, of course, is due to the charismatic performance of its star and Rock's skillful manipulation of it.

Within the video, Bowie's movements are carefully controlled. There are, in Mick Rock's words, "no distractions ... just David": this video features no interaction or juxtaposition with his (absent) band or with dancers, as in the "John, I'm Only Dancing" video.[25] Instead, the focus is on Bowie, his face, his body, and his interaction with the camera and, by extension, the viewer. This is a formula to which Bowie would return, most notably in the "Be My Wife" and "Heroes" videos: both feature blank backgrounds that offer little distraction and show similar editing choices. Bowie frequently embraced the tactic of direct address, staring straight into the camera. This is notable also in his breakout *Top of the Pops* performance of "Starman" from 1972. Though that performance has become legendary for his interaction with guitarist Mick Ronson (seen at the time as quite homoerotic), one of its more striking aspects is his comfort with

---

[24] Once again, the similarity to Berkeley's treatment of the body and space is striking.
[25] Michael Hann, "Watch the Reworked Video for David Bowie's Life on Mars," *The Guardian*, November 4, 2016, https://www.theguardian.com/music/musicblog/2016/nov/04/david-bowie-life-on-mars-watch-reworked-video-mick-rock Accessed February 19, 2021.

playing to the audience, both in studio and at home.[26] This is most notable in the second verse. Bowie begins the verse gazing straight ahead, in the direction of one of the two main cameras used to capture the performance. When he reaches the line "so I picked on you," he turns to the second camera, staring down its barrel and pointing directly to "you," the viewer and listener. Marking you as his chosen confidante in the performance, Bowie brings the spectator into his world, making the homoeroticism of the rest of the performance that much more personal and titillating. He turns the power of the video apparatus to his purpose.

This ability to create immediate, unselfconscious intimacy with the viewer was a great skill, and one used repeatedly throughout his career. In "Life on Mars?" it is present from the very first shot: as Rock pans down Bowie's face, the singer unabashedly stares back. Though a similar stark white studio setup was used in Bowie's *Love You till Tuesday* promotional film, this sort of direct address was much less frequent in it. Instead, those videos sought to capture or recreate live performance much more than they explored the unique, intimate possibilities of music video as a form. The creation of intimacy within "Life on Mars?" is likely aided by the actual intimacy of the set: only two cameramen were used, both of whom Bowie had working relationships with (Rock himself was second camera on the shoot).[27] Rock makes much of the fact that the video was shot on a shoestring budget.[28] They had no money for a larger crew or more help. The setting, too, feels at once close and vast, with its limitless expanse of white. Rock's framing choices help to heighten the spectator's closeness to Bowie, both in terms of his use of actual, tight closeups and in the way he controls the camera's movement toward and around his subject. It is obvious that he and Bowie knew each other and their common visual style well enough to play on tropes established in their earlier videos.

We might see the collaborators on this video as being more than just Bowie and Rock, though. Pierre Laroche's makeup design is of central visual importance, as is designer Freddie Burretti's suit. They, too, were longstanding collaborators.

---

[26] Bowie and Ronson were not the first frontman/guitarist duo to attract such attention. Bob Dylan and Robbie Robertson also sparked this kind of reaction during their 1965–6 tour. Still Ronson and Bowie's interaction was performed for the camera and broadcast around the nation, unlike Dylan/Robertson. For more on this interaction, see Howard Sounes, *Down the Highway: The Life of Bob Dylan*, New Updated Edition (New York: Grove Press, 2021), 198.

[27] Hann, "Watch the Reworked Video."

[28] Ibid.

Burretti designed many Ziggy Stardust-era costumes, while Laroche is perhaps best known for his makeup design featured on the *Aladdin Sane* album cover. Both are frequently cited in Bowie tributes. Laroche's work, in particular, clearly shows the main effect of this video: an intense focus on the features of Bowie that make up his popular culture iconography. Laroche's design consists mostly of highly pigmented blue eye shadow, stark light or white foundation, and a glossy lip. (Laroche also uses an orangey blush to accentuate Bowie's cheekbones, but this element is sometimes rendered invisible in the original, washed out color of the 1973 video. In Rock's 2016 edited reissue, the color is more saturated and this makeup choice more evident.) The effect is to break down Bowie's face into a combination of highly recognizable features, with his eyes as the most prominent. This focus would prove fruitful in the long run. Bowie's different sized pupils (frequently misattributed to heterochromia) became an indelible element of his public image.

In their intense focus on Bowie, his body, and his face, Rock and Bowie also helped to establish this narrow focus on certain iconic elements. Rock alternates between intense closeups and wider shots of Bowie within the empty studio space. This juxtaposition makes the eyes yet more striking when isolated. Beyond these shooting choices, though, Rock's processing of the film footage also helps to amplify this focus on Bowie's features. The original, 1973 release of the video features a washed-out color palette. Laroche's makeup and Burretti's designs share three colors: light blue, an orange-red, and white. Shot against a white backdrop, the two other colors pop yet more. Bowie's face is made to blend into the white of the studio backdrop, truly isolating his features as stark blue and orange spots within a field of white. Rock's 2016 re-edit of the video adds back much of the saturation. While it is beautiful, the effect accomplished by the original is somewhat dulled. Bowie becomes more complete, more human, and thus less like the amalgamation of features that "Life on Mars?" first celebrated. Bowie, the surveyed object regains some of his subject position and wholeness, and in this, the illusion of the video is weakened. It is worth noting, though, that Rock lists the 2016 version as his favorite.[29] In this, we might see the different goals Rock and Bowie had for the work. Rock's recent re-edit is undoubtedly more vivid and, in some ways, more visually striking. The 1973 release, though, fundamentally alters its subject in the ways analyzed above. Both are effective, but serve different purposes.

---

[29] Email message with the author, April 2, 2021.

The great accomplishment of "Life on Mars?" is its translation of Bowie's creative approach into video. More than in "John, I'm Only Dancing," here Bowie and Rock show an innate understanding of the power of video to complement and truly complete a musical expression. As Stan Hawkins writes, "with [video] recording, then, the magnification of the star, aurally and visually, reveals in close-up the body as much as its temperament."[30] Indeed, "Life on Mars?" magnifies its star in this video revelation. Bowie and his iconography become yet more solidified and easily communicable through their translation to video. In their approach to the burgeoning format, Rock and Bowie show that they understood its potential in ways that others would not for almost a decade.

"Ashes to Ashes": Recycling and Rebirth in Video Form

The music industry began to truly understand the power of music video in the 1980s, with the birth of MTV and the more widespread broadcasting of videos. Music videos were already promotional tools, but as Rock and Bowie's accounts above show, they were not always well supported financially. This is perhaps unsurprising: their reach could be somewhat limited, since there was not a centralized, dedicated broadcasting home for the music video. Once the cable channel MTV (and VH1, a year later) provided that home in the United States, music videos became much more elaborate and expensive affairs. The shift is visible in Bowie's work: we need only compare something like "Heroes" to *Jazzin' for Blue Jean* to see it.

"Ashes to Ashes," though it predated the birth of MTV, sums up some of the network's style features succinctly. Kay Dickinson writes of the connection between music video style and film editing style more generally, highlighting the shorter shot length and somewhat frenetic editing for which MTV's videos would become known.[31] In Dickinson's formulation, this editing and a focus not on narrative but on mood or lyrical content are paramount. "Ashes to Ashes" features many of these aesthetic considerations while also continuing the stylistic hallmarks evident in Bowie's early music video offerings. In particular,

---

[30] Stan Hawkins, *The British Dandy: Masculinity, Popular Music and Culture* (New York: Routledge, 2009), 62.

[31] Kay Dickinson, "Pop, Speed, Teenagers, and the 'MTV Aesthetic,'" in *Movie Music: The Film Reader*, ed. Kay Dickinson (New York: Routledge, 2003), 143–52.

the video plays to important visual signs in Bowie's personal iconography. Bowie's eyes feature prominently in closeup, as do various Bowie personae of the 1970s. Costuming and setting for each of these personae is clear, differentiated, and given ample screen time. In other words, these are signs intended to be understood. They are a part of the shared encyclopedia of Bowie fandom circa 1980. This focus is in keeping with the visual style developed in "Life on Mars?", but here "Ashes to Ashes" takes the established encyclopedia of visual signs that communicate Bowieness and plays with them, altering their context and their relationship to the broader world. The effect is both familiar and alien. For Bowie's ideal viewer, one steeped in his iconography, the video is a cornucopia of signs. To unpack them is to delve more deeply into the way Bowie's video style centered on the hauntological, haunted by others' works as well as his own.

Overtly, the song "Ashes to Ashes" makes reference to Bowie and his past. Major Tom of "Space Oddity" returns in lyrical form, his memory tarnished and haunted more than a decade after his first lyrical appearance. Similarly, the video for "Ashes to Ashes" plays on Bowie's established visual tropes, most prominently the Pierrot. A favorite of Expressionists like the composer Arnold Schoenberg, Pierrot's nineteenth- and twentieth-century history is rich.[32] The *commedia dell'arte* character not only has a long cultural history, but is also entwined with Bowie's onscreen persona. Aileen Dillane, Eoin Devereux, and Martin J. Power track the Pierrot in Bowie's career, noting its importance from the 1960s through the artist's final albums and videos.[33] As they note, "Ashes to Ashes" seems to "ostensibly have been about Major Tom, but the video is dominated by the Pierrot figure."[34] That figure, instantly recognizable in his white makeup and costume, appears on the album's cover as well. For Bowie devotees, the character was not new. Bowie appeared (as a different character, Cloud) in an early Lindsay Kemp production, *Pierrot in Turquoise*. In addition, the Pierrot is included on an early Bowie album cover. The first Phillips pressing of *Space Oddity* featured a pop art-inspired front cover, as well as an intricate back cover illustration designed by Bowie's friend George Underwood. There, Pierrot walks with his arm around an elderly lady—an image echoed directly in

---

[32] See, for example, Alexander Carpenter, "'Give a Man a Mask and He'll Tell You the Truth': Arnold Schoenberg, David Bowie, and the Mask of Pierrot," *Intersections* 30, no. 2 (2010): 5–24.
[33] Aileen Dillane, Eoin Devereux, and Martin J. Power, "Culminating Sounds and (En)visions: *Ashes to Ashes* and the Case for Pierrot," in *David Bowie: Critical Perspectives*, ed. Aileen Dillane, Eoin Devereux, and Martin J. Power (New York: Routledge, 2015), 35–55.
[34] Dillane, Devereux, and Power, "Culminating Sounds," 44.

the "Ashes to Ashes" music video. In ways both direct and oblique, Bowie points to his own iconic past as a way of reinventing himself for the 1980s.

The video is indeed a reinvention, for as much as it invokes and plays on Bowie's history. The visual style of the video was groundbreaking. Co-directing with David Mallet (with whom he had worked on the video for "Look Back in Anger," among other projects), Bowie helped to shape a visual style that played to the strengths of his earlier videos while exploiting new technological possibilities. In particular, the colorized sections of the video are striking, especially in contrast with the black-and-white sections of the whole. While the exaggerated color feels very era-appropriate, the lucky accident of the video's black sky effect is more disorienting. This effect, discovered by Mallet during the shooting of another project and put to compelling use here, serves to turn Pierrot's seaside scenes dark, both literally and figuratively.[35] It was not an original part of Bowie's planning, but became an important aspect of the video's visual contrasts.

This stark contrast is eased by the use of long, slow dissolves throughout—another difference from earlier Bowie videos that relied more heavily on quick, hard cuts. Some of these slow dissolves serve to transform Bowie and his visage, forcing visual connections that turn Bowie into an object onscreen, rather than a unified human subject. "Life on Mars?" accomplished a similar feat through its visual fracturing of Bowie, but here the filmic grammar asks the viewer to see Bowie as an extension of inanimate objects, and vice versa. For example, on the first appearance of the "Ashes to Ashes" chorus, the video dissolves from a tight closeup of Bowie's face as Major Tom into a wide view of Pierrot Bowie, the New Romantic extras, and a bulldozer pushing toward camera. Disorientingly, Bowie's eyes in the first sequence slowly dissolve into the headlights of the bulldozer which, in the second shot, threatens to overtake Pierrot and his coterie. A similar dissolve transitions into the second chorus, again using Bowie's eyes as the focal point. At the start of the next verse, the camera focuses on Pierrot Bowie's hand in extreme closeup. As Pierrot's fingers spasm, Mallet uses a long dissolve to take the viewer into the barred, padded cell occupied by yet another Bowie. The long dissolve creates another unlikely match cut: Pierrot's fingers become the Expressionist shadow of bars in the cell, diagonally slicing the frame.

In each of these moments, Bowie's own body is transformed into a threatening or stifling visual element for another version of the artist. His eyes become

---

[35] "David Bowie Episode of Video Killed the Radio Star" uploaded by Richard's David Bowie Channel, February 15, 2020, https://www.youtube.com/watch?v=QY59_Dgp7EI Accessed March 13, 2021.

headlights, his hands bars. As Bowie sings, "to get things done, you'd better not mess with Major Tom." That is, Bowie's own past forms a threatening presence in the lyrics of "Ashes to Ashes." Visually, the video transforms Bowie's body into the threat present in the song's lyrics. In doing so, it employs the strategy of visual fragmentation present in "Life on Mars?". Rather than presenting Bowie's face and body as an unproblematic object of pleasure, here the video troubles that notion, again paying close visual attention to the aspects of Bowie's physicality that are famous and revered, but transfiguring them into the objects by which Bowie is restrained or threatened. This unsubtle visual transformation speaks directly to the lyrical content of the song and, perhaps, the pressures felt by Bowie on the cusp of the 1980s.

A third long dissolve takes the viewer from a drowning Pierrot to the roiling, billowing set of Major Tom's captivity. This is the only one of the dissolve matches that plays on the setting rather than Bowie himself as the point of connection; it is worth noting, though, that both the Pierrot and Major Tom characters in this dissolve are shown to be trapped in their surroundings. Thus, these three different dissolve scenarios highlight the theme of the intrusion of the past and the inescapable pressures of the public star images Bowie had so carefully crafted. It serves as a commentary on stardom and persona in a multimedia setting (favored themes throughout Bowie's career, of course). Even though this final dissolve does not turn Bowie's own body into an object of fear or confinement, it does put the visual focus squarely on the things that threaten the existence of each character. The video shows familiar Bowie personae in precarious states, their precarity seemingly caused by the other characters themselves (through visual analogies). The end result is disorienting despite and *because of* its play with familiar signs. Sunil Manghani aligns "Ashes to Ashes" with Roland Barthes's idea of a text of bliss rather than one of pleasure.[36] He calls it "visually ambivalent," pointing at least in part to the "solarized" color as an unmooring technique.[37] We might see the above editing moments as similar pieces in this textual bliss, moments that complicate its reading. Here Bowie and Mallet combine the familiar with the intensely unreal to create a startling visual world.

Archival materials show that that visual world was at least partially conceived by Bowie himself. Hand-drawn storyboards for this video show that the color,

---

[36] Sunil Manghani, "The Pleasures of (Music) Video," in *Music/Video: Histories, Aesthetics, Media*, ed. Gina Arnold, Daniel Cookney, Kirsty Fairclough, and Michael Goddard (New York: Bloomsbury, 2017), 33–4.

[37] Manghani, "Pleasures of (Music) Video," 34.

camera angles, and more were carefully planned preproduction, a clear departure from the working style of the early 1970s Mick Rock videos. Such alteration in practice can be attributed to a number of factors: Bowie's growing knowledge of and comfort with film technology, the development of the music video as a form, and the increased budget for such experiments no doubt played a role. Indeed, the "Ashes to Ashes" video is frequently cited as one of the most expensive videos ever made, at the time of its production.[38] To plan carefully, then, would be of paramount importance. These planning materials show the control with which Bowie approached the dissemination of his public image. The Pierrot appears in these storyboards, almost identical to his costuming in the final video (created by Natasha Korniloff, who also costumed Bowie, Kemp, and company for the aforementioned *Pierrot in Turquoise*). Similarly, Bowie makes notes on the color manipulation he expects for certain sequences. In other videos throughout the 1980s, Bowie exercised a similar level of control. Julien Temple, with whom Bowie worked on the feature film *Absolute Beginners* (1986) and the videos for "Blue Jean" and "Day In, Day Out," described the musician as one of the most involved collaborators with whom he had worked.[39] His practice of storyboarding ideas for music videos seems to have continued throughout his career; the *David Bowie Is* exhibition in Brooklyn featured one of Bowie's last notebooks, in which were displayed storyboards for his final music videos "Blackstar" and "Lazarus." In "Ashes to Ashes," we can see an early indication of this burgeoning film style.

Bowie does not play himself in "Ashes to Ashes," but rather multiple characters. We see him as Pierrot, Major Tom, and other, unnamed personae in the three-and-a-half minutes runtime. Though this is unsurprising for a performer well known as a chameleon, it does subvert some of the expectations of the music video form. As Vernallis writes, "the conventions of rock and roll imply that the singers in music videos are trying not to act but to speak truthfully."[40] This is, perhaps, true of other rock stars, but by 1980, one could assume that Bowie was always already acting. As far back as his *Love You till Tuesday*, he embodied multiple roles in promotional shorts (frequently, but not always, multiple roles *within one* short). Here, then, we see Bowie slipping back into his actorly vestments.

---

[38] "ANCIANT Video Focus: 'Ashes to Ashes,'" *DavidBowie.Com*, September 27, 2017, https://www.davidbowie.com/blog/2017/9/27/anciant-video-focus-ashes-to-ashes Accessed October 4, 2021.

[39] Charles Shaar Murray, "Sermon from the Savoy," in *Bowie on Bowie: Interviews and Encounters with David Bowie*, ed. Sean Egan (Chicago: Chicago Review Press, 2015), 171.

[40] Vernallis, *Experiencing Music Video*, 56.

This shift is facilitated by the different voices Bowie utilizes throughout the video. Pierrot leads us into the song with a higher, reedy voice, referring to Major Tom lyrically. Each aside is given in a different voice: "oh no, not again" not only *sounds* separate from Pierrot, but is presented as such visually, with Mallet's use of the freeze frame. Throughout the video, this gambit continues, emphasizing the persona shifts that are audible within Bowie's vocal line.[41] While various changes in setting align with structural markers in the song's form, it is this persona division that is most important, as the visual confirms our aural understanding of Bowie's performance. In combination with the dissolves, Mallet creates a compelling corollary to Bowie's song, deepening its meaning through the visual depiction of its characters. In editing choices, Bowie and Mallet turn the video's separate scenarios into parts of the same unified story, turning individual characters into facets of the same whole, though they never interact directly on screen.

Darryl Perrins sees these actorly roles as a "video exorcism," freeing Bowie of his dead, formerly inhabited characters.[42] Dillane, Devereux, and Power counter that the video is "as much about Bowie's future as his past."[43] Given Bowie's direction in the years that followed, it is tempting to see the video as a moment of escape from a flamboyant, othered past. I wonder, though, if it is not more of a conjuring than an exorcism. Bowie was always already free of these characters, as they were never truly *him*, but clothes that he put on for a time. By recalling them here, Bowie is not so much running away from them as calling them up and putting them in their place within his semiotic encyclopedia. Though he publicly bemoaned being seen for decades as the alien figure Ziggy, whom he had inhabited for mere months, Bowie also played with that alien figure repeatedly. As we have seen in earlier videos, Bowie was interested in the establishment of a personal iconography as much as in its reinvention. His videos are texts that reward close reading, much like his music. They are created through a complicated *bricolage*, borrowing and repurposing from a shared cultural past. By 1980, Bowie's own professional past is a well-established component of his audience's shared culture. Thus, the hauntological moments

---

[41] For more on these vocal characters, see Kevin Holm-Hudson, "'Who Can I Be Now?': David Bowie's Vocal Personae," *Contemporary Music Review* 37, no. 3 (2018): 214–34.

[42] Darryl Perrins, "'You Never Knew That, That I Could Do That': Bowie, Video Art, and the Search for Potsdamer Platz," in *Enchanting David Bowie: Space/Time/Body/Memory*, ed. Toija Cinque, Christopher Moore, and Sean Redmond (New York: Bloomsbury Academic, 2015), 325.

[43] Dillane, Devereux, and Power, "Culminating Sounds," 36.

of "Ashes to Ashes" are in keeping with what came before: Bowie remains a consummate borrower, though this time he borrows from himself to create new, complex semiotic systems.

"Just Walking the Dead": Bowie's Late Music Video Style

When, in January 2013, Bowie released the video for "Where Are We Now?", it caught the world unawares. Since his health scare in the early 2000s brought an end to his live performances, Bowie had remained quiet, not sharing any new music or performing publicly. In fact, his film cameos were his only notable presence in popular culture. With "Where Are We Now?", Bowie reasserted his position as an elder statesman of rock, not only by releasing new music but also by explicitly calling on his past in visual, lyrical, and musical ways. Bowie's time in Berlin, his earlier music, and his own embodied persona are central foci for the video, connecting to threads apparent in the previous case studies, too. Here, though, the reflective mood is yet more obvious and has been read, retroactively, as a sort of meditation on death in light of Bowie's passing.[44]

As with "Life on Mars?" and "Ashes to Ashes," the Bowie visual encyclopedia is once again in play. References abound and, given the video's chronological distance from previous works, seem to comment on the whole of his career in a retrospective way. From a "Song of Norway" T-shirt to the city of Berlin itself, the video is bursting at the seams with hidden references to be understood by the ideal viewer. In terms of visual style, too, we can see some of the same concerns returning. Bowie is again treated as object, though through different visual devices than in the videos analyzed above. Here it is the work of another artist, Tony Oursler, that transforms Bowie.

The video was created in secret, with the help of director Oursler. Oursler is perhaps best known as a video artist in the installation sense of the word. Bowie and Oursler met in the mid-1990s; Bowie, always interested in visual art, reached out to Oursler after both were featured in an art and fashion exhibition.[45] The

---

[44] To be clear, there is no evidence that Bowie's cancer was diagnosed as terminal at the time of the recording and release of *The Next Day* or its lead single. Nonetheless, public reception has retroactively linked the song and album to Bowie's declining health and a final reevaluation of his work and career. For a more nuanced discussion of Bowie's last period, see Leah Kardos, *Blackstar Theory: The Late Works of David Bowie* (New York: Bloomsbury Academic, 2021).

[45] Boris Kachka, "Bowie Collaborator Tony Oursler on the Icon's Art-World Ties, Generosity, and Final Years," *Vulture*, February 1, 2016, https://www.vulture.com/2016/02/tony-oursler-on-david-bowies-art-world-ties.html Accessed October 4, 2021.

friendship led to collaboration, first on Bowie's 1997 Earthling tour, then on his fiftieth birthday concert at Madison Square Garden that year, and in the Floria Sigismondi-directed video for "Little Wonder" (also from the *Earthling* album). Each featured Oursler's signature approach, which he calls electric effigies. These effigies are puppets onto which faces, in whole or in part, are projected. In "Little Wonder," Bowie's entire face is shown on one effigy, while his mouth and a single eye are isolated on others. This approach carries some of the fragmentary power of the closeup in early Bowie videos. Through visual isolation, these aspects of Bowie's appearance are objectified. The objectification is quite literal in the case of Oursler's work: features are projected onto objects, forced out of their physical context and into a sort of talismanic embodiment in a puppet. Though Oursler did not direct a music video for Bowie during the 1990s or 2000s, the two remained in contact, attending art exhibitions together and discussing their work. Bowie sustained his interest in Oursler's approach and, by the time of *The Next Day*'s recording, had found another suitable application for Oursler's effigies within his own work. "Where Are We Now?" would take that approach even further, making it the main focus of the video rather than an ancillary feature.

Stylistically, "Where Are We Now?" differs greatly from the nascent MTV aesthetic seen in "Ashes to Ashes." Gone are the altered and exaggerated colors—here, we see only black-and-white footage of Berlin alongside sunlit studio images in unaltered color. Despite this stylistic difference, Bowie appears to have planned this video frame by frame, too, much in the same way his storyboards show the development of "Ashes to Ashes." Oursler recalls his first meeting with Bowie about the video, stating that,

> David had a fully articulated vision in his head. It was an exercise to tease this vision out, which was quite easy, and articulating it fast. I asked him what he saw and he described it all: the figures, the screen, the size of the screen, how much material to use. It was a crystal vision of what it was going to look like.[46]

This clear planning combined with collaborative realization is, as we have seen, typical of Bowie's music video *modus operandi*. Where this particular project is unique, then, is in its style.

---

[46] Paul Gallagher, "Tony Oursler: David Bowie's Latest Work Is Astounding. There's a Level of Detail and Variety in It with the Highest Level of Production," *Independent*, January 13, 2013, https://www.independent.co.uk/news/people/profiles/tony-oursler-david-bowie-s-latest-work-astounding-there-s-level-detail-and-variety-it-highest-level-production-8449414.html Accessed October 4, 2021.

Given the lyrics of the song, it is not surprising that the video itself feels deeply nostalgic. Bowie refers to places in the city of Berlin, a location deeply entwined with his own career and life. Bowie left Los Angeles for Berlin at the height of his mid-1970s cocaine addiction and, while in Europe, created the trio of albums colloquially referred to as the "Berlin trilogy." At the same time, he was also producing some of Iggy Pop's most exciting solo work. These Berlin references, then, read not only as love letter to an important location, but also as a remembrance of a previous life. This nostalgia is accomplished through a number of means, but its specific manipulation of moving image formats is striking. The video begins with digital video shots of an artist's studio, presented in the high definition format expected in 2013. Images of Berlin street scenes are intercut with this contemporary footage. The difference in image quality is striking. While neither Oursler nor Bowie has spoken about the source of this footage, it appears to be decades-old video (or is processed to appear as such in this projection). Tony Visconti, *The Next Day*'s producer and a longtime Bowie friend, reinforced such an interpretation, affirming that "the footage of Berlin is very old footage before the Wall came down."[47] Visconti does not expand on the film's origins, but it is clear that it is meaningful, particularly for him as an active participant in Bowie's Berlin years.

Whether or not the footage is actually old is almost immaterial: its meaning is coded as old and, within the context of the song, it becomes as close to a memory made manifest as the artists could accomplish. The footage capitalizes on what Roland Barthes has called film's "third meaning," its details that point to the real.[48] For Barthes, such a detail may be a headscarf, a gesture, or another small moment that takes a viewer out of the narrative of a film for a split second, emphasizing instead the film's documentation of a real moment, acted by humans. The grain of the images of Berlin might act similarly, taking us out of the city as shown and instead emphasizing the city as *remembered*, as chronologically distant from us thanks to the perceived age of the media that recorded it. We see, then, the contemporary artist's studio, the effigies with their projected faces, and the otherworldly remembrances of Berlin, all intertwined throughout the music video itself.

---

[47] Quoted in David Buckley, "Revisiting Bowie's Berlin," in *David Bowie: Critical Perspectives*, ed. Eoin Devereux, Aileen Dillane, and Martin J. Power (New York: Routledge, 2015), 216.

[48] Roland Barthes, "The Third Meaning: Research Notes on Some Eisenstein Stills," in *Image-Music-Text*, translated by Stephen Heath (New York: Hill and Wang, 1977), 52–68.

The editing of these various kinds of footage is markedly different from that of "Ashes to Ashes," or even many Bowie videos of the intervening decades. Oursler moves between handheld footage of the studio, a stationary view of the effigies with Berlin footage projected behind them, the Berlin footage alone, and tighter, individual shots of the heads of the effigies. These transitions seem to happen independently of the music. The edits do not seem motivated by the song's form or lyrics, despite the fact that those lyrics are superimposed on the footage throughout. Save for a few formal convergences (as at the start of the first chorus, for example), Oursler transitions freely between these types of footage. In most music videos, particularly of the MTV golden age, editing emphasized form or rhythm quite clearly, drawing an even tighter relationship between the image and the music it accompanied. The result here is more contemplative than propulsive in its trajectory, a move that aligns with the nostalgia woven into the song and video.

Bowie's Berlin connection is well documented and well researched. For my purposes, the iconography of the city (and Bowie's time in it) is of greatest importance. As Susan Ingram has shown, many threads connect Bowie and his particular kind of stardom to Berlin, showing what she calls an elective affinity.[49] Bowie chose this city as a backdrop and continued to return to it, enmeshing its future with his own. As important as Berlin and its associations undoubtedly are for Bowie, this video shows some fault or distortion in memory. As Ingram and others have noted, place names in the song are frequently misspelled. (Since the lyrics are superimposed on the image, this is more apparent than it might otherwise be, if one were forced to instead check the lyrics in the official paratext of the CD booklet.) In and of itself, a misspelling is not surprising in Bowie's output. His many handwritten lyric sheets show plenty of spelling mistakes, as do some of his letters, but the translation of such an error into the planned visual language of the video seems more intentional.[50] The fact that Bowie's pronunciation of "Böse brucke" is close, while its spelling is incorrect, is even more notable. At the risk of reading too much into a small detail, one might see these misspellings as errors of memory: while the body remembers speaking these names, they have faded a bit. The place names we see are ghosts of their

---

[49] Susan Ingram, "Constellating Stardom, Berlin Style: Bowie, Christiane F., Hedi Slimane," in *David Bowie and Transmedia Stardom*, ed. Ana Cristina Mendes, and Lisa Perrott (New York: Routledge, 2020).

[50] See, for example, "emerged" in his handwritten lyrics for "Lady Stardust," in *David Bowie Is Inside*, ed. Victoria Broackes and Geoffrey Marsh (London: V&A Publishing, 2013), 183.

originals, resurrected for the purpose of this memorative journey. In their imperfection, they speak of the passage of time.

This mismatch implies a sort of distortion of memory that comes with temporal distance. These places existed for him in his experience of 1970s Berlin and, in the 2010s of "Where Are We Now?" they have faded and broken apart. Similarly, the visual distortion of the projected Berlin footage implies chronological distance. Whether actually aged or not, its difference in processing and presentation give that appearance. While Perrins assumes that the Berlin footage and the artist's studio of "Where Are We Now?" video show the same physical spaces (that is, that the projected footage depicts spaces just outside the studio), I would argue that the entire video is predicated on a strategy of self-conscious distancing and remembrance. Even the editing of the video supports such a reading. Transitioning smoothly between different vantage points, Oursler makes notable use of slow dissolves throughout. While hard cuts move us, the audience, to different views of the effigies, dissolves are reserved for transitions between the Berlin footage and the "present" of the artist's studio. Such use of cinematic grammar allows us to understand that footage as memory: we dissolve into it from images of Bowie's effigy, and out of it to the same (or, later in the video, into images of the man himself within the studio). In almost all cases, the visual transitions seem to move at their own pace, again unmooring the visual from strict alignment with the musical and formal content. Bowie is, as he sings, "walking the dead" as we walk through his memories, real or constructed.

In this way, the video becomes an embodiment of the process of memory, and indeed a meditation on the complexities of remembrance and self-storytelling. This is not new territory for Bowie, as the previous case study shows, but this video is much more self-consciously a memorative construction. Where, in "Ashes to Ashes," Bowie presented his past to be viewed and moved beyond, here he invites the audience into his remembrance, creating a participatory rather than presentational performance. Perrins notes that the inclusion of a second effigy head (with projection of Jacqueline Humphries's image) creates a sort of dialogue within the video.[51] Perrins quotes Oursler's assertion that Bowie "wanted a *doppelgänger* [double], appendage, or mirror character."[52] Where Perrins reads Humphries as a Yoko Ono analogue, I see her presence as less explicitly referential. Though she does not speak or directly respond to

---

[51] Perrins, "Bowie, Video Art," 330.
[52] Quoted in Perrins, "Bowie, Video Art," 330.

Bowie's words, the woman's face presents a silent, immobile opportunity for the audience to insert themselves into this intimate performance of remembrance. Where direct address broke down the performer-audience barrier in "Life on Mars?" and the use of a common semiotic language drew the viewer into "Ashes to Ashes," here Bowie combines both strategies, adding an audience insert. His autohistoriography becomes more intimate in its telling, since it is told to a figure in whom the audience may see themselves.

At play in this video is an extended rumination on the signs that make up Bowie's long career. Indeed, popular press accounts of the video and the album point to a similar understanding. Tom Hawking proclaims that Bowie's latest persona, premiering on *The Next Day*, is "meta-Bowie, David Bowie playing with the idea of 'David Bowie.'"[53] As the above video analyses have shown, this meta-Bowie strategy has been employed by the artist for decades. However, as Hawking and others have noted, here in "Where Are We Now?" and the rest of *The Next Day*, it takes on an almost elegiac tone. Lisa Perrott writes of this musical and visual hauntology as an engagement with the ghost of past performers and past selves that permeates much of Bowie's work. Perrott explicitly connects this hauntological approach to the way Bowie creates his personae, stating that it "underscor[es] the fluidity and multiplicity of identity."[54] To see Bowie as haunted by the past—his own and a broader cultural past—is particularly fitting in "Where Are We Now?", with its explicit sense of loss and nostalgia. Shelton Waldrep and others have written of a "future nostalgia" in Bowie's work, a sort of sense of loss of a possible future. Such concerns swirl in *The Next Day*, but most explicitly in this video.

Conclusion

Throughout his decades-long career, Bowie played with the music video apparatus in ways that would change the form itself. It is tempting to see his work as unique and iconoclastic, separate from others' experiments in the form.

---

[53] Tom Hawking, "'The Next Day': Meet David Bowie's Final Incarnation, Meta-Bowie," *Flavorwire*, March 11, 2013, https://www.flavorwire.com/376749/the-next-day-meet-david-bowies-final-incarnation-meta-bowie Accessed February 10, 2021.

[54] Lisa Perrott, "Time Is out of Joint: The Transmedial Hauntology of David Bowie," in *David Bowie and Transmedia Stardom*, ed. Ana Cristina Mendes and Lisa Perrott (New York: Routledge, 2020), 117.

Of course, this would ignore Bowie's very working procedure. Borrowing freely in a sort of *bricolage*, Bowie turned the music video into a hybrid form, taking from and breaking down many of film's stylistic norms. Bowie's music videos wore their influences on their sleeves and worked, at least in part, because of that transparent reference. This same approach would inform Bowie's planned films.

Apart from referentiality, the most marked feature of these decades of music video is certainly their treatment of their subject, Bowie himself. These case studies show a slow development, whereby Bowie and his director-collaborators form a distinctive approach to filming his own body and personae. Throughout, he is transformed by the filmic apparatus, made into something other than David Jones. He is made into a cultural object and is visually treated as such. In the closeups and framing of "Life on Mars?", the evocative transitions of "Ashes to Ashes", and the transformation into effigy of "Where Are We Now?", we can find a strategy of literal objectification. Bowie is viewed as and transformed into an object—or indeed, many objects. His personae coalesce into solid objects, displayed on film and in conversation with each other.

This is shown yet more directly in the music video for "Love Is Lost (Hello Steve Reich Mix by James Murphy for the DFA)," released in October 2013. The remix for a new song from the album *The Next Day* features musical returns: James Murphy interpolates the hook from "Ashes to Ashes" in this remix, appropriate for a song so lyrically concerned with the past.[55] This musical choice is echoed in the video's content and tone. Much like "Where Are We Now?", this video features Bowie in electric effigy. However, it also incorporates elements from the earlier videos discussed in this chapter. Like "Life on Mars?", the video fragments Bowie's body—this time, with particular focus on the eyes and hands. Like "Ashes to Ashes," various earlier personae show up physically. Bowie is not dressed as these characters, though. Instead, the video incorporates dolls of the Thin White Duke and Pierrot, lurking in the shadowy environment of the video. Unlike the stark white spaces of early Bowie videos, here we find the negative image, all shadows and hauntings.

"Love Is Lost" serves to illustrate the consistency across the artist's music video output. It is telling that we see such a direct distillation of his style in this video: in fact, Bowie shot it himself, not working with any director or budget

---

[55] In fact, Devereux, Dilliane, and Powers note that the "Ashes to Ashes" connection goes deeper and can be found in the harmonic progression of the verse in "Love Is Lost." Eoin Devereux, Aileen Dillane, and Martin J. Power, "Say Hello to the Lunatic Men: A Critical Reading of 'Love is Lost,'" *Contemporary Music Review* 37, no. 3 (2018): 264–5.

(beyond the reported $12.99 USB drive the video was saved on).[56] Shot at home, the video's production was assisted by Jimmy King (credited with many of the publicly released images of Bowie in his final years) and Coco Schwab, Bowie's longtime friend, confidante, and personal assistant. With this skeleton crew (none of them music video professionals), "Love Is Lost" seems the closest of Bowie's videos to his own conception and execution. It features his history and style in an undiluted way. It is interesting to note that the effigies and ventriloquist doll in the video were objects created for an earlier, never-realized music video; Bowie preserved them in his personal archive.[57] That archive formed much of the *David Bowie Is* exhibition and, it seems, is painstakingly complete. Bowie's use of it here, in a music video that was entirely his own conception, is exactly in keeping with the style seen in his earlier music video work. Much like the musical return of "Ashes to Ashes" in this "Love Is Lost" remix, Bowie resurrects his own visual history in a new setting.

Film is an important tool for him, as it captures and records his personae and visual hallmarks in much the same way that his albums capture musical transformations. Just like the production on those albums shaped each era's sound, so did the editing, framing, and stylistic choices in these music videos serve to shape the public's audiovisual understanding of Bowie. "Love Is Lost" encapsulates this in a project that was truly Bowie's own: conceived, shot, and edited in house in much the same way that his 1970s film projects would be conceived.

The seeds of those film projects can be seen in Bowie's music videos. Though Mick Rock emphasizes Bowie's deference in their video projects, it is clear that the artist became more vocal and collaborative in his videos as he gained more experience. Using his visual art training and his years of cinephilic knowledge, Bowie treated his work in the moving image much as he did his musical work. Where there, one might use Philip Tagg's concept of the museme to understand Bowie's musical borrowing, here we must turn to the pillars of the moving image: framing, lighting, editing styles, and more. Having seen these influences made manifest in his decades of music videos, one can also find them in his planned film projects.

---

[56] "Watch David Bowie's $12.99 Love Is Lost Video Here Now," *DavidBowie.Com*, October 31, 2013, https://web.archive.org/web/20131105001515/http://www.davidbowie.com/news/watch-bowie-s-1299-love-lost-video-here-now-52201 Accessed March 13, 2021.

[57] Devereux, Dillane, and Power, "Say Hello to the Lunatic Men," 262.

4

Screen Dreams: Theatrical Staging, Film, and *Diamond Dogs*

"One can't fight the urge to play around with film and video—it's a magic world, when you can create that little world and portray its environment and the characters in it. It becomes obsessive."

—David Bowie, *Bowie 83* promotional material[1]

Sometime in 1974, David Bowie procured a camera from his record company RCA. The camera came to New York's Pierre Hotel and was put to use shooting the opening sequence of a new film. The project showed the dystopian future world depicted in the album *Diamond Dogs*, a desolate city populated by roving packs of humanoids, though at this stage characters were only represented by hand-drawn miniatures. That the film's plot and the title borrowed from Bowie's most recent album was not surprising. The artist had toyed with the medium of film for years, adopting the music video format early in the 1970s. It was with *Diamond Dogs*, though, that Bowie's film ambitions reached a new level. He had carefully planned a complete visual world for a feature film, not just a three- to four-minute-long music video. The *Diamond Dogs* project united music, film, stagecraft, and visual design. In his planning, Bowie accounted for every aspect of the production, acting as a true auteur.

Among fans, the footage shot on that RCA camera and the possibility of a *Diamond Dogs* film have long been enticing enigmas.[2] Bowie spoke of his

---

Research for this chapter would not have been possible without the support of a fellowship from Case Western Reserve University and the Rock and Roll Hall of Fame Library and Archive in Summer 2017. Special thanks to Rock Hall archive librarian Jennie Thomas for all of her patience and help through the research process. Thanks also to the participants at the David Bowie Interart | Text | Media conference in Lisbon, Portugal, September 2016 for their comments on an early draft of this work, and their generosity in sharing rare sources.

[1] *Bowie 83* promotional material, Jeff Gold Collection ARC-0037 Box AF3, Folder 18, Rock and Roll Hall of Fame Library and Archives, Cleveland, Ohio.
[2] The film will be referred to hereafter as *Hunger City*, in order to differentiate it from the *Diamond Dogs* album and tour.

filmic vision in interviews, though it never materialized in a public form.³ This in and of itself was not uncommon: Bowie had a habit of expanding on the truth in interviews, and frequently referenced projects that were allegedly in production, yet never came to fruition.⁴ For the *Diamond Dogs* project, though, more evidence existed, giving the public a taste of what Bowie had planned. Importantly, this *Diamond Dogs* endeavor took multiple forms, each one interconnected and revealing of the others. *Diamond Dogs* exists as an album, a touring stage show based on that album, and a planned feature film project. Of these, only the album remains well documented. The tour traveled Canada and the United States; though two live albums from the tour have been released, neither documents the earliest and most complete version of the tour's narratively organized set list. To date, no complete, extended footage is available of either the film or the stage show.⁵ However, through analysis of footage recently released by the David Bowie Archive, in combination with archival materials about the tour and personal interviews with Bowie's collaborators, this chapter works to reconstruct the stages of the project, shedding new light on Bowie's multimedia vision. This chapter analyzes three manifestations of the project: 1973's *1980 Floor Show* television special, a predecessor of the album and tour; 1974's Diamond Dogs, the stage show; and *Hunger City*, the film. Each is analyzed for its narrative choices, planning, construction, and visual language. By treating each of these iterations as complete and nuanced artworks in their own right, we are able to more fully understand Bowie's conception of his art as multimedia work and to make sense of the many projects through which he engaged the film, dance, theater, and visual art worlds.

This multipronged *Diamond Dogs* project, though ultimately a failure, represents a watershed moment for Bowie as artist. The threads of visual style already apparent in his earliest music videos, personal styling, and album artwork come to bear with the more extended narrative of the *Hunger City* film. On the heels of success with *The Rise and Fall of Ziggy Stardust and the Spiders from Mars* (1972) and *Aladdin Sane* (1973), Bowie undertook *Diamond Dogs* at a moment of unprecedented artistic freedom. He had the means to expand his

---

[3] Michael Watts, "Confessions of an Elitist," in *Bowie on Bowie: Interviews and Encounters with David Bowie*, ed. Sean Egan (Chicago: Chicago Review Press, 2015), 77–101.

[4] See, for example, Cameron Crowe, "David Bowie: Ground Control to Davy Jones," *Rolling Stone*, February 12, 1976, https://www.rollingstone.com/music/music-news/david-bowie-ground-control-to-davy-jones-77059/ Accessed November 20, 2021.

[5] Bootleg copies of some show footage do exist, but most are snippets and do not present a complete, clear idea of staging and transitions.

vision for the album and, though the final realizations do not match his early plans, through those plans we can see the way Bowie had hoped to create the world of Hunger City.

This chapter is divided into two large sections, each concentrating on one main manifestation of the *Diamond Dogs* endeavor. First, the earlier stagecraft: *The 1980 Floor Show* and Diamond Dogs touring stage show, both musical, narrative, and visual events, the full scope of which can now only be accessed through archival materials and interviews. Second, the film project, referred to here as *Hunger City* rather than *Diamond Dogs,* for clarity's sake. With the release of new materials in the evolving *David Bowie Is* exhibition, recent documentary films, and the "David Bowie Is" augmented reality app, a much clearer image of the film and its planning can be constructed. These materials, held by the artist's own, private David Bowie Archive, show that the film was much more thoroughly planned than may have been generally understood. Drawing together this new information about both *Diamond Dogs* projects, this chapter shows the possibility of the stage show and film as they *might have been,* unencumbered by the burdens of budget or feasibility. In these hypothetical iterations, the close connection between image and sound across the *Diamond Dogs* constellation of projects is striking; music and moving image could have worked in tandem, had Bowie's ambitious plans been fully realized. As such, the planning materials give a purer understanding of Bowie the musician and auteur.

Halloween Jack in America: *The 1980 Floor Show* and the Diamond Dogs tour

In the spring of 1974, going to a David Bowie concert meant you were in for a fantastical experience. The show would have no opening act, but instead a carefully plotted performance centering around Bowie's latest album *Diamond Dogs*, complete with elaborate choreography, cityscape stage sets, movable catwalks, streetlamps, and mirrored eggs. As a highlight, Bowie himself would be suspended over the audience for "Space Oddity" in an office chair held by a cherry picker, singing into a red telephone.

Of course, some nights he would get stuck there.

This Diamond Dogs tour of 1974 is legendary among Bowie fans for many reasons. First, the elaborate design was unlike any seen before. With set designer Mark Ravitz, lighting and production designer Jules Fisher, and choreographer

Toni Basil, Bowie created a carefully plotted, beautifully designed world for the tour. Second, the tour was exclusive to North America: Bowie's British and European fan base would only experience second-hand accounts, furnished through grainy photographs and bootleg audio recordings. Third, and perhaps most importantly, the tour was plagued by an almost comical number of mishaps. Bowie would get stranded in the "Space Oddity" set piece, needing to clamber back on the cherry picker's arm. The moving catwalk once collapsed with Bowie atop it for his "Sweet Thing"/"Candidate" performance. And, of course, parts of the elaborate set itself met a tragic end: on the way to the July 4, 1974 gig in Tampa, the set ended up in the swamps of Central Florida, ending the experiment of the original Diamond Dogs tour plan.[6]

The mistakes and mishaps of the tour were well-known at the time, and might account for its lukewarm reception in the press. To take only one such example, John Rockwell's *New York Times* review recognizes the potential in Bowie's combination of rock and theater, though he does not think it entirely successful.[7] What is less well documented, though, is the planning that went into this tour, and the way it changed based on the challenging circumstances that went along with implementing such a complex show on a tight tour schedule. The details of this stage show are fascinating not only for their complexity, but also for their originality; indeed, curator Kathryn Johnson described the show as "theatrical, operatic, even," in its design.[8] Though the idea of a pop star mounting a carefully choreographed tour with a complex set is now quite common, it was innovative at this point in David Bowie's career. He embraced the idea that "you could do something more interesting on stage than just wear blue jeans."[9] Acts like Genesis, the Who, and Alice Cooper were already exploring this theatrical tour idea, to some extent. Bowie would take that theatricality yet further. This tour was, in many ways, the genesis of a project and a style that would continue throughout

---

[6] Christopher Spata, "Bowie's Stripped Down Tampa Tour Stop in 1974 Still Resonates," *Tampa Bay Online.* http://www.tbo.com/events-tampa-bay/bowies-stripped-down-tampa-tour-stop-in-1974-still-resonates-20160111/ Accessed May 17, 2018. The tour continued on after this point without these pieces of the set. Bowie himself told a different story in later years, asserting that he tired of the project and scrapped the set. Paul du Noyer, "Contact," in *Bowie on Bowie: Interviews and Encounters with David Bowie*, edited by Sean Egan (Chicago: Chicago Review Press, 2015), 373.

[7] John Rockwell, "Pop Music: Bowie Puts on Lavish Show at the Garden," *New York Times* July 21, 1974, https://www.nytimes.com/1974/07/21/archives/pop-music-bowie-puts-on-lavish-show-at-garden-good-moves-pacing-add.html Accessed November 21, 2021.

[8] "David Bowie Is ... Gems of the Exhibition: Diamond Dogs," uploaded by AMCI, September 27, 2015, https://www.youtube.com/watch?v=an797gMuCpo Accessed February 7, 2021.

[9] Du Noyer, "Contact," 373.

Bowie's later work. Here we see a conscious construction of a narrative setlist, the collaboration of artists across different fields in the service of a single vision, and the idea that a tour was more than the simple, straightforward public performance of songs already familiar to fans. Archival materials highlight the artistic influences visible in these tours, and allow us a new avenue by which to understand David Bowie as a multimedia artist, as well as the historical context of this groundbreaking but ultimately flawed stage show.

Beyond this importance for Bowie studies, though, the tour also presents an interesting moment in the performance and touring of pop and rock musicians. Bowie's use of theatrical elements and a cohesive conception of the show all point to important threads that continue in pop star showcases. The fusion of Fisher's musical theater expertise and Bowie's vision for his stage show are precursors for massive tours by the Rolling Stones, KISS, and others, which would come to define the genre's performance practice. Importantly, Bowie's interest in incorporating film *onstage* and in a potential adaptation of the album and stage show provides an early example of such multimedia projects as Beyoncé's *Lemonade*/Formation tour and Janelle Monáe's *Dirty Computer* emotion picture and tour. As Landon Palmer notes, these projects show new horizons for pop stars: filmed performance that differs from a music video or a narrative film role in important ways.[10] It is striking that Bowie foresaw this as a possibility long before the video and streaming technologies that allowed *Lemonade* and *Dirty Computer* to find broad audiences. Previously unstudied aspects of the Diamond Dogs tour, made clear in these planning documents, give new insight into this performance tradition and the development of a filmic counterpart for audio albums.

The Year of the Diamond Dog

The year of *Diamond Dogs* stands out as a bit of an enigma. 1974 falls between two better loved eras of Bowie's output: it is bookended by the extraterrestrial incarnations that brought Bowie to international superstardom (Ziggy Stardust and Aladdin Sane) and 1976's *Station to Station*, which featured Bowie's Thin White Duke persona, a threatening European character who dabbled in Nazi imagery and references. The two eras are markedly different not only in these characters, but also in the music that defines them. Ziggy and Aladdin Sane are emblematic

---

[10] Landon Palmer, *Rock Star/Movie Star: Power and Performance in Cinematic Rock Stardom* (New York: Oxford University Press, 2020), 215–21.

of Bowie's glam rock era, while the Thin White Duke takes stylistic influence from more experimental rock, foreshadowing the albums of Bowie's Berlin years.

The year 1974, then, is a bit of boundary, and was even recognized as such at the time. As an October *Melody Maker* feature shows, 1974 Bowie was seen as a *"new,"* different, and newsworthy Bowie, no small feat for a musician already known for his constant changes.[11] The year 1974 included both the release of *Diamond Dogs* and the tour supporting that album. Among all that activity, Bowie was recording songs that were planned for the album *The Gouster* in Philadelphia's Sigma Sound Studios; this project eventually turned into *Young Americans*, his plastic soul album.[12] In style and location, then, 1974 shows Bowie striking out in new directions.

Despite its outlier status, *Diamond Dogs* seems to have held an important place in Bowie's creative consciousness. Well after 1974, Bowie continued to address this album in interviews. In a 1992 conversation with Kurt Loder, Bowie stated that, although a musical based on Orwell's novel *1984* was his original plan for the album, he quickly found that his management, MainMan, had not secured the rights, and so the project needed to change to avoid conflicts with the Orwell estate. As Bowie said, "they [MainMan] really didn't do much."[13] Despite the fact that Orwell's widow wouldn't grant Bowie the rights to adapt the novel, vestiges of that *1984* plan permeate the final version of *Diamond Dogs* (most obviously in the songs "Big Brother" and "1984"). Bowie's fascination with his Hunger City setting for the album and its associated iconography continued to resonate through later tours like Serious Moonlight and Glass Spider in the 1980s. The show and its ideas, which found expression in projects from television to stage to film, represent an important phase in Bowie's growth as auteur.

The 1980 Floor Show

Months before the Diamond Dogs show took flight as a tour, Bowie tested some of his new material in a more controlled environment. At the end of 1973, he was asked to create a musical event for television, which would air in the United

---

[11] "The New Bowie," *Melody Maker*, October 12, 1974, 39.
[12] *The Gouster* was finally released as part of the 2016 box set *Who Can I Be Now*, though some of the songs recorded in those sessions, including "Shilling the Rubes," were not included and have yet to receive an official release.
[13] Kurt Loder, "David Bowie: Stardust Memories," *Rolling Stone*, April 23, 1987, https://www.rollingstone.com/music/news/david-bowie-the-rolling-stone-interview-19870423 Accessed May 17, 2018.

States as an episode of *Midnight Special* on NBC. *Midnight Special* was a new variety show, one that featured performances from popular pop and rock artists as well as some comedy. Such variety shows had been popular since mid-century and tended to be weekly events hosted by famous entertainers. Norma Coates addresses the rise of rock music on such shows as *Shindig!* and *Hullabaloo* after the cultural impact of the British Invasion.[14] *Midnight Special* was a bit different, airing late at night and targeting a young, rock-loving audience. Notably, *Midnight Special* performances were typically live in studio, a factor that differentiated them from other longstanding musical showcases like *Top of the Pops*. This special episode of *Midnight Special* featured not only Bowie and his band, but also Marianne Faithfull, Carmen, and the Troggs. Amanda Lear was also present as part of Bowie's performance of "Sorrow" and a presenter, trading lines with Bowie. In all, the show would feature some ten songs and interstitial banter.

The invitation to design a *Midnight Special* episode offered Bowie a prime opportunity to test his *Diamond Dogs* material for an American audience. His performance would not be live in studio, but instead filmed at London's Marquee Club. It seems that Bowie and company had greater visual control than they would have had in studio, a real coup for an artist planning an elaborate stage show. This meant an opportunity to share Bowie's theatrical vision with an audience who may not have been able to see him in person before; even better, the televisual medium provided a level of control previously unavailable to Bowie in stage shows. His planning for the performance reveals a grasp of this possibility: the David Bowie Archive holds costume sketches, set designs, and more, created in preparation.[15] Each number would have a costume change and a different visual approach. Some used scaffolding as a set, while others incorporated dancers. In each number, Bowie crafted a distinct visual that, together with the rest of the show, created an odd and unique world.

The 1980 Floor Show is most interesting, though, as a gestational artifact. It shows, in embryonic stage, the *Diamond Dogs* theatrical project. Some of its ideas came to be a part of the final tour. Even more than this, *The 1980 Floor Show* hints at the way Bowie saw and controlled his audiovisual works. As Camille Paglia writes, that special showed "Bowie's genius for using the camera the

---

[14] Norma Coates, "*Hullabaloo*: Rocking the Variety Show in the Mid-1960s," in *The Bloomsbury Handbook of Popular Music Video Analysis*, ed. Lori A. Burns and Stan Hawkins (New York: Bloomsbury Academic, 2019), 111–28.

[15] See, for example, the "1980 Floor Show" section of the "David Bowie Is" augmented reality app.

way others use a paintbrush or chisel—not from behind the camera but before it."[16] We might, in fact, see it in both ways. From some of his earliest television appearances, Bowie evinced a clear understanding of the medium and its gaze. His music video work, analyzed in the previous chapter, shows this command of the camera yet more clearly. *The 1980 Floor Show* was shot with two cameras only (due in part to the size of the venue). Because of this, each number was shot many times from a variety of angles. The goals were twofold: complete coverage as well as the ability to shape the performance and the audiences' apprehension of its various details. Like his 1970s music videos, *The 1980 Floor Show* exhibits some of Bowie's broader auteurist tendencies, with archival materials showing his input in costuming, set design, and framing, rather than just his own performance in front of the camera.

In its title, the show hints at its purpose: when spoken, *The 1980 Floor Show* can be heard as a play on *1984 Show*. The set list for the TV special includes numbers from Bowie's previous albums *Aladdin Sane* and *Pin Ups* as well as new *Diamond Dogs* compositions, some in early stages. *The 1980 Floor Show* version of "1984/Dodo" in particular shows the album concept's evolution. The "1984" section of the song features all the main formal sections of its final album version, with the interpolation of the song "Dodo," which would be excised before the album. (See Table 4.1 for formal comparison of "1984/Dodo" with the album version of "1984.") Though "1984" features overt Orwellian references, most especially in its title, "Dodo" is yet more clearly aligned with the novel.[17] It has an even more direct narrative, perhaps pointing to Bowie's original intention of creating a stage musical. Lyrical allusions abound: the novel's protagonist, Winston, refers to the fear of being turned in by one's own children, who are trained to be zealots for Big Brother's cause. This precise scenario shapes the verses of "Dodo."

Beyond the inclusion of songs from the *1984* project, Bowie also drew on inspiration that would continue to shape his visual and theatrical language. Most notably, his sketches for *The 1980 Floor Show* set feature the distinctive scaffolding and lighting first seen in the "John, I'm Only Dancing" video (1973). That theatrical set existed at London's Rainbow Theater, where Bowie had seen

---

[16] Camille Paglia, "Theater of Gender," in *David Bowie Is Inside*, ed. Victoria Broackes and Geoffrey Marsh (London: V&A Publishing, 2013), 86.
[17] A studio recording of "Dodo" is included as bonus material on the second disc of the *Diamond Dogs*, 30th Anniversary Edition (Virgin 77857).

Table 4.1 Formal structure of "1984/Dodo": *Diamond Dogs* versus *1980 Floor Show*.

"1984/Dodo," *The 1980 Floor Show* (1973)	"1984," *Diamond Dogs* (1974)
Intro (saxophone, no strings)	Intro (strings)
Verse 1 "Someday they won't let you"	Verse 1
Verse 2 "They'll split your pretty cranium"	Verse 2 "pretty cranium"
Pre/Chorus "Come see, come see"	Pre/Chorus
	Interlude
"Dodo" intro (saxophone)	
"Dodo" Verse 1 "confidence"	
"Dodo" Verse 2 "well screened"	
"Dodo" Chorus	
"Dodo" Verse 3	
"Dodo" Chorus	
"Dodo" Bridge	
"Dodo" Chorus x 2	
	Bridge
	Pre/Chorus
Interlude	Interlude
Pre/Chorus	
Final vamp "1984" to end	Final vamp "1984" into "Big Brother"

a London production of *Cabaret* in 1968.[18] That production's themes and visual language would provide critical inspiration for Bowie, as shown in the notes Mark Ravitz and Jules Fisher took in preparation for the later tour.[19] In *The 1980 Floor Show* as well, the cabaret-style performance aesthetic is strong. Rather than simply presenting a series of song performances straight to camera, Bowie provides interesting staging choices (as in the use of scaffolding for Amanda Lear in the "Sorrow" number) and some banter between tunes (with both Lear and Marianne Faithfull). Glenn Hendler points to the format's prevalence in 1970s television, calling Bowie's special a "hilariously demented parody of a variety show."[20] Indeed, Bowie takes the trappings of something like CBS's *Cher* series and turns it on its head.

Many preparatory sketches for the visual style of *The 1980 Floor Show* survive. Visible in the *David Bowie Is* exhibit and augmented reality app, these sketches show a very well-defined vision for the show's appearance. As would later be the case in the design for the Diamond Dogs tour, stylistic elements of *Cabaret*

---

[18] Paglia, "Theatre of Gender," 72.
[19] Victoria Broackes, "Putting Out Fire with Gasoline: Designing David Bowie," in *David Bowie Is Inside*, ed. Victoria Broackes and Geoffrey Marsh (London: V&A Publishing, 2013), 130.
[20] Glenn Hendler, *Diamond Dogs* (New York: Bloomsbury Academic, 2020), 3.

abound throughout. However, George Grosz's artistic style is perhaps an even more prominent influence. In his depictions of interwar German culture, we find the same decadence and decay that Bowie highlights in this and other *Diamond Dogs* projects. By way of comparison, we might juxtapose Grosz's *Berlin* or *Twilight* (1922) with Bowie's stage sketches. In addition to the similarity of their subjects, each takes a similar canted perspective on the decaying decadence it depicts. Bowie's use of the camera to control audience perspective is particularly notable in the outtakes for the *Floor Show*: he made sure each performance was captured from a variety of stylized angles, rather than simply performing straight on for a single stationary camera.

Though somewhat restricted by the stage setup for the show, Bowie still incorporates movement throughout *1980 Floor Show*, a central link to his live performance. In "Sorrow" and other numbers, this movement only takes the form of walking within the set. However, "1984/Dodo" and "Time" show greater attention to the idea of choreography and point toward the movement style of the Diamond Dogs tour. "1984/Dodo" in particular shows the dual role played by backing singers in Bowie's tours. Here, the Astronettes serve in multiple capacities, providing vocal harmonies while also fleshing out the physical world of Bowie's *1984* vision. Ava Cherry and Jason Guess sing backing vocals while also helping in the visual reveal central to the number: when Bowie changes characters in the transition from "1984" to "Dodo," a costume change accompanies. In keeping with the Japanese *hayagawari* quick-change style he incorporated into the Ziggy Stardust tour, Bowie loses his large outer garment to the dancers' pulls and appears in a keyhole jumpsuit as this new character (Figure 4.1).[21] A similar move accompanies his changing voices in the "Sweet Thing"/"Candidate" suite in the eventual Diamond Dogs tour, though here Bowie undresses himself without assistance (Figure 4.2). Many of his dramatic conceptions of movement and character first tested in this *1980 Floor Show* performance are later perfected in the Diamond Dogs stage show. Despite the fact that choreography for "1984" would differ in the tour, the development of this concept is clear.

Though *The 1980 Floor Show* lacks a clear narrative structure, it does point to many of the defining features of the *Diamond Dogs* multimedia projects. First, its use of the camera shows an auteurist sensibility in Bowie, one that will

---

[21] Glenn Hendler also points out the relationship of this staging choice to the style of Black performers like James Brown. Hendler, *Diamond Dogs*, 65.

Figure 4.1 Stills from *The 1980 Floor Show* (1973).

Figure 4.2 Stills from *Cracked Actor* (1975, dir. Yentob).

continue in the remainder of the project. Second, the choreography and staging, not typical of a *Midnight Special* performance, point to a desire to augment straightforward musical performance with a theatrical framing. Finally, the musical additions present in these early *Diamond Dogs* works point even more directly to a narrative involving clearly defined characters moving in a detailed diegetic world. From this first televisual experiment, Bowie would move on to partner with experienced collaborators in an effort to bring *Diamond Dogs* to greater, more visually fantastic life.

Diamond Dogs Tour Stage Show

Following *The 1980 Floor Show*, Bowie continued planning for his largest, most elaborate tour yet. The Diamond Dogs tour's most prominent players included Jules Fisher, set designer Mark Ravitz, and choreographer Toni Basil. Fisher and Basil had experience working on Broadway productions. Indeed, many of the stylistic markers of such a Broadway show can be found in the initial leg of the Diamond Dogs tour. This was combined with the more experimental set, designed by Ravitz. Consisting of buildings bleeding in bright colors, this set borrows heavily from the visual language of Weimar Germany, as

Ravitz's notes on the set indicate.[22] These notes specifically reference Fritz Lang's *Metropolis* and George Grosz as important visual precursors. Mentions of works like *Cabaret* also abound, showing the highly referential nature of Bowie's stated vision for the tour as well as its connection to the earlier *Floor Show*. Not all these allusions would be realized in the final tour design, but their influence was clearly a matter of discussion among the collaborators at this stage in planning.

Of these collaborators, Jules Fisher and Mark Ravitz are the most important for our purposes. Fisher left detritus of the tour in archives, while Ravitz has, through personal communication, helped to illuminate some of the more opaque aspects of the tour's planning. Fisher and Ravitz's preparation process and notes are revealing, showing more of the finished product than any other non-photographic sources. It is through Fisher's eyes, as production and lighting designer, that we find a clearer image of Bowie and company's intent in the stage tour. Since the actual production was plagued by so many problems, these documents and interviews are unique in their ability to shed light on the conception of the *Diamond Dogs* project in ways even video evidence could not.

Jules Fisher had long worked as a producer and lighting designer. During his student days at Carnegie Mellon, Fisher took time off to work in New York City as a lighting designer. His credits include various New York stage productions, in both theater and musicals; by the mid-1990s, he had lit more than 140 Broadway shows, and continues to work today.[23] In addition to this theater work, Fisher also operates an architectural lighting business.[24] (The connections between this field and the cityscape of Bowie's Hunger City are striking.) By the time Bowie's management, MainMan, approached Fisher about the 1974 tour, he was already an established producer, lighting designer, and teacher, having worked in New York for a decade and taught at New York University's School of the Arts for five years.[25] It was there that Fisher and Ravitz connected, when Ravitz enrolled as a student at NYU. When Fisher was hired as production designer for the tour, he reached out to former student Ravitz to design the set. This pairing was fortuitous, as Ravitz's visual language clearly spoke to Bowie: the two would work together for more than a decade after the 1974 tour. Following his collaboration with Bowie, Fisher would do even more lighting design for

---

[22] Broackes, "Putting Out Fire," 130.
[23] Florence S. Daniels, "Jules Fisher: Oral History Memoir," William E. Wiener Oral History Library of the American Jewish Committee at New York Public Library (February 1993), 12.
[24] Daniels, "Jules Fisher," 13.
[25] Ibid., 23.

rock tours, working with KISS and Parliament-Funkadelic, among others. For this Bowie tour, though, Ravitz and Fisher's creative impulses seem to be closely linked to their work on the stage.

Judging by MainMan's promotion of the tour, this Broadway cachet was Fisher's main draw. In an undated MainMan fan club letter (based on content, probably sent between the album's release and the beginning of the tour), the author "Stellar Steele" hypes Bowie's upcoming album and tour. Stating that she has seen a rehearsal, presumably during the week of final rehearsals in Port Chester, New York, Steele writes, "Not only was he [Bowie] great musically, he gave a tremendous theatrical performance. The concerts, the perfect vehicle for Bowie's multi-faceted talent, are very much presentations of theater quality. The sets and special effects are out of this world. The whole effect is really show-biz, worthy of Bowie and his top-notch Broadway set designer, Tony award winner [sic] Jules Fisher."[26] While these details are interesting for a general audience, their focus on production rather than performer is odd for a (largely young adult) fan club.

This highlighting of the theatrical is in keeping, however, with Bowie's conception of the tour, and with the area into which MainMan was funneling money. A MainMan newsletter from April 1, 1974, shows a similar interest in the theatrical aspects of Bowie's new project. Before any mention of *Diamond Dogs* or the attendant tour, the newsletter informs the reader that Bowie is "currently in France conferring with John Dexter (the director of the National Theater in London and the Metropolitan Opera House in New York)," although it does not specify any project the two may be working on.[27] The upcoming tour is then referred to as "an extensive series of theatrical presentations," which "have been designed and staged by Bowie in collaboration with Jules Fisher (Tony Award winning lighting designer whose vast credits include 'Pippin', 'Lenny', 'Seesaw' and 'Hair')."[28] No mention of the upcoming *Diamond Dogs* album, then a month from its release, is made until paragraph three of the newsletter. In its publicity, the Diamond Dogs tour is framed mostly as a stage production; to judge from MainMan's press releases, the idea that the tour is promoting an album is of secondary or tertiary importance.

---

[26] MainMan Bowie fan club letter, 1974, Jeff Gold Collection ARC-0037 Box AF3, Folder 53, Rock and Roll Hall of Fame Library and Archives, Cleveland, Ohio.
[27] MainMan newsletter, April 1, 1974, Rolling Stone Collection ARC-0114 Box A18, Folder 2, Rock and Roll Hall of Fame Library and Archives, Cleveland, Ohio.
[28] Ibid.

A November 1974 RCA publicity biography of Bowie also hammers home the idea of the theatrical nature of his performances. It opens with a paragraph that marks a change from previous RCA press bios, and is worth quoting at length.

> A Bowie concert is like no other. Onstage, splendidly costumed, he moves with spellbinding animal grace. And when the icy sharpness of his voice soars through the auditorium, even the most jaded rock cynics in the audience cannot help but be captured by the aural and visual drama that unfolds. This, then is Bowie, the man who grabbed music by the neck and dragged it into a new era.[29]

Where previous releases quoted Oscar Wilde and positioned Bowie as an *artiste* with a pedigree, this 1974 statement is geared to show the musician as consummate multimedia performer. As this release was timed to coincide with the *David Live* album and the end of the Diamond Dogs tour, the shift in focus makes sense. Interestingly, the press release does more than hail Bowie as a great live musician. Later in the release, he is described as achieving an "electrifying fusion of total musicality, theatrical flair, and visionary genius."[30] In the Diamond Dogs tour, Bowie and his management intend to show the performer's vision as a kind of *gesamtkunstwerk*, bringing together the most innovative and exciting aspects of a variety of art forms.

Advertisements for the tour show a similar intent to celebrate a theater show built around Bowie. In newspaper tour ads, stylized cartoon dogs flank text that states only, "BOWIE, Diamond Dogs, designed by Jules Fisher."[31] Apart from ticket prices, little else is listed. The focus is clear: this is a bona fide theater production, with the pedigree to prove it. RCA even writes of the 1974 tour as a "TheaTour" titled "The Year of the Diamond Dogs."[32] Thus theatrical framing and staging were at the forefront of both planning and promotion of the tour, thanks in no small part to the work of Jules Fisher.

Planning Stages

While RCA and MainMan were presenting the idea of this TheaTour to the public, Fisher and Ravitz were helping to plan it. Fisher was the first to be approached

---

[29] RCA biography of David Bowie, November 1974, Jeff Gold Collection ARC-0037 Box AF3, Folder 53, Rock and Roll Hall of Fame Library and Archives, Cleveland, Ohio.

[30] Ibid.

[31] Diamond Dogs tour advertisement designed by Roger Sheperd, 1974, Jeff Gold Collection ARC-0037 Box AF1, Folder 18, Rock and Roll Hall of Fame Library and Archives, Cleveland, Ohio.

[32] RCA biography of David Bowie, November 1974, Jeff Gold Collection ARC-0037 Box AF3, Folder 53, Rock and Roll Hall of Fame Library and Archives, Cleveland, Ohio.

by MainMan, and he brought former student Ravitz into the production. Ravitz recalls his first meeting with Bowie as taking place on April 14, 1974—Easter Sunday. Prior to this meeting with the Bowie entourage at the Pierre Hotel, Ravitz was given three keywords to guide his proposal: "Metropolis, power, Nuremberg."[33] *Metropolis* was clearly identified as the 1927 Fritz Lang film, a classic of German Expressionism. In its eventual realization, the visual and promotional style of *Metropolis* permeates Ravitz's set. Power and Nuremberg were (purposefully, it would seem) a bit more nebulous. Ravitz interpreted the concept of power in both literal and figurative ways. As his posterboards from this initial meeting show, he invoked the image of the power station, sketching various tubes and machines to conduct power. Few of these specific elements would be retained in the final stage set, but one can see the role they played in the development of style throughout.

Ravitz's proposed set designs also included overt Nazi imagery, likely because of the "Nuremberg" suggestion. Ravitz admits that this was the most surprising of the three inspirational words given to him for visual design. Perhaps it should not have been, given the turn toward overt Nazi imagery that came only a year later in Bowie's 1975–6 Thin White Duke character. Even more so, the *Cabaret* inspiration gives a clear link to the fascist underpinnings of the world of *Diamond Dogs*. While such symbols did not appear in the Freddie Burretti-designed outfits Bowie wore on stage, Ravitz did make every effort to translate this inspiration into clear visual cues in the set design. Most notably, lightning bolt banners feature prominently in the proposed designs. These lightning bolts very closely resemble Nazi SS insignia, while also echoing the Ziggy Stardust iconography. Though these banners do not seem to be present in the final stage set, it is clear from planning documents that they were considered throughout the process. Some of Fisher's later budgets even include a line item for an inflatable lightning bolt, indicating the popularity of this design element.

Perhaps the most striking element of Ravitz's design is the inclusion of large-scale image projection. Though, by his own recollection, this was not a continuing element in the planning of the tour, many of his painted set design boards show large, television-like screens. The scale of these screens must have been enormous: in one depiction, a small figure stands astride the screen, dwarfed by its size. Ravitz prepared this set idea in multiple colorways, giving options for its implementation into the final design. The purpose of this screen

---

[33] Mark Ravitz in conversation with the author, October 18, 2019.

is not fleshed out in the design papers, but other archival materials hint at the development of a video plan. In my interpretation, it seems this screen idea connects directly to the telescreen in all homes in *1984*, as do the budgetary items that flesh out the needs to bring such projection to life. With these screens, Bowie and company would turn a live show into a mediated theater event. While Hegarty and Halliwell see such mediatization and theatricality as a feature of prog rock rather than glam, this failed plan for Bowie's 1974 tour shows the importance of media integration and the moving image to his particular brand of rock, which was expanding beyond glam by 1974.[34] Its plans show the blossoming of a new pop star showcase: one that is inherently multimedia, and would dominate world tours in coming decades, even if it didn't make it to the stage for Bowie. As this plan was complex and, eventually, deemed too expensive, we do not have any final indication of its importance to the overall plot of the show. However, Jules Fisher's papers do give more information on its proposed role.

Narrative Structure

Diamond Dogs itself was structured as a narrative in many ways, and its tour continued this conceit. It would certainly be reasonable to view the work as a concept album, though it is not as straight-forwardly narrative as something like *Jesus Christ Superstar* (1971). Still, the tour program for *Diamond Dogs* refers to it as a "concept album." Like *The Rise and Fall of Ziggy Stardust and the Spiders of Mars* before it, *Diamond Dogs* tells its story obliquely: characters are named and Bowie clearly adopts different voices, but the storyline itself is a bit more nebulous than it is clear. In fact, Hendler states that "while *Diamond Dogs* lacks anything like narrative continuity, it does have two other elements of a story: setting and characters."[35] Indeed, setting and characters are finely drawn within the album. Beyond this, however, the album shows the influence of another specific musical drama in its overarching structure in ways that help to make its narrative clear. That template is the musical *Cabaret*.

Cabaret was an important visual influence for the *Diamond Dogs* project. Bowie's appreciation for both stage and film versions is well documented.[36] Previous

---

[34] Paul Hegarty and Martin Halliwell, *Beyond and before: Progressive Rock since the 1960s* (New York: Bloomsbury Academic, 2011), 122–3.
[35] Hendler, *Diamond Dogs*, 128.
[36] See, for example, Kevin Cann, *Any Day Now: The London Years 1947–1974* (London: Adelita, 2011), 264.

scholarship has not, however, addressed the important similarities between the narrative structures of *Cabaret* and *Diamond Dogs*. Traditionally, *Diamond Dogs* has been viewed as being influenced by three literary sources, as Shelton Waldrep lists: *1984*, *Oliver Twist*, and Burrough's *The Wild Boys*.[37] Hendler focuses on similar influences in his study of *Diamond Dogs*.[38] The basis for these designations is, of course, lyrical references to *1984*, but also Bowie's own interviews and comments on the album. While these works are certainly present in many ways, it is fruitful for us to look beyond Bowie's (sometimes prevaricating) interviews to take greater stock of the work itself and the newly available materials that reflect on *Diamond Dogs*' development.

The structural similarities between *Diamond Dogs* and *Cabaret* are striking. Take, for example, the opening number of *Cabaret*, "Willkommen." Sung by the emcee of the Kit Kat Club (the center of the action in *Cabaret*), this song evolves from a solitary singer's introduction, into a world-building number that incorporates the Kit Kat band and lets the audience know what to expect: we are within the free-wheeling, licentious world of 1930s Weimar Republic cabaret. With a simple, singable, oft-repeated melody and frequent spoken-word insertions, "Willkommen" catchily does the work of setting the stage for the audience, directly introducing the musical's characters and setting.

Similarly, *Diamond Dogs* opens first with "Future Legend," in which a lone narrator's speech introduces us obliquely to Hunger City, the album's setting. (Hendler identifies this as a Tony Visconti addition that points to the influence of Burroughs.[39]) With the crashing opening riff of the title track, though, Bowie brings us a fuller image of *Diamond Dogs*' world. It is the imagery and catchy, repeated tune (used for various repetitions of the title phrase) that most define this song. From "Diamond Dogs" opening salvo, the dystopian imagery of Hunger City intensifies. Within the first verse, Bowie introduces us to the city with its oxygen tents and grotesque characters with "a silicone hump and a ten-inch stump" (like "Todd Browning's *Freaks*") who will shortly be "crawling down the alley on [their] hands and knees." Through the course of the song, we meet Halloween Jack ("a real cool cat"), as well as the Dogs themselves in the gloriously evocative phrase "mannequins with kill appeal." In short, Bowie creates and populates a world for us within the space of a five-minute song, in

---

[37] Shelton Waldrep, *Future Nostalgia: Performing David Bowie* (New York: Bloomsbury Academic, 2016), 151.
[38] Hendler, *Diamond Dogs*, 102.
[39] Ibid., 20.

much the same way we might expect a musical to drop us into a fully formed and nuanced world through its opening number.

Jack Viertel writes of the importance of a clear and cohesive opening number for the success of a musical, citing examples like the changed opening of *A Funny Thing Happened on the Way to the Forum*. Without this strong opening, which sets the tone for the show and allows the audience to form expectations that will shape their experience, Viertel argues that the show would never have achieved its eventual success.[40] Bowie's world building here can be seen in the same way. *Diamond Dogs*'s opening is markedly different from those of earlier Bowie concept albums like *The Rise and Fall of Ziggy Stardust and the Spiders from Mars*, or *Aladdin Sane*. Though both are built around main characters and loose narratives, just like *Diamond Dogs*, those albums open with much more impressionistic songs. The character of Ziggy is not even mentioned by name until late in that album, and *Aladdin Sane* can only be viewed as narrative in the very loosest sense. *Diamond Dogs*, then, shows structural differences that are important for our understanding of its lost afterlife as a film; indeed, the album itself shows the importance of visual and narrative elements, even at that relatively early stage in the project.

The album continues to take structural hints from musical theater, especially *Cabaret*, as in the centerpiece of its first side, the "Sweet Thing"/"Candidate" suite. Structurally, these songs appear immediately after the title track and serve to flesh out the characters and dilemmas of the album's world. Bowie voices more than one character in the suite, differentiated by both the musical form of the songs and Bowie's expressive timbral shifts. The "Sweet Thing" suite can be seen as the emotional center of the album, or at least of its first side. It acts in a way analogous to something like "Maybe This Time," a number that fleshes out the character of Sally Bowles in *Cabaret* after her bombastic introduction ("Mein Herr"). Like "Maybe This Time," "Sweet Thing" gives Bowie a moment alone in the spotlight, emoting and showing his expressive and vocal range. Both expand on characters' inner lives and showcase the performer.

The first half of the album trades in oblique references to its source material, but *Diamond Dogs*' second side is much more clearly *1984*, as many authors have shown. The final songs on the album's second side—"1984," "Big Brother," and "Chant of the Ever-Circling Skeletal Family"—all make clear the ideological

---

[40] Jack Viertel, *The Secret Life of the American Musical: How Broadway Shows Are Built* (New York: Sarah Crichton Books, 2016), 20.

basis of the dystopian society of Bowie's Hunger City. This sequence of songs serves a similar purpose to "Tomorrow Belongs to Me," the Nazi sing-along late in *Cabaret*. Both are melodically straight-forward, repetitive, and steady in their driving rhythms. Maybe more importantly, though, the suite at the end of the album, like "Tomorrow Belongs to Me," seems to capture the mob mentality described by Orwell in the Two Minutes Hate practiced by all good party members in the world of *1984*. Many commentators have pinpointed the similarity between these final songs and Orwell's Two Minutes Hate. In Orwell's novel, our protagonist, Winston, at first feigns participation in this demonstration of hatred in order to avoid arousing the suspicion of those around him. As the two minutes progress, though, he is drawn in to their virulent expression of anger, only to find himself fully and violently participating by its end. Bowie's compositions here accomplish a similar feat: beginning with "1984," this section builds in intensity till it is hard not to join in exultation of Big Brother. Hendler focuses on the way Bowie manipulates pronouns to implicate the listener in the narrative. While many previous songs used "you" in a way that could be understood as referring to the listener, "Big Brother" instead implicates the listener in a collective "we," which Hendler calls "a dystopian extinction of individuation."[41] The song "Big Brother" illustrates this particularly well in its music, denying the resolution of its chorus three times before we finally reach the section's release, with the words "we want you, Big Brother." We can see in the album, then, a progression from the individuality of our hero, through his temptation, into his eventual subsumation under the party line, as the listener too feels the drive to join in the celebration of Big Brother's control. Though plot is not explicit in the songs' lyrics, the structure of the album betrays the influence of familiar musical theater frameworks, providing a clearer throughline for the story.

Technical Staging Concerns

Bringing that musical theater structure to the stage, though, was a fraught journey. The Rock Hall's archival holdings show important moments in the development of the stage show. Fisher was brought on quite early in the process, working with the tour from the beginning conceptual stages. Bowie first thought of the *Diamond Dogs* material as a stage musical, and early tour planning notes show an attention to blocking, choreography, and staging that might be expected of more traditional musical theater. Given Fisher's professional experience, this is not surprising.

[41] Hendler, *Diamond Dogs*, 129.

The multiple versions of Fisher's lighting notes on each song betray a close attention to stage elements and to song structure. In a recent interview, Fisher discussed his experience lighting musical works, stressing that, while he connects to musical structures, his understanding and interpretation are not immediate, but carefully considered.[42] Fisher's notes for the 1974 tour show this careful examination of the music. Multiple lyric sheets for each song are included in the files; these appear to be from different legs of the tour. As Bowie's conception of the show as a whole changed, so too did Fisher's lighting design for each song. Throughout, Fisher has corrected small misprints in the lyric sheets.[43] See, for example, his notes on "Rebel Rebel": the printed lyrics do not include the opening "Hot tramp, I love you so," but Fisher inserts it, also noting that the printed lyrics for the second verse are incorrect. While the first correction is undoubtedly important for Fisher's cuing as those lyrics mark the beginning of the song, the latter is less essential to the song's formal structure. Rather, it shows Fisher's attention to the lyrical content as a sort of plotline in the show: were the second verse to be an exact replication of the first, the lighting's role would be quite similar. Instead, Fisher is meticulous in his attention to lyrical detail and the visual plotting of this stage show.

Beyond notations on the timing and blocking of the show relative to the lyrics, sheets included among Fisher's papers hint at a broader, narrative interpretation of the songs. Songs like "Changes" list descriptors for the mood or theme of the song.[44] Written in all caps, the annotator labels the first verse of "Changes" as "HONEST" while "these children that you spit on" is labeled "HEAVY" and the final iteration of the chorus "EXPANSIVE." While these notes don't tell us exactly what was planned for the narrative of "Changes" within the show, the notations hint toward a broader understanding of the songs. Beyond just the lyrics, there is a focus on the import or affect of each song as well. Thus, the production design takes into account the broader picture of Bowie's oeuvre, expanding the show's narrative beyond just the lyrically linked *Diamond Dogs* material.

Fisher speaks of the show as being narrative, a feature he notes as quite different from earlier rock shows. Fisher, who had by this point worked on tours for musicians like Laura Nyro, emphasizes the importance of story to

---

[42] Jules Fisher, interview with the author, August 11, 2020.
[43] Lyric sheet for "Rebel Rebel," Jules Fisher Papers, ARC-0098, Box 1, Folder 7, Rock and Roll Hall of Fame Library and Archives, Cleveland, Ohio.
[44] Lyric sheet for "Changes," Jules Fisher Papers, ARC-0098, Box 1, Folder 7, Rock and Roll Hall of Fame Library and Archives, Cleveland, Ohio.

the Diamond Dogs tour. In our interview, Fisher made a point to mention "story meetings" in which he and Bowie would discuss the trajectory of the stage show.[45] Despite the fact the set lists would differ from night to night, Fisher maintains that the narrative thrust of the show remained important and differed from the structure of the album discussed above. He says that the planning process never involved the sort of book that one might expect to accompany a stage musical, but Bowie was intent on what Fisher calls a "mood story."[46] Fisher's notations on lyric sheets point to exactly this: a story told in broad strokes, one that leaves interpretive room for the audience and for the performer.

A MainMan memo from September 1974 shows that these details of plot were of the utmost importance to all involved. The memo discusses changes to be made on subsequent shows, which would eventually come to be known as the Philly Dogs or Soul leg of the tour. It was during this time that Bowie, working on the *Young Americans* album, made personnel and set list changes to reflect his new musical direction. With the addition of Ava Cherry, Robin Clark, Luther Vandross, and others on backing vocals, as well as Carlos Alomar on guitar, the original *Diamond Dogs* material was integrated into a new, more soul-inflected set. Given this new focus, the narrative established in the tour's early shows needed to be changed. The aforementioned memo gives rare insight into Bowie's conception of the set list, laying out some of the possible permutations that could shape the new song order. Essentially, Bowie saw these songs as operating in discrete units, each one a musical and narrative moment. The groups span different eras and albums, combining, in the case of the first group, songs from *The Rise and Fall of Ziggy Stardust and the Spider From Mars, Aladdin Sane, Diamond Dogs,* and the new soul album he was recording. These moments, the memo explained, could be reordered within the grand scheme of the set list, but would remain in their groups, maintaining their relationship to each other. The anonymous author of the MainMan missive recognizes the convoluted nature of this semi-organization, writing that "Bowie has separated the songs into four groups. He doesn't know which of these groups he will perform first or in what order he will perform the songs within the group (confused?)."[47] While Fisher may have been confused (and we along with

---

[45] Jules Fisher, interview with the author, August 11, 2020.
[46] Ibid.
[47] Memo from MainMan to Jules Fisher, September 1974, Jules Fisher Papers, ARC-0098, Box 1, Folder 4, Rock and Roll Hall of Fame Library and Archives, Cleveland, Ohio.

him), this sort of structure hints that Bowie may have been using a favorite compositional technique in the ordering of his set lists: the cut up.

In 1973 and 1974, Bowie began openly discussing his use of this technique, made famous by Beat author William S. Burroughs. Most famously, Bowie shared his thoughts on the concept in a *Rolling Stone* interview with Burroughs, as well as in the 1975 BBC documentary *Cracked Actor*, which took audiences inside the world of the 1974 *Diamond Dogs* tour. To create a cut up, any text may be used: the author should disassemble the text in the manner of their choosing, and then recombine it. Burroughs and Brion Gysin, in their *The Third Mind*, cite this technique as a way to reveal new, extant but obscured meanings in material.[48] The cut up may be divided in any way the author prefers (Burroughs and Gysin show some by paragraph, phrase, or geometric shape) and should be randomly recombined, in order to tap into the "third mind" which exists outside the author and the text.[49] In the documentary *Cracked Actor*, Bowie discusses his own cut up process. He shows how diary entries can be turned into lyrics through the transformative process. Though he literally cuts up these words for the purposes of the documentary film, it seems that the procedure may have been used on a broader scale in this set list construction. Here, too, we find Bowie dividing up his materials, and setting parameters by which to recombine them.

Such a technique would make sense in this particular case: Bowie, presented with circumstances vastly different from the start of the tour, now needed to find a new way of making sense of the combination of his *1984*-inspired material, and his newer "plastic soul." Burroughs' cut ups show one way to integrate independent texts. In this memo, then, we can see the process by which Bowie is attempting to make disparate works communicate with each other. "Confused," as our MainMan memo asks? Certainly a little, but this process would be in keeping with Bowie's known working patterns at the time.

Film and Video in the World of Diamond Dogs

Apart from his role in designing and adapting the tour's lighting to match the narrative, Fisher was tasked with other responsibilities in bringing the tour to fruition. Early planning documents seem to show Fisher and company planning preliminary budgets and contacting a variety of potential venues to ensure that the technical specifications of the tour's equipment could be met. The initial

---

[48] William S. Burroughs and Brion Gysin, *The Third Mind* (New York: Viking Books, 1978).
[49] Burroughs and Gysin, *The Third Mind*.

planning stage of the tour is revealing for the aspects that did not come to pass: a planned large Aladdin Sane style lighting fixture, for example.[50] Even more importantly, though, these documents show that Bowie, Ravitz, and Fisher had planned the inclusion of film and video projection.

In the modern pop star's tour arsenal, video is an unsurprising tool. Whether projecting closeup views of the performer or ancillary imagery, video screens have long been a staple of touring shows. In 1974, though, they were less so, and in this project in particular, the inclusion of projection is striking. As noted, Bowie had conceived of this project as a film—possibly before the tour began—even shooting some rough footage and storyboarding scene ideas. Thus, the inclusion of a film artist and film projection equipment in the tour's initial budget is tantalizing for its possibilities. Could Fisher and Bowie have intended to include some of that footage in the tour?

Bowie's 1974 tour comes at an important moment in rock history and performance practice. Michael Walker labels 1973 as the year the Sixties died and a new sort of rock stardom was born. Though his work focuses much more on the shenanigans that marked 1973-4 tours by Led Zeppelin, the Who, and Alice Cooper as separate and different from the hippie-infused 1960s rock scene, there is a yet more important aesthetic consideration to these tours.[51] That is, the theatricality that 1973-5 would bring to the rock stage. Each of the three acts discussed by Walker shows just this theatricality, though in different ways. Alice Cooper's makeup and sets are quite different from the physical theater of a Led Zeppelin performance (as described by scholars like Susan Fast[52]), but they are united by an approach to rock as spectacle. That spectacle sometimes involved multimedia approaches—we could think, for example, of the Who's *Tommy* (1975) or the Led Zeppelin concert film *The Song Remains the Same* (1976). Both films capitalize on the power of the moving image to enliven and enhance the band's performances, though that focus does not appear as directly in their stage shows of the era.

This time period is one of technological change, and the concerts of the era can be seen to incorporate those technologies in a variety of different ways. From the expanded possibilities of live sound manipulation to the introduction of the

---

[50] Jules Fisher budget, April 13, 1974, Jules Fisher Papers, ARC-0098, Box 1, Folder 2, Rock and Roll Hall of Fame Library and Archives, Cleveland, Ohio.
[51] Michael Walker, *What You Want Is in the Limo* (New York: Spiegel and Grau, 2013), ix–xii.
[52] Susan Fast, *In the Houses of the Holy: Led Zeppelin and the Power of Rock Music* (New York: Oxford University Press, 2001).

Sony Portapak in the late 1960s and the VCR in the mid-1970s, this time period provided many new tools for multimedia and video artists. The rise of video art was not lost on Bowie, who would go on to collaborate with artists Nam June Paik and Tony Oursler at later stages in his career.[53]

Thus, the mid-1970s are a sort of perfect storm of influences. The theatricality and excess of 1970s rock, with its concept albums and larger-than-life personae, seemingly begged for more intricate staging in live shows. The development of video technology and the slow lowering of projection costs met this need. In theater productions, both rock music and these various new technologies were already being explored. In order to put it into practice on tour, though, theater professionals' expertise was needed on tour staff. Coupling soundboard advances already in use *and* the lighting and staging experience of seasoned Broadway professionals, the mid-1970s birthed a new sort of rock concert.

Apart from the Diamond Dogs tour, many other touring productions help illuminate this era in rock, technology, and theatrics, some of which have been studied in great depth. Genesis's *Lamb Lies Down on Broadway* tour of 1974–5 fits the bill, with its use of costumes and projected slides to depict the concept album's narrative. Kevin Holm-Hudson calls it "the culmination of Genesis's contributions toward an emerging sense of rock theater," noting a similarity between Bowie and Gabriel in their approach to this aspect of rock.[54] Greater mediatization was also occurring in stage shows like the Grateful Dead's use of light, or the slide projection that Paul Hegarty and Martin Halliwell address in Hawkwind's mid-1970s tours.[55] But an even more successful example might be the Rolling Stones' 1975 Tour of the Americas. Production designer Fisher was also hired for this tour, and with the Stones' greater popularity (and money) he was able to accomplish much that was floated for Bowie's tour but never happened. Hendrik Hertzberg of *The New Yorker* described the tour's Madison Square Garden stop as a Futurist extravaganza, highlighting the projected images of flying eagles on the walls, and the mechanical stage set up that slowly revealed Mick Jagger within a large lotus flower.[56] This is quite a departure from tours of the 1960s, when their

---

[53] See, for example, Darryl Perrins, "'You Never Knew That, That I Could Do That': Bowie, Video Art, and the Search for Potsdamer Platz," in *Enchanting David Bowie: Space/Time/Body/Memory*, ed. Toija Cinque, Christopher Moore, and Sean Redmond (New York: Bloomsbury Academic, 2015), 323–36.
[54] Kevin Holm-Hudson, *Genesis and the Lamb Lies Down on Broadway* (New York: Ashgate, 2008), 29.
[55] Hegarty and Halliwell, *Beyond and before*, 122–3.
[56] Hendrik Hertzberg, "Three Musical Situations," *The New Yorker*, June 30, 1975, https://www.newyorker.com/magazine/1975/07/07/three-musical-situations Accessed November 30, 2021.

use of stage design and technology was much less integral to their performances. In each of these instances, we can see the slow integration of video and film into the stage rock star showcase. The Diamond Dogs planning documents show that it would have been yet more advanced in its use of both film and video onstage.

The details of this planned film and video are sparse. Initial budget projections written in Fisher's hand from April 13, 1974 (about a month before the release of the *Diamond Dogs* album and two months before the beginning of the tour) list a film artist as well as a video artist.[57] The inclusion of both is telling. While Bowie could have used clips from existing films, projected from a film print, the video artist may point to other possibilities. In Ravitz's initial planning boards, there is reference to a large screen on stage.[58] That screen seems to have been conceived of as a sort of "Telescreen" in Orwell's *1984*: like the screen installed in all homes, this screen would show *and* tell, watching those who attended the concerts. Ravitz's drawings seem to show the potential for live edited video that would bring the audience directly into the narrative Bowie was crafting onstage by juxtaposing video images of the audience with pre-recorded video of Bowie and others. This gambit was not entirely new. In fact, the Rolling Stones famously accomplished a similar feat in their 1969 tour. Turning on the house lights during "Little Queenie," the Stones made their audience "conscious of itself *as* a crowd," as Steve Waksman put it.[59] Bowie and company intended to take this a step further: not only would they show the crowd *as crowd*, they would put the crowd *on stage*. This speaks directly to the plot and construction of *Diamond Dogs*, the album the tour was meant to support. As Glenn Hendler and Shelton Waldrep have shown, Bowie's invocation of the world of *1984*, his free shift between different voices, and his frequent use of direct address all help to create an immersive audience experience.[60] With the help of his theater design crew, Bowie's tour could have done the same. The possibility of this sort of integrated audiovisual storytelling is enticing—it would have allowed an immersive experience for the audience and an additional level of narrative engagement with the *Diamond Dogs/1984* world.

---

[57] Jules Fisher budget, April 13, 1974, Jules Fisher Papers, ARC-0098, Box 1, Folder 2, Rock and Roll Hall of Fame Library and Archives, Cleveland, Ohio.

[58] Victoria Broackes, "Putting Out Fire," in *David Bowie Is Inside*, ed. Victoria Broackes and Geoffrey Marsh (London: V&A Publishing, 2013), 132.

[59] Quoted in Steve Waksman, "The Road to Altamont: The Rolling Stones on Tour, 1969," in *Beggars Banquet and the Rolling Stones' Rock and Roll Revolution: "They Call My Name Disturbance,"* ed. Russell Reising (New York: Routledge, 2020), 178.

[60] Hendler, *Diamond Dogs*, 73–4.

In Ravitz's personal sketches, elevations for the construction of such a rear projection video screen exist. The screen looks as though it features inflatable and/or silk-screened components; such devices were considered for other aspects of the staging, including buildings that were silkscreened. Though Ravitz himself has no detailed memory of this filmic aspect of the project, archival materials show that it must have progressed at least far enough to warrant detailed sketches as a prelude to construction. The evidence from Fisher's budgets corroborates such an interpretation.

It is feasible that Bowie's own homemade *Hunger City* videos may have been planned as a part of the tour. Perhaps the budget line item for a video artist could have been intended to flesh out this project, though Bowie has spoken about the *Hunger City* film as a separate entity. Unfortunately, the documentary evidence is sparse, so it is impossible to know for sure. It is clear, though, that in the planning stage both film and video were conceived of as a part of the tour, and that they served distinct purposes from one another. In later Bowie tours, both formats would have a role. As soon as 1976's Isolar tour, Bowie would project film. Those concerts would open with Buñuel and Dalí's *Un chien andalou* (1929) in its entirety before the performer took the stage with his band. This 1976 tour uses only film projection, without needing rear projection or live video editing. The setup can be seen in fan-shot Super 8 footage: the screen served almost like a curtain, rising at the end of the film as guitarist Stacy Heydon began playing "Station to Station."[61] The idea of setting the stage through the inclusion of filmic inspiration is not far-fetched for Bowie, then.[62] Given Ravitz and Fisher's notes, one could easily compile a list of potential films for inclusion on the Diamond Dogs tour: Robert Wiene's *The Cabinet of Dr Caligari* (1920) is an obvious choice, as is Fritz Lang's *Metropolis* (1927). As both are quite long films, it seems unlikely that they would have been considered for inclusion without substantial editing, which may have been the plan for the "film artist" line item in Fisher's budget. Later tours, including the 1990 Sound + Vision retrospective, would use video to show Bowie in close up, while other sequences would incorporate the projection of set pieces like his "Look Back in Anger" feature with dancers La La La Human

---

[61] See, for example, "David Bowie • Station to Station • Live 1976," Nacho Video, uploaded July 1, 2016, https://www.youtube.com/watch?v=XAj2iX9xqCo Accessed December 6, 2021. The video incorporates footage shot by Phillippe Bergeron at the Montreal Forum in 1976.

[62] Indeed, Bowie opened *Ziggy Stardust* shows with the Wendy Carlos version of the "Ode to Joy" from Beethoven's Symphony No. 9 as a nod to Kubrick's *A Clockwork Orange* (1971). This can be heard at the opening of the *Live Santa Monica '72* album (a recording of Bowie's October 20, 1972 show), as well as in *Ziggy Stardust and the Spiders from Mars: The Motion Picture* (dir. Pennebaker, 1973).

Steps. The possibilities in the Diamond Dogs tour are many, considering Bowie's ongoing *Hunger City* film project and his choreography work with Toni Basil for the tour.

Neither film nor video would be seen in the eventual 1974 tour, though. The video artist and projection were the first to be excised from the budget, as is shown in the typewritten version of Fisher's initial budget. This is likely because of their exorbitant expense: the video projection alone shows a budget of $2,000, more than that of the lighting for the tour. This makes sense given the advancement of video technology in 1974. It would still have been prohibitively expensive to project video in a large format, and would have required its own equipment separate from the film projector. That film projection remained in the budget, though, as Fisher researched and included projection choices (specifically, a "16 mm –Zenon Arc—Remote Control" projector[63]). Fisher also included a provision for three prints of whatever was intended for this film projection. Given the equipment, that could be still images or film clips. The projection of still images, either on a scrim or on the venue's ceiling, was similarly a staple of Bowie concerts throughout his career. From the 1971–2 projections of photographs and visual artworks (both Bowie's own and that of other artists) to the intricate projected stagecraft of the 1990 Sound + Vision tour, this idea remained important for Bowie. Either way, in the initial stages, it is clear that the Diamond Dogs tour was conceived of as a multimedia event, and one that would bring together various aspects of Bowie's planning on this broader project.

Thus the 1974 Diamond Dogs tour shows an important moment in the development of Bowie's performance style, and the style of rock arena shows more broadly. Many of the innovations planned for Bowie's tour would not be realized, but in future productions designed by Fisher, they would come to take center stage. Even one year later, technology and prices for that technology had changed enough to allow for a much more elaborate show to be planned for the aforementioned Rolling Stones' 1975 Tour of the Americas. Also designed by Fisher, this tour would feature large arena shows (both indoors and out), with elaborate lighting and a specially designed stage shape. From the lotus flower stage, Mick Jagger and company performed amid large inflatable puppets. Interestingly, the idea of "inflatable sculpture objects" was also in play in the

---

[63] Jules Fisher budget, 1974, Jules Fisher Papers, ARC-0098, Box 1, Folder 2, Rock and Roll Hall of Fame Library and Archives, Cleveland, Ohio.

early stages of *Diamond Dogs* planning, as Fisher's papers show.[64] Whether this idea was simply *en vogue* at the time, or a favorite device of Fisher's (the common link between the two productions), remains unclear. What is clear is that the increased budget and advanced technology of the Stones' 1975 tour allowed these ideas to be implemented.

The Rolling Stones' 1975 tour was much more grand than Bowie's 1974 outing, though they share a similar theatricality. In a Jules Fisher memo to Mick Jagger, he explains the various lighting innovations that will be used on the tour. These include more automation than on the Bowie tour, as well as a wider variety of lights. This difference is due, at least in part, to budget: the Stones were a much bigger, more established act in 1975 than was Bowie. Beyond that difference, though, the Stones had the benefit of quickly evolving technology. Many of the innovations Fisher suggests for the Stones would have been fitting for Bowie's "TheaTour," but were not as widely available only a year earlier.

We can see, in Bowie's stage show, the roots of a developing rock performance style. Informed by theatrical conventions, this style is spectacular in its nature: it aims not just to show you the performer and their skills, but also to present a cohesive, multimedia experience. Today, this seems like a given. Earlier rock shows, though, focused almost solely on the performer, without the benefit of extravagant lighting, staging, or choreography. Taking cues from more flamboyant performers of the past, glam rockers like Bowie embraced the theatricality of Little Richard and his contemporaries. In the hands of glam performers like Alice Cooper and Bowie, Little Richard and Jerry Lee Lewis's flamboyant dress morphed into elaborate stage shows like that planned for *Diamond Dogs*.[65] While not everything worked in that 1974 Bowie tour, it is still a clear example of changing performance practice.

In discussions of Bowie's performance practice, theatricality is often a focus. Philip Auslander uses the better-documented Ziggy Stardust tour as the prime example of this flaunting of the rock tradition of "authenticity" in Bowie's stage shows. Auslander is quick to point out, though, that Bowie did not stage the *Ziggy* album as a sort of rock opera.[66] Instead, Bowie and company used

---

[65] Auslander also discusses the connection between these early rock and roll musicians and glam stage presentation. See Philip Auslander, *Performing Glam Rock: Gender and Theatricality in Popular Music* (Ann Arbor: University of Michigan Press, 2006), 139.

[64] Jules Fisher budget, April 13, 1974, Jules Fisher Papers, ARC-0098, Box 1, Folder 2, Rock and Roll Hall of Fame Library and Archives, Cleveland, Ohio.

[66] Auslander, *Performing Glam*, 138.

stark lighting and stage blocking to convey a drama and excitement, playing the various band members off each other in stage movement that went beyond their musical interplay. The *Ziggy* shows included dramatic set pieces, as in the "Width of a Circle" battle between bassist Trevor Bolder and guitarist Mick Ronson.[67] Such set pieces are also present in the 1974 tour, but it is clear that Bowie and company sought to add the overarching narrative connection that the *Ziggy* shows lacked.

Reviewers of the tour noted the change and placed it within a new direction in rock performance. John Rockwell's *New York Times* review of the first Madison Square Garden show, for example, names Bowie a "self-professed bisexual glitter-theater wizard."[68] Though the label and some of the commentary sound a mocking tone, Rockwell nonetheless positions Bowie's theatricality as a harbinger: "More and more rock hands [*sic*] have lost interest in the more bovine kind of concert, wherein bands stand in stoned stolidity and just play."[69] The Diamond Dogs "TheaTour" was certainly conceived as a move in this direction. As Rockwell's review shows, even after the extensive movable sets were damaged and retired, Bowie retained the theatrical bent of the original tour plan. The dancing "Dogs" Gui Andrisano and Warren Peace (Geoff MacCormack) were used to dramatic effect. Extant recordings show the playful interchange between Andrisano, Peace, and Bowie on numbers like "Jean Genie."[70] With dramatic and responsive lighting, backup dancers acting out a narrative, and a carefully ordered setlist, the 1974 Diamond Dogs tour signals a move toward a theatricality focused on narrative rather than simply spectacle. Film and video were, it seems, the missing pieces in its final iteration.

Hunger City Film Project

While Bowie's stage show made waves across the country, another branch of the large-scale conceptual work progressed. The world of *Diamond Dogs* was a rich one, and Bowie intended to bring it to life as fully as possible. The stage show represented one such approach: with its *Cabaret* structure and careful

---

[67] For a full analysis, see Auslander, *Performing Glam,* 139.
[68] John Rockwell, "Pop Music: Bowie Puts on Lavish Show at the Garden," *New York Times* July 21, 1974.
[69] Rockwell, "Bowie Puts on Lavish Show."
[70] See *David Bowie: The Last Five Years* (dir. Whately, 2017).

choreography, the tour in its ideal form captured Hunger City in a visceral way. However, the loss of much of the stage set in July 1974 necessitated a change in plans. Bowie would later refer to the shift as a moment when he lost interest in the project,[71] but evidence indicates that this may be a reshaping of the facts. Personal interviews with other collaborators suggest that the visual elements created for the *Hunger City* film do not predate the tour, indicating that the film's conception may have followed the destruction of the stage set.

By mid-summer 1974, the film project had advanced to rough video shoots of the opening credits, as shown in the 2017 documentary *The Last Five Years* (dir. Whately). This sparse footage presents a tantalizing view of Bowie's directorial vision, a window into the vision of Hunger City that had developed in Bowie's imagination since the inception of the *1984* adaptation. Beyond this, it is not known how much footage was shot, or how far the plan for that specific footage went.[72] The *Hunger City* film was clearly deeply important to Bowie. Speaking in 1980, he recalled, "I wanted to make a film of 'Diamond Dogs' *so* passionately, *so* badly."[73] He describes his process of creating miniature sets for the film in his New York hotel, manipulating the camera through these small, ramshackle streets. This 1980 interview, six years after he abandoned the project, shows some of the allure it still held.

We do have evidence, however, that Bowie had very carefully planned beyond this opening sequence, detailing a course of action to continue shooting the film. Within the David Bowie Archive, materials like sketches for scenery and characters show such a plan.[74] The sketches are frequently small (smaller than an 8.5 × 11-inch sheet of paper) and are sometimes on lined notebook paper. These material choices are consistent with other Bowie documents, like lyrics in process, and suggest that the sketches were intended for planning only. Were they to be filmed or shown as part of a presentation, they would likely have been larger, cleaner, and more detailed. This is the case for the materials that were filmed as opening credits, as well as the sketches and painted miniatures Mark Ravitz created for the planning of the 1974 tour. Some character drawings and settings are rendered in full color, on more sturdy materials. These seem

---

[71] Du Noyer, "Contact," 373.

[72] The only publicly available information about this film project can be found in *The Last Five Years* and the Victoria and Albert Museum's *David Bowie Is* exhibition and its catalogue.

[73] Angus MacKinnon, "The Future Isn't What It Used to Be," in *Bowie on Bowie: Interviews and Encounters with David Bowie*, ed. Sean Egan (Chicago: Chicago Review Press, 2015), 123.

[74] These materials, owned by the David Bowie Archive, were exhibited in the *David Bowie Is* exhibition and app, but are not available for reproduction here.

to have been constructed for use: specifically, for use in the test footage Bowie shot on videotape. The full extent of these drawings is unclear, as the Archive remains closed to researchers and the general public. However, materials from the *Hunger City* project have featured in each iteration of the *David Bowie Is* exhibition, in that show's catalogue, and in the accompanying augmented reality app released in January 2019. In the app, *Diamond Dogs* has its own dedicated section, with many of the film materials displayed and discussed at length. Given the prominence of the materials in these, the first public glimpses of Bowie's collection, we can safely assume that the project held some significance for Bowie himself.

The sketches show a visual world similar to that of the stage design for the Diamond Dogs tour. As in the design of that set, Bowie uses vibrant colors and a dilapidated cityscape that speaks of decay and danger. It is notable that the collaborators responsible for that stage design were not aware of the film plans at all. In our personal communication, Ravitz did not remember any discussion of a film project and had no familiarity with Bowie's marker sketches shown in the *David Bowie Is* exhibition.[75] Given that lack of direct collaboration and the clear influence of Ravitz's visual style, it seems probable that these sketches were made after the initial plans for the tour and perhaps even after the tour's storytelling potential seemed compromised. The visual similarities are too striking to be mere coincidence, and there would have been little time between the April 1974 meeting with Ravitz and the start of tour rehearsals for any extensive film planning. It is likely, then, that these sketches and the footage could both date from August 1974, when Bowie was on break from the tour, and the set had been decimated the month before. With the stage show no longer able to accomplish its goals, the *Hunger City* film project came into being, reviving the dramatic potential of *Diamond Dogs*.

That potential was carefully fleshed out by Bowie himself. In a synopsis, character sketches, and storyboards, he created an extended narrative that expanded upon the *Cabaret*-structured story of the album and the stage show's "mood story." Some connections remained. The main character Halloween Jack appears in planning documents, as do Harpie and the "Dogs" themselves. Interestingly, Bowie gives a tentative cast list in the opening titles he shot: he himself will play Harpie, while friends and collaborators, like Cyrinda Foxe (who appeared in the "Jean Genie" video), Ben Gyn, and more, round out the

---

[75] Mark Ravitz in email communication with the author, November 3, 2019.

cast of characters. Specific scenarios for these characters are less clear. Still, from the available documents, we might piece together some of *Hunger City*'s story, visual language, and place within Bowie's moving image oeuvre.

Unfortunately for our knowledge the film's story itself, a complete synopsis is not available. There is, however, a handwritten description of the world of *Hunger* City, as well as a rundown of the planned opening of the film. These planning documents evince more careful, sustained attention than do available documents from other planned film projects. For example, the 1975 *Major Tom* planned film seemed to consist of little more than a few sketches and some loose narrative planning. Drawings are not on separate, dedicated pages and, while there is some engagement with the planned use of the filmic apparatus, it is not particularly detailed.[76] With *Hunger City*, Bowie seems to have written much more material. All is in his hand, rather than typewritten, which seems to suggest that the plan had not moved to more formal stages that would have required the circulation of memos within a production unit. Indeed, the handwritten pages include scratched out words and the sort of misspellings that are characteristic of Bowie's writing. They appear to have been written by and *for* himself, rather than for collaborators or a production company. All indications show that, while this project captivated Bowie, it remained informal and personal.

The dating of this material is a matter of debate. While I contend that the visual planning documents, including the sketches, are likely from August 1974, the David Bowie Is app labels one written planning document as originating in 1973. Such a date would be fascinating, as it would predate the entirety of the *Diamond Dogs* album, as well as the evolution of the stage show detailed above. This would link it more closely to *The 1980 Floor Show*, that earlier iteration of the Orwellian concept. In that case, it could be a script treatment for a stage adaptation. If it is indeed a film script, though, we might understand it as having been composed after the MainMan meeting with George Orwell's widow, when adaptation rights to *1984* were denied. The script does not bear the title of that book, nor does it reference characters or settings within it. Rather, like the album and the touring stage show, the inspiration is more loose. In addition to this "First Page of Diamond Dogs Script, 1973," the *David Bowie Is* exhibition also featured a written treatment of the film's opening. Some of the visuals described are similar to what was shot on video, indicating that this detailed description

---

[76] Materials from this project were shown in the *David Bowie Is* exhibition's Brooklyn Museum iteration.

likely dates from around the same time as the video. In it, Bowie not only describes what will be shown on screen, but also details the way each object will move, and the framing of each shot.

The archive has also displayed documents that point to specific characters and settings that make up the planned *Hunger City*. Character sketches and small miniatures show the tattered wardrobe of the world; oddly, the Dogs are depicted on roller skates in these miniatures and some marker sketches. Beyond this, Bowie created an extensive chart showing the planned scenarios of the film. Little narrative information is visible in it, but he does specify settings and characters, plotting out who would appear in what setting in which scene. This planning appears to be extensive. Thirty-four different scenes are plotted; it is unclear whether these numbers correspond to the storyboard cells discussed below. Regardless, it is clear that Bowie approached this film with more than a passing interest: he planned, plotted, and drew this world into being.

Analyzing the Film

It is a strange project to analyze an unrealized film. To do so, I draw on the archival materials as well as the audiovisual style information we have about Bowie. He spoke about films (his own and those he liked) in many interviews. His visual art gives clues to the styles for which he felt an affinity, as does his extensive art collection. The music videos discussed in the previous chapter show his auteurist tendencies. In the end, however, much of this analysis takes the form of informed reconstruction. My conclusions are reached via close attention to the album itself and the most specific of the film planning materials. Despite my best efforts, this analysis will necessarily owe as much to my reading and understanding of Bowie's *modus operandi* as to Bowie himself. However, there is still much to be learned from the detritus of this abandoned *Hunger City* project, and close analysis shows the common threads of Bowie's manipulation of the moving image.

Of all these materials, the only extant, readily available footage is of the opening credits. Fanmade videos identify this footage as being shot on an RCA video camera with the assistance of cameraman John Dove, though this is difficult to confirm.[77] Dove is also noted as the cameraman for the only extant

---

[77] David Cantello, "Diamond Dogs—an Unfinished Film by David Bowie," *Dailymotion*, https://www.dailymotion.com/video/x59bv6m Accessed December 2, 2021.

professionally shot footage of the Diamond Dogs tour. That footage, parts of which were screened in the *David Bowie Is* exhibition, gives the clearest image of the Diamond Dogs tour that exists. Dove's apparent knowledge of the *Diamond Dogs* material and familiarity with Bowie (he had also helped to shoot the "Life on Mars?" video) would have made him an obvious choice for this stripped-down attempt at filmmaking as proof of concept for *Hunger City*.

Given the likely equipment used and the lack of access to an editing suite, it seems probable that the effects achieved in these opening credits were the product of in-camera techniques. In this, Bowie also drew on German Expressionist filmic style. Fritz Lang's *Metropolis*, noted as a source of visual inspiration for the tour's style, also featured innovative in-camera effects to bring its titular city to life. Lang used the Shuftan process, described by film historian Siegfried Kracauer as "an ingenious mirror device permitting the substitution of little models for giant structures."[78] Introduced by Eugene Schuftan in the early days of German film experiments, this process uses a mirror to reflect a drawn or painted model of the setting of the scene to be shot. A section of that mirror's surface is scratched away, allowing the camera to see through the mirror and capture the movement of the human subjects of the scene, seemingly placed within the drawn or painted setting. We can see this effect in the *Hunger City* test footage, as a miniature Bowie himself is placed within the cardboard setting he created. Such an effect could also be achieved using matte paintings, a common practice in Hollywood filmmaking. However, that process typically relies on paintings on glass; the archival evidence shows that Bowie's settings were not created in this way. Indeed, the process used in *Metropolis* seems a likely candidate for Bowie's experiments. It is easily accomplished in camera and requires none of the repeated exposure that was typical of the use of mattes. It is very possible that Bowie or his cameraman was aware of the Shuftan process; Kracauer and others wrote about it as early as the 1940s, and Bowie was an infamously voracious reader. Regardless of whether or not he was copying the *technique*, the final product was similar in *effect* to Lang's legendary *Metropolis* innovations.

The miniature sets themselves also show this German Expressionist influence. Bowie's treatment for the opening of the film describes a tower, quite similar to *Metropolis*'s Tower of Babel (see Figure 4.3). This tower is revealed in the filmed opening, though Bowie's notes give much more detail about its potential use in

---

[78] Siegfried Kracauer, *From Caligari to Hitler: A Psychological History of German Film*, Princeton Classics Edition (Princeton: Princeton University Press, 2019), 149.

Figure 4.3 Still from *Metropolis* (1927, dir. Lang).

Hunger City. Introduced as a monolith at sunrise, the tower's initial appearance could be a reference to Kubrick's *2001: A Space Odyssey* (which was, of course, a favorite visual touchstone for Bowie), or indeed the towers of *A Clockwork Orange*, another favorite. Like that *2001* monolith, *Hunger City*'s tower is at first shiny and beautiful. In Bowie's imagining, this tower was white with chrome balconies, shown in glowing sunlight. The tower was then to rotate slowly, aging as it moved. With each revolution, the tower became shabbier and more dilapidated; the daylight was intended to wane in tandem. In Bowie's film, the tower would be used as an avatar for the rot and decay of Hunger City's society. Much like the ultimately doomed tower of its Biblical and filmic predecessors, *Hunger City*'s tower seems to represent the fatal flaw at the heart of its society.

Despite Bowie's description of the tower's color and materials, the treatment for this opening specifies, at its heading, that the opening was to be in black and white. Partway through this sequence, a hand in "modern colour" enters the frame to place letters spelling out "BOWIE" and "DIAMOND DOGS." A shift into full color is not labeled, but the later storyboard cells are rendered in color and seem to imply that the contemporary world of the film would be presented in lurid, full-color detail. Bowie's plan implies a division between the black-and-white opening sequence and the full color of the world of the film's narrative; via color, he is specifying two different chronological story spaces. This choice is also in keeping with the German Expressionist influence of stage set and story conception. As Thomas Elsaesser notes, a common device among these Weimar era films was fluid narrative movement between discrete temporal moments and framing scenarios.[79] Much like in *Caligari* or *Metropolis*, here Bowie proposes an introductory framing section, meant to give clarity and structure to the narrative that follows. *Caligari* begins with just such a device, as we are invited into the world of the film through a conversation. *Hunger City* does the same with an introduction to the setting of the film. This clear connection to Expressionist cinema is perhaps expected, given Bowie's professed interest in the stylistic movement, but to see such clear structural similarity allows us to analyze other such connections throughout the production material.

Storyboards and Narrative

While some of Bowie's planning documents are idiosyncratic, others show the kind of visual and narrative planning that is typical of a film production. The archive's framing of these materials seems to imply that there exists a complete script for the film. Even without such a script, Bowie's hand-drawn storyboards show a level of detailed planning that suggests extended engagement with this filmic project. Though only nine cells were published in the exhibition catalogue, Bowie's graphic organizer chart for the project seems to reference at least thirty-four discrete scenes.

Bowie's storyboards are among the most illuminating archive material pertaining to *Hunger City*; they reveal more of the nascent filmic style visible in *1980 Floor Show*. While certain cells are directly evocative of Weimar-era German Expressionist cinema, all give an idea of how Bowie intended to use the camera as an integral component of his storytelling. His cell labels not only quote potential dialogue, but also intimate the style of editing and camera movement that might have been found in a fully realized *Hunger City* film. Bowie's labels describe close, intense focus on images of suffering in Hunger City: one reads "close-up of teeth, sideways on, pulls back to reveal two victim

---

[79] Thomas Elsaesser, "Germany: The Weimar Years," in *The Oxford History of World Cinema*, ed. Geoffrey Nowell-Smith (New York: Oxford University Press, 1996), 143.

children fighting."[80] These cells, reproduced in the *David Bowie Is* catalogue, show an active, mobile camera. In this way, they differ from the style of most German Expressionist cinema. In landmark films like *The Cabinet of Dr. Caligari* and *Metropolis*, the camera is largely stationary. This is unsurprising in film of this era and is perhaps not an essential aspect of Expressionist style. It is clear, at least, that Bowie did not see it as such.

In terms of framing and treatment of the bodies of Hunger City's denizens, we can see some similarity to Bowie's early music video style. Videos like "Life on Mars?" treated Bowie's body as a conglomeration of parts: his eyes, lips, hair, and hands were each isolated and highlighted in turn. The segmentation of Bowie's body served not only to highlight the iconic aspects of his appearance, but also to turn him into an object of visual fascination, rather than a unified human subject. The framing and editing choices of those early videos shaped the way people viewed and related to Bowie. Likewise, his storyboard cells betray a similar treatment of the downtrodden masses in Hunger City.

A similarity of style is visible in the light and shadow present in these storyboard cells and the setting and character sketches. Bowie creates for *Hunger City* a starkly lit world wherein shadow cuts across spaces and faces. Much like in Wiene's *The Cabinet of Dr. Caligari*, Bowie uses lighting as an extension of the interiority of his characters, crafting an Expressionist filmic space redolent of psychological torment. In her study of German Expressionist film, Lotte Eisner points to a characteristic "leaning toward violent contrast … the inborn German liking for chiaroscuro and shadow, [which] obviously found an ideal artistic outlet in the cinema."[81] That chiaroscuro is present in all the released storyboards, most especially in cells like #29. The image depicts Jack, in three-quarters view looking over his shoulder to deliver a line. Jack's face is partially shaded, and the background appears to show light obstructed by blinds. In combining deep shadow with the graphic, slightly askew pattern of these blinds, Bowie plays into yet another visual trope of Expressionist cinema: what Lotte Eisner calls "an eerie gift for animating objects."[82]

In her writing on *Caligari*, Eisner highlights the importance of the sets in the film, finding their power in their ability to unsettle the viewer. This is in part due to their unbalanced lines, but also the falsity of their spaces (see Figure 4.4).

---

[80] Broackes, "Putting Out Fire," 132.
[81] Lotte H. Eisner, *The Haunted Screen: Expressionism in German Cinema and the Influence of Max Reinhardt*, trans. Roger Greaves (Berkeley: University of California Press, 1973), 17.
[82] Eisner, *The Haunted Screen*, 23.

Figure 4.4 Still from *The Cabinet of Dr. Caligari* (1920, dir. Wiene).

Bowie borrows this approach, sometimes in quite obvious ways. In addition to the askew blinds of cell 29, many of Bowie's unnumbered set drawings show a similar reliance on sets and props with uneven, tilting angles that seem to enliven and possess the sets. In canted angles and vibrant color, these drawings connect not only to the visual world of *Caligari*, but also to contemporaneous painting styles. In particular, the work of Grosz seems to be a progenitor of Bowie's *Hunger City* style. Grosz's *Metropolis* (1917), for example, creates just such a claustrophobic city, with signs and carriages askew amid a crush of humanity. This same visual approach was clear in the set for the Diamond Dogs tour, where none of the buildings featured perpendicular lines. Those buildings, covered in paper that would be dramatically torn down at the end of each show, took on symbolic importance within the narrative Bowie and company crafted. That angular feature of set design is even more pronounced in Bowie's preparatory drawings for the film. In his test shots, the world of the film is yet more false and disorienting, thanks in part to the use of in-camera effects. The result is a world that feels like an unreal drawing, much like the setting that envelops *Caligari*'s somnambulist. Kracauer notes that these "settings amounted to a perfect transformation of material objects into emotional ornaments."[83] As in the German Expressionist style, sets here were more than mere backdrops. They served to bring the fear and futility of life in Hunger City to more palpable embodiment.

We might assume that the world of a finished *Hunger City* film, then, would be very like that of *Caligari*, where walls seem to close in and buildings themselves appear as reaching, grasping fingers. In fact, the most clearly defined aspect of the failed film project is its world. This is in keeping with the prominence given to the setting of *Diamond Dogs* in the album's lyrics. "Future Legend" opens the album by describing the city itself, and the subsequent title track gives more detail to the world of Halloween Jack. While none of the other characters are named within the album's lyrics, different voices appear throughout, placed within these physical spaces of Hunger City. We can hear more than one permutation of Bowie's voice in the transition from "Sweet Thing" to "Candidate," and the aural setting of those voices changes, too. We can hear within the album different worlds, settings wherein the singer is closer to us, more intimate in address and others that imply a communal boisterous celebration. Settings are given pride of place throughout *Diamond Dogs*. Rooftops, hills, ditches, stairs, curtains, and more populate the album's lyrics. Indeed, the settings themselves *become* characters, seeming to act upon the album's speakers and situations through the manipulation of the soundbox. It is little wonder, then, that Bowie's drawings give so much focus to the abstract, expressionist world of *Hunger City*: it shapes the action of the album and the film in important ways.

Conclusion

This *Hunger City* project is fascinating for its detail and ambition. It is clear from the planning materials that Bowie found the project compelling. Those materials also show the close link between the proposed film and the album as it existed. In fact, many of the visual elements that appeared in the *Hunger City* materials resurfaced in later projects. The Expressionist lighting of the storyboards can be found in the "Ashes to Ashes" video, as well as later music videos. Even the appearance of roller skates, seen on the Dogs in some character sketches, would

---

[83] Kracauer, *From Caligari to Hitler*, 69.

return. "Day In Day Out" shows Bowie on roller skates, gliding through Los Angeles's Skid Row to create an image not too far divorced from 1974's film plan.

In the end, of course, *Hunger City* was never made. It would later be joined in the proverbial dustbin by a number of projects Bowie began to plan: a Major Tom/*Young Americans* film, a Ziggy project in the 2000s, and an unnamed film project around the time of *Tin Machine II*, to name only a few. Though none of these directorial impulses came to fruition, it is striking that Bowie continued to plan them. Even with decades of unrealized screen dreams, the pull of a truly multimedia expression for his work was strong. He storyboarded, created long-running characters and references within music videos, and took on co-director roles in some of his music videos. (It would seem he unofficially co-directed many more, to the joy or chagrin of his credited directors.) He continued to mention his desire to direct, bringing up the subject in interviews from the late 1970s through 2000 at least. While no feature film was ever made, he brought many of these auteurist impulses to his work in other ways, including photography and involvement in video games via *Omicron, BowieWorld*, and more. Had technological constraints been different in 1974, it is tantalizing to consider what *Hunger City* could have looked like.

Part Two

Bowie as Sign

5

Hollywood Highs: Acting Roles and Bowie's Star Image

In an internal Capitol/EMI memo dated April 20, 1978, business affairs manager Arnold Holland approached chairman and CEO Bhaskar Menon with a thorny issue. The company was attempting to sign David Bowie to a record contract through Capitol, but Holland had been told that an EMI Films issue could complicate matters. Bowie, then with a budding film career, was attached to the film project *Walley*, which had been offered to EMI Films. (*Walley* never came to fruition as a feature film.) Per Holland, the company's executive Michael Deeley was vehemently against the project, reportedly stating "If Bowie's in it, I don't want to get involved." Holland voiced concerns about the potential conflict this could cause with the Capitol deal, asking Menon "if EMI Films considers Bowie a viable actor."[1]

Such a question may seem unthinkable now, as some younger audiences know Bowie best through his screen roles. The memo highlights an important tension within Bowie's output, though: the public image Bowie had constructed for himself in the arena of rock would not necessarily transfer directly to film stardom, and his acclaim earned playing the role of "David Bowie" throughout the 1970s did not necessarily mean that he could successfully act on screen. As Serge Denisoff and William Romanowski note, "musical charisma does not always translate onto the big screen," and many musicians' film vehicles bombed at the box office in the early 1980s.[2] More than questioning Bowie's acting ability, the EMI memo seems to pinpoint one essential difference between musical and movie stardom. Embodying a character is necessary for both, but creating a stable star image seems much more important for sustained film stardom. Bowie's film

---

[1] Arnold Holland memo to Bhaskar Menon, April 20, 1978. Jeff Gold Collection ARC-0037 Box AF3, Folder 52, Rock and Roll Hall of Fame Library and Archives, Cleveland, Ohio.
[2] Serge Denisoff and William Romanowski, *Risky Business: Rock in Film* (New Brunswick: Transaction Publishers, 2016), 452.

career is of particular use in analyzing his multimedia work because it brings the tensions of his career into stark relief: celebrated as a rock chameleon, Bowie needed to align his musical star image with an actorly one. As the EMI memo shows, a film career posed challenges for Bowie's money-making ability as well as his skill. The film industry put different pressures on his construction of self than did the music industry; in probing these pressures, we can see Bowie's nuanced approach to star image in the context of films controlled and created by others.

Bowie in Film

Almost as soon as David Bowie began recording music, he also began to act in films. We may take, as a representative example, one such early film credit: his role in *The Image* (1969, dir. Armstrong). Young Bowie appears in this wordless short as the living embodiment of an artist's painting. Birthed of the painter's artistic impulse, the creation works its way into the reality of its creator. The artist is hounded by his creation, which pursues him through his home, violently confronting him. In some ways, this first film role is emblematic of Bowie's many personae. Whether we're discussing those of the stage like Ziggy Stardust and the Thin White Duke, or the screen like Thomas Jerome Newton and Jareth the Goblin King, for many, Bowie the artist seems inseparable from his creations, who are multitudinous and vastly different. These creations sometimes confront Bowie and his newer work in hostile ways.

As previous chapters have discussed, Bowie the musician was active in the creation of his own star image, consciously masking David Jones under each new persona. This masking included a variety of means—vocal, physical, and personality transformation accompanied each shift. A chameleonic approach became something of a calling card for Bowie as, in a paradoxical way, changeability became one of his most defining features. His record company emphasized that characteristic: a 1980 RCA press release touts Bowie's longevity, crediting him with "extending his Warholian fifteen minutes in the limelight by changing character every quarter hour."[3] In press materials for *The Man Who Fell to Earth*, Bowie's first lead film role, that same rhetoric continued. These

---

[3] RCA Records Public Affairs, "Feature Story: David Bowie – A Man for All Decades," December 1979, Rolling Stone Collection ARC-0114 Box A18, Folder 1a, Rock and Roll Hall of Fame Library and Archives, Cleveland, Ohio.

materials refer to the way Bowie has "'reincarnated' himself repeatedly … This time as an actor."[4] For many entertainers, such malleability of not only character but self would be seen as a liability. Bowie sought to capitalize upon it.

In adopting characters on film, Bowie was essentially pursuing the same sort of expression that he did in his musical stage characters. As he said in 1976, "I've been making films on records for years now."[5] *Diamond Dogs* is perhaps the clearest example of such a cinematic record, as it very nearly made the transition to film. When working on Hollywood studio films, though, he created cinematic characters within large productions and a film industry over which he had relatively little influence or control, despite his musical stardom. These film roles, then, give an important window into Bowie's career: the roles he chose reflect his own proclivities, but the way those characters are depicted in the films' final edit and marketed to the public can tell us something about the way the film industry and the world at large wished to understand Bowie. Joshua Gamson has referred to the star image as a negotiation between publicist and media outlets.[6] We might amend that formulation to address Bowie's auteurist tendencies, as established in previous chapters. Rather than publicist and media, here I analyze the interplay between Bowie himself and the film industry writ large. Between performance and marketing, we can see the tension inherent in the creation of an actorly Bowie star image.

Bowie's filmic star image is complex and should not be viewed as authored by him and him alone, though he exerts great control over the musical aspect of his image. Though Richard Dyer does write of some stars whom we might analyze as their own personal auteurs, I understand Bowie as operating a bit differently when he parlays his music stardom into the world of film.[7] We might view Bowie as a blend of the ways he seemed to see himself (not as an overdetermined sign, but as a sort of palimpsest or blank slate), and the way the broader entertainment industry and society sought to see him (as the embodiment of a particular kind of rock star cool, uncomplicated by some of Bowie's more difficult aspects).

The idea of a Bowie star image has been invoked in previous studies, including those by Philip Auslander and Julie Lobalzo Wright. Auslander's work on

---

[4] John Springer Associates *Man Who Fell to Earth* Press Release, Jeff Gold Collection ARC-0037 Box AF1, Folder 18, Rock and Roll Hall of Fame Library and Archives, Cleveland, Ohio.
[5] RCA Press Biography, December 1976, Rolling Stone Collection ARC-0114 Box A18, Folder 1a, Rock and Roll Hall of Fame Library and Archives, Cleveland, Ohio.
[6] Joshua Gamson, *Claims to Fame: Celebrity in Contemporary America* (Berkeley: University of California Press, 1994), 79.
[7] Richard Dyer, *Stars* (London: BFI, 1979), 174.

theatricality in glam rock is particularly relevant. As Auslander notes, it is quite common to hear and read Bowie in an actorly way. On these early albums, such vocal shifts frequently involve direct mimicry of other artists, such as Anthony Newley and T. Rex frontman Marc Bolan.[8] Later in his career, we can hear the assumption of different vocal timbres as clear indicators of persona shifts. In fact, on his 1990 retrospective Sound + Vision tour, Bowie adopts different voices for different periods and songs; a clear example is audible in live recordings of "Rock and Roll Suicide," when the more nasal vocal timbre of Ziggy Stardust takes over from 1990 Bowie. Auslander's focus in his study is restricted to the glam era, and is largely concerned with the idea of theatricality in performance rather than the construction of the public self, but his analytical tools are applicable in a broader analysis of Bowie's performances.

Wright, though, is directly concerned with the concept of star image. In her study, she pinpoints the alienness and otherness of Bowie's acting roles and his public image. Analyzing a variety of film roles, Wright concentrates on a sort of overdetermined outsider star image for Bowie, consistent throughout various eras. Elsewhere, she also approaches Bowie's music videos through the lens of star image.[9] Alien roles, like that of Thomas Jerome Newton in *The Man Who Fell to Earth* (1976, dir. Nicolas Roeg), are emblematic of such consonance in star image. Where early 1970s glam Bowie embraced the extraterrestrial identity of Ziggy Stardust, so too does *The Man Who Fell to Earth*. In fact, the origin story of *The Man Who Fell to Earth*'s casting supports such a reading. Director Roeg saw Alan Yentob's BBC documentary *Cracked Actor*, which followed Bowie on the West Coast leg of the Diamond Dogs tour in 1974.[10] The performance Bowie gave, both on stage and for Yentob's camera, is said to have inspired Roeg to bring him in for a screen test. Bowie's 1974 appearance, as a skeletal, British fish out of water in the American West, suggested many of the traits Roeg sought to bring to life in *The Man Who Fell to Earth*. Writing of this casting choice, Sean Doyle notes the distinct "blurring [of] the line between character and reality."[11] It is true

---

[8] Philip Auslander, *Performing Glam Rock: Gender and Theatricality in Popular Music* (Ann Arbor: University of Michigan Press, 2007), 110–11.

[9] Julie Lobalzo Wright, "The Boy Kept Swinging: David Bowie, Music Video, and the Star Image," in *Music/Video: Histories, Aesthetics, Media*, ed. Gina Arnold, Daniel Cookney, Kirsty Fairclough, and Michael Goddard (New York: Bloomsbury Academic, 2017), 67–8.

[10] Sean Doyle, "Video Essay: The Soundtracks of the Man Who Fell to Earth," *Film Comment* Accessed March 22, 2021, https://www.filmcomment.com/video-essay-the-soundtracks-of-the-man-who-fell-to-earth/

[11] Doyle, "Video Essay."

that a fair amount of Bowie's screen roles accomplish precisely this: they build off of the public's perception of him in a way that seeks to extend and deepen that perception.

While my analysis is indebted to this work, I view Bowie's actorly relationship to the constructed character of "David Bowie" as operating slightly differently. Certain roles do seek to capitalize on Bowie's existing and deeply engrained musical star images, but several other important roles are incongruous with our understanding of the artist. This chapter takes Bowie's acting roles of the mid-1980s as its main focus, and seeks to suss out the tensions between the Bowie constructed in film industry publicity and the Bowie we see in performance, making his own presentational choices. *The Man Who Fell to Earth* and *Merry Christmas, Mr. Lawrence* (1983, dir. Ōshima) have already been masterfully analyzed by Wright, Palmer, and Waldrep, among others, so I do not address them here. Much as in Roeg's earlier *Performance* (1970), *The Man Who Fell to Earth* capitalizes on congruences between musical star image and film role. The otherworldly character Thomas Jerome Newton aligns with the public's understanding of David Bowie in the mid-1970s: an alien rock star plays a literal alien. The film was also initially advertised as featuring Bowie's music. Some 1976 editions of the Walter Tevis novel on which the film is based featured film information on their back covers, including the promise of "music by David Bowie ... Album available on RCA."[12] Of course, that Bowie score never materialized, but the close linkage between his musical and filmic persona in this case is clear. *Merry Christmas, Mr. Lawrence* similarly toys with Bowie's public persona, though here by concentrating on the charisma and allure of the rock star. The eroticized nature of Bowie's depiction on screen tracks nicely with a consistent aspect of his star image: whether appearing as the alien Ziggy Stardust or a *Let's Dance*-era heartthrob, sexuality was central to Bowie's public persona. Both of these performances, as Waldrep points out, achieve their success largely through reliance on the same tools of gesture and image that defined Bowie in the realm of musical performance, too.[13] My two case studies, in contrast, investigate moments of tension between Bowie's established musical star image, the role performed in each film, and the way that role was marketed or communicated to the public. In these films, there is an inherent tension between

---

[12] Walter Tevis, *The Man Who Fell to Earth* (London: Pan, 1976).
[13] Shelton Waldrep, *The Aesthetics of Self-Invention: Oscar Wilde to David Bowie* (Minneapolis: University of Minnesota Press, 2004), 118–19.

Bowie's outsider, cult status and the mainstream success he found in the mid-1980s. In *The Man Who Fell to Earth* and *Merry Christmas, Mr. Lawrence*, Bowie still traded on the cult appeal of his Ziggy Stardust fame. As Jamie Sexton has shown, working with independent, arthouse directors such as Roeg and Ōshima can solidify this aspect of a star's persona, even in the face of more mainstream acceptance.[14] Analyzing his roles in *The Hunger* and *Labyrinth* in comparison to Bowie's musical identities, this chapter instead addresses the purposefully fluid nature of Bowie as star.

Star Image in Film

In this context, I am not concerned with David Bowie (or more accurately, David Jones) as a man, but rather as a sign. Richard Dyer's seminal 1979 monograph *Stars* provides an example of how we might analyze and understand Bowie's carefully crafted public personae. Dyer notes that multiple aspects of a star's output play a role in the construction of a star image; promotion, publicity, films, and commentary are central to this process. Taking Classic Hollywood stars as his examples, Dyer delves into the multifaceted process by which, for example, Lucille LeSueur *becomes* "Joan Crawford"—not only by changing her name, but by the careful control of photographs, gossip, publicity, and roles that the studio system used to craft the idea of Joan Crawford. Given Bowie's cinephilic approach to his art and clear understanding and manipulation of stardom, it is easy to see many of the same facets at play the construction and public promulgation of the "David Bowie" star image. I use "star image" here in the sense that Dyer does: not as literal image alone, but "rather a complex configuration of visual, verbal, and aural signs."[15] Acting roles, appearance, publicity, and personal background (as communicated to the public) all contribute to this star image.

The complex configuration of a star image can take a variety of forms. In particular, Dyer highlights the way the star images can play with or against types.[16] This aspect is especially interesting in the case of Bowie, as typology may be one of the few unifying factors in his ever-changing star image. It is rare

---

[14] Jamie Sexton, "Prisoner of Cool: Chloë Sevigny, Stardom, and Image Management," in *Cult Film Stardom: Offbeat Attractions and Processes of Cultification*, ed. Kate Egan and Sarah Thomas (New York: Palgrave Macmillan, 2012), 78–9.
[15] Dyer, *Stars*, 38.
[16] Ibid., 53.

that a star is seen as a pure type—this would dilute their power as an individual. However, association with a type allows the audience to make sense of and relate to a given star. Dyer uses the examples of Marilyn Monroe and Katharine Hepburn as stars whose multifaceted person and persona become flattened (to a certain extent) in order to facilitate marketing and audience affiliation.[17] Typology allows for more ready identification of the star as well as quicker understanding and appreciation.

Aligning with a type may seem antithetical to the Bowie approach, as much of his media narrative has been concerned with his chameleonic, ever-changing physical appearance and style. However, that very changeability and lack of conformity are themselves a kind of type. In Bowie's case, we may see him as an example of Dyer's anomic type, embodying both the "rebel" and (to an extent) the "independent woman."[18] These types are typically outsiders in some way, struggling against the constraints of dominant society. Dyer lists Marlon Brando, Katharine Hepburn, and Marlene Dietrich as examples.[19] Connections to Bowie are abundant: beyond his direct references to and channeling of each of these stars in his work, there is the clear, consistent framing of Bowie as Other. This tactic began under Bowie's early 1970s manager, Tony DeFries, and continued throughout the 1970s. In fact, Bowie's record label RCA identified and sought to capitalize on this outsider status. In ads for Bowie's *"Heroes"* (1978), the record company asserted "There's old wave, there's new wave, and there's David Bowie." The print ad shows the *"Heroes"* album cover, as well as another photo of a leather-jacket clad Bowie, louchely leaning against a piano. His wardrobe and nonchalant pose evoke the iconic images of fellow anomic type Brando used to advertise *The Wild One* (1953, dir. Benedek). In text and in costuming, the message is clear: David Bowie is not your average, categorizable rocker. Both ads prioritize star image over the work itself. Rather, the idea of Bowie and Brando as emblematic of a rebellious, unique type is foregrounded. Audiences are encouraged to view each work as a vehicle for that star and for that *particularly understanding* of that star: Bowie could not create *"Heroes"* if he were like everyone else, and Brando could not carry *The Wild One* if he did not possess his unique brand of rebellious appeal. Thus, Bowie manages to invoke an existing star type (and marketing strategy) while simultaneously emphasizing the fact of

---

[17] Ibid.
[18] Ibid., 59–60.
[19] Ibid.

his otherness. This strategy of star typing became even more prominent in the promotional materials for Bowie's acting roles.

Dyer lists a variety of factors that determine a star image, among them roles or characters, physical appearance, publicity, and personal background. For our purposes, we will expand the "roles" category to encompass more of Bowie's creative output. This is a particularly interesting area of analysis because of the tension that sometimes existed between Bowie's musical and actorly star images. By analyzing contemporaneous publicity materials from his music and film projects, this study seeks to investigate those tensions. In their occasional lack of congruency, such contradictory attempts to define Bowie help us to get closer to an idea of a stable or consistent Bowie star image.

The strength of Bowie's musical and personal star image casts a long shadow in his filmic work. In a *New Yorker* article appearing the week after Bowie's death in 2016, Anthony Lane surveyed the artist's cinematic legacy. Like many, he labels Bowie an underwhelming leading man, but points to the power of a few onscreen Bowie moments. Lane writes "His cameo in 'Zoolander,' whipping off his shades and guying his own status as a lionized legend beside the catwalk, is not only more entertaining, but more tightly bound to Bowiehood than his entire leading role in 'Merry Christmas, Mr. Lawrence.'"[20] Here, Lane identifies the power of Bowie as undiluted image. For Lane and others, then, Bowie works best when left to his own devices: the semiotic pieces that served Bowie so well throughout his musical career. This "Bowieness" comes through most clearly in roles like his *Zoolander* cameo because the apparatus of the film industry is largely separate from such small roles. Though Bowie is acting in a large budget, major studio release, he is intended to play himself and, as such, has less shaping or amplifying of his star persona from the film and the press surrounding it. It works, Lane seems to argue, because Bowie is presenting and poking fun at his own image. Following Sean Redmond, we might see Bowie as "always *in cameo*" onscreen.[21]

We could see a similar thread between the *Zoolander* appearance and Bowie's other, smaller roles: as Nikola Tesla in *The Prestige* (dir. Nolan, 2006) or a hitman in *Into the Night* (dir. Landis, 1985). Each film allows Bowie to enter the film and rely more on his own charismatic star presence than on his ability to transform into a character. Each emphasizes the things for which rock star

---

[20] Anthony Lane, "David Bowie in the Movies," *New Yorker*, January 13, 2016, https://www.newyorker.com/culture/cultural-comment/david-bowie-in-the-movies Accessed October 6, 2021.

[21] Sean Redmond, "David Bowie: In Cameo," *Cinema Journal* 57, no. 3 (Spring 2018): 150.

Bowie was known: innovation, danger, and (in *The Prestige*, at least) a sort of "elder statesman" presence. *Into the Night* features a series of such "insider" cameos, including directors like John Landis himself, Roger Vadim, Jim Henson, and Amy Heckerling. Still, Bowie is given more screen time than most others and exudes a slickness and appeal that align with his musical star image in 1985. As such, his cameo is among the more successful in a film packed with them, causing *New York Times* critic Vincent Canby to note with regret that Bowie is "on and off too quickly."[22] On the strength of his Bowieness, the cameo succeeds and ties into his current public persona. Even his styling in *Into the Night* echoes Bowie's 1980s stagewear through tailored suits worn with an air of informality, and the casual homoeroticism of Bowie's interaction with star Jeff Goldblum (at one point, Bowie inserts his gun into Goldblum's mouth in a threatening joke) plays on the sexual ambiguity of Bowie's musical star image (see Figure 5.1).

These cameos operate in much the same way as the music video.[23] Without extended exposition, cameo characters are created largely on the strength of their visual presence and charisma—aspects at which Bowie excels. Lane may have been reacting to the connection between the immediate impact of such

Figure 5.1 Still from *Into the Night* (1985, dir. Landis).

---

[22] Vincent Canby, "Film: John Landis' *Into the Night*," *New York Times*, February 22, 1985. Section C Page 8.

[23] While Bowie is, frequently, treated as an object to be viewed in much the same way as his music video presentation, the framing of his body is quite different. The isolating close shots highlighted in Chapter 3 are not present here (and, indeed, would not be particularly fitting for a narrative film.)

cameos and the immediate, visual communication style Bowie honed through decades of music video experimentation. This is not to say that Bowie was not a capable actor, but rather that, for a wide audience familiar with his musical personae, roles that emphasized his established strengths resonated with the most power.

Wright and Rosalind Galt similarly start from an understanding that Bowie's star image works best in certain films: for them, those films that capitalize on his otherness or homoeroticism.[24] In his leading roles, though, Bowie on screen is not *just* Bowie, but rather the version of him that the film wishes to use and coopt. There are many instances in Bowie's cinematic oeuvre that show precisely the congruence to which Galt and Wright attest, but other projects wish to use Bowie in different, more broadly marketable ways. For example, Bowie's role in *The Linguini Incident* (1991, dir. Richard Shepard) is out of step with an alien, outsider understanding of the star. The film (also, hilariously, known as *Shag-o-Rama*) is a romantic caper comedy in which Bowie plays a charming leading man. The plot plays on Bowie's easy charisma, allowing him to win over costar Rosanna Arquette and the audience simultaneously. *The Linguini Incident* was produced by Bowie's Isolar production company; interestingly, although it did not align with the general public's understanding of him as an alien, outsider star, it *did* align with Bowie's own persona shifts during that period. He was engaged to supermodel Iman (who appears briefly in the film) and working on *Black Tie White Noise*, a poppy break from some of his more outré musical endeavors like the Tin Machine albums that preceded it. *The Linguini Incident* matched real-life Bowie, but not the generally accepted star image of Bowie. We might see this disconnect as part of the reason that many of Bowie's leading roles tend to be derided: they do not show us the musical star we know, because that Bowie is a bit too contradictory to comfortably assume a static, marketable filmic star image. How, then, might we measure success in Bowie's screen acting, and what relationship does it have to his musical success?

The struggle in reconciling a pop star's musical image and their filmic star persona is not new, as Landon Palmer has shown in the case of Elvis Presley's image shift around the time of his film stardom.[25] Palmer's approach to transmedia stardom studies through Elvis's film roles is illuminating: the apparatuses of

---

[24] Rosalind Galt, "David Bowie's Perverse Cinematic Body," *Cinema Journal* 57, no. 3 (Spring 2018): 131.

[25] Landon Palmer, "'And Introducing Elvis Presley': Industrial Convergence and Trans Media Stardom in the Rock'n'Roll Movie," *Music, Sound, and the Moving Image* 9, no. 2 (Autumn 2015): 177–90.

multiple industries must be taken into consideration when approaching a musician's foray into the acting realm. Presley's pivot to cinema was orchestrated as a way to amplify his musical stardom; the two were intrinsically linked. Unlike Elvis, though, Bowie seems to avoid the concerted effort to match his musical and filmic personae in this type of transmedia star image. In interviews, he spoke of a desire to distance himself from a strictly alien persona. While doing press for *Just a Gigolo* (1978, dir. Hemmings), Bowie answered questions about his rumored involvement with a *Stranger in a Strange Land* adaptation. He had turned down the role, realizing that if he did appear in it, "I'd be alien for life. I'd just be stuck out there. All I'd be offered would be people with green skins and varying hair colour—that would be the only character change I could make, hair colour."[26] Unlike Presley, Bowie sought to use film stardom as a way to expand and diversify his already complex star image, rather than a way to solidify and consolidate it. Of course, such a gambit carried its own difficulties. Though he was not stuck in green skin for his entire cinematic career, Bowie was subjected to a manipulation of his star image, in order to capitalize on what the public already knew of him. As the EMI memo suggests, this tension between star and image, and particularly between *musical* and *filmic* star images, would prove to be one of the central concerns of Bowie's acting career. In his appearances in *The Hunger* and *Labyrinth*, this negotiation shows particularly interesting aspects of Bowie's persona, as understood and marketed in the year of each film's release.

Palmer also addresses Bowie's film career, this time with an eye toward the industry trends reflected in his film treatment. Bowie's first decade of starring roles in feature films coincides with a time of great change in the film industry's relationship to music and music stardom.[27] Specifically, this period marks a move away from compilation scores and toward the outsized aesthetic influence of the birth of MTV in 1981. Each of these factors combines to shape Bowie's onscreen presence and its reception in the years from *Man Who Fell to Earth* through *Labyrinth*. As Palmer notes, in Bowie's first film roles, his musicianship is not an active part of the role and he does not perform his music onscreen. However, his star image and star power are quite important, as can be seen in the way these film appearances are advertised. Concentrating on Bowie's first decade of starring roles, Palmer analyzes many of the same movies that this

[26] Michael Watts, "Confessions of an Elitist," in *Bowie on Bowie: Interviews and Encounters with David Bowie*, ed. Sean Egan (Chicago: Chicago Review Press, 2015), 84.
[27] Landon Palmer, *Rock Star/Movie Star: Power and Performance in Cinematic Rock Stardom* (New York: Oxford University Press, 2020), 136.

chapter addresses. Our approaches differ in their focus: while Palmer looks to Bowie and these films as exemplars of the changing film industry, I analyze them for the insight they can give into Bowie's construction of self and the way that construction is mediated by others. Our studies complement each other, together forming a nuanced view of Bowie in this specific moment of film and musical stardom.

Both *Labyrinth* (1986) and *The Hunger* (1983) fall into a period of increased synergistic film/music crossovers. As Denisoff and Plasketes have shown, the symbiotic use of compilation soundtracks as marketing for films was wildly popular during the early 1980s.[28] Examples ranging from *Flashdance* to *Footloose* to *Top Gun* show this approach. According to Denisoff and Plasketes's research, though, this popular gambit was not ultimately successful in increasing box office returns. (Though I do not address the film at length here, Bowie's involvement in *Absolute Beginners* [1986, dir. Temple] can be seen as part of this trend. Bowie's brief role features a performance of the song "That's Motivation." He also provided the title song for *Absolute Beginners*. Palmer presents a detailed analysis of this film.[29]) It did not necessarily produce the highest art, either. Bowie himself acknowledged that, of his 1983 efforts, *Merry Christmas, Mr. Lawrence* is certainly the stronger film.[30] In fact, Roger Ebert called *The Hunger* "an agonizingly bad vampire film, circling around an exquisitely effective sex scene."[31] Similarly, *Labyrinth* is celebrated more for its nostalgic significance for audiences than its deep artistic achievement. Despite this almost universal assessment of their relative weakness as art, *The Hunger* and *Labyrinth* help to illustrate a tension that Bowie's more prestigious films do not.

The Hunger: David Bowie's Dead?

Bowie's second major star turn (after *The Man Who Fell to Earth*) came in the form of director Tony Scott's 1983 film *The Hunger*. Bowie had appeared in other films in the 1970s, notably *Just a Gigolo*, but that effort had not seen the same wide

---

[28] R. Serge Denisoff and George Plasketes, "Synergy in 1980s Film and Music: Formula for Success or Industry Mythology?," *Film History* 4, no. 3 (1990): 257–8.
[29] Palmer, *Rock Star*, 164–8.
[30] *Bowie on Bowie*, 151.
[31] Roger Ebert, "The Hunger (1983), " *RogerEbert.com*, originally published May 3, 1983, https://www.rogerebert.com/reviews/the-hunger-1983 Accessed April 14, 2020.

distribution or cultural significance as *The Man Who Fell to Earth*. In *The Hunger*, Bowie plays John Blaylock, the companion of Catherine Deneuve's powerful vampire Miriam. Unlike Miriam, John is starting to age, and has been unable to find a way to stop it. The plot of the film centers around this struggle, and the couple's relationship with a doctor, played by Susan Sarandon, who is brought in to help solve John's problem. While Blaylock ages and becomes an unsuitable partner for Miriam, she finds a new love interest in Sarandon's doctor. The film is stylishly shot, with visual language influenced by the burgeoning MTV aesthetic of the 1980s. The opening scene comprises impressionistic glances, bold color, and freeze frames. Miriam's home is all shadows and billowing curtains. It is a visually striking vampiric love story gone wrong. It is also a complex portrayal of Bowie. At once a powerful, dangerous creature and an ailing, fragile lover, Bowie and *The Hunger* play with and trouble the public's understanding of him as a star. This tension is explored in the film's plot and Scott's visual choices in particular.

The Hunger begins with a scene in a club, which features the band Bauhaus performing "Bela Lugosi's Dead" as John and Miriam hunt for new blood. Director Scott shoots this stylish sequence with stark lighting, exaggerated and unnatural colors, and quite short shot length—as a result, it is somewhat disorienting. The opening credits play over images of Bauhaus's Peter Murphy, usurping the role of the rock star here, though the credits announce Bowie's presence prominently (he is second billed, after Deneuve). Murphy is given the majority of this sequence's screen time, his appearance taking precedence over anything else, including other band members (see Figure 5.2). Following introductory shots of Murphy and brief establishing shots of the club's interior, Miriam and Blaylock enter, stalking for potential victims. They spot a couple on the dance floor and proceed to take them home in a sequence featuring almost no dialogue. Bowie is treated in mid-shots and obstructed views for the first three minutes, though each other character is given slower panning shots to reveal their face, body, and role in this seduction and ambush of the clubgoers. You could be forgiven for not fully recognizing David Bowie: his discernible features (including his voice) are denied to us for a full three and a half minutes. This delayed reveal is typical of the visual treatment of a cameo appearance, but here Bowie is supposed to play a main character.[32] His presence is not a surprise to be withheld. Oddly, the opening sequence seems unsure of whether to treat

---

[32] Redmond, "David Bowie," 151.

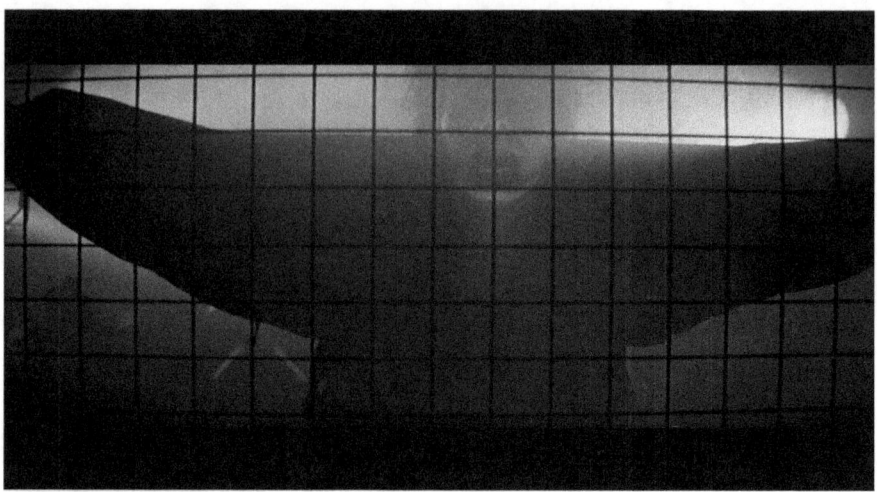

Figure 5.2 Still from *The Hunger* (1983, dir. Scott).

Bowie *as Bowie*, internationally famous rock star and sex symbol appearing onscreen, or as John Blaylock, nuanced main character. Upon closer inspection, Scott's choices throughout are instructive of the interplay between star images that shapes Bowie's role in the film.

The entire sequence is scored by Bauhaus's performance. Musically, this "Bela Lugosi's Dead" differs from both the album version and the 12" single extended version. Director Scott requested a new recording unique to the film; Bauhaus supplied a live version from their November 1981 performance at Hammersmith Palais.[33] While much of the musical material remains the same, important formal differences bind the visual and aural aspects of *The Hunger*'s opening. The first forty-five seconds of the film begin with the extended opening of "Bela Lugosi's Dead," layered with nonmelodic guitar effects. Unlike the album version, this recording extends the introduction, denying clear tonal or pitched material for the better part of a minute. In this nonmelodic stasis, Scott holds a stationary shot on Peter Murphy, lit in blue and interrupted only by the titles announcing the film's cast. That static shot is broken musically and visually with the entrance of the bass, at which point Scott inserts shots of the clubgoers, filmed inside London's legendary Heaven nightclub. The bass ostinato

---

[33] Jason Pettigrew, "Goth Inventors Bauhaus Recall the Night They Met David Bowie," *Altpress*, January 23, 2018, https://www.altpress.com/features/bauhaus_undead_met_david_bowie_the_hunger/ Accessed July 1, 2020.

provides some harmonic framework and motion as the camera starts to define the space of this nightclub setting. Scott maintains a style reminiscent of the MTV aesthetic, with quick transitions and freeze frames highlighting Murphy's performance. Though the bassline gives more tonal guideposts than did the drum introduction, the song's vocal melody remains absent, as does a full view of our lead actors.

Aural and visual alignment continues as the song enters its verse. Here, the camera moves for the first time, pushing in to a closer shot of Deneuve and Bowie, though their faces remain partially obscured. Music and image intersect, as Murphy's lyrical invocation of Lugosi's monster of Hollywood lore introduces our own movie monsters, here shown as mysterious and alluring. The camera even approaches them differently, treating them with more dynamism and interest than its other subjects. The increased visual rhythm and movement throughout this first verse continue as the song expands aurally, gaining textural complexity to match Scott's increasing visual pace. By the time Murphy and company reach the second verse, both the visual and aural registers of the opening sequence have reached a more frenzied intensity: Bowie and Deneuve have spotted their prey in the club and initiated contact, just as Murphy's voice has risen out of its low tessitura to repeatedly emphasize "undead" in the verse's lyrics.

Violent aural and visual disruptions mark the transition from club to car as Deneuve and Bowie take their conquests home. Scott maintains the quick visual transitions that marked the first verse, but here they are matched by jarring sound transitions. Interrupting Bauhaus's performance, the soundtrack is punctured by droning, synthesized sounds as a mode of transition from club to seduction scene. The film preserves its jarring nature through the unpredictability of these transitions. Though they begin with the start of the second verse, these interpolations happen at different and unpredictable formal intervals, keeping the spectator on edge. Eventually, the droning material supplants Bauhaus and takes over the soundscape of the seduction. The final Bauhaus moments again punctuate "undead" repeatedly, emphasizing the vampiric nature of Bowie and Deneuve before their attack is even complete. This opening uses music and visuals in convergent and divergent ways to increase interest in our leads while also undercutting the spectator's sense of security. It sets the stage for the unorthodox vampire narrative to follow, and for the film's surprising presentation of Bowie himself.

This sequence serves as a blueprint for the way the film would like us to see Bowie in particular, as he is shot differently than costar Deneuve here. Even in his introduction, he is shielded from our view, held apart from the camera. Shots focus in either intense closeup or obscured midshot, with neither giving a clear, satisfying view of Bowie. The effect here is twofold: first, it amplifies our desire for the full reveal of Bowie. Secondly, though, it *undercuts* the importance of Bowie as actor and as character. He is seen in bits and pieces; we are denied the sight of his most famous feature (his mismatched pupils), and his face is first shown beneath dark glasses. His visage is of secondary importance in this scene, and is first shown as Bauhaus announces the death of the cinematic star Bela Lugosi. In this musical introduction, we can read directly the death of Hollywood's vampire prototype (we will not see Lugosi's powerful, alluring Count here), but also of the leading man star image with which Bowie might be most closely associated in 1983, and indeed in his other film performance from that year, *Merry Christmas, Mr. Lawrence*.

Of course, the layered personae on display in this scene become yet more fraught once Bauhaus and Peter Murphy himself are taken into account. The choice of music and performer is important here, as again we find a link to Bowie's offscreen star image. Goth progenitors Bauhaus and the goth scene in general were influenced by Bowie. Alexander Carpenter notes the frequent comparisons between Bowie and Murphy in press coverage, as well as the role that Bowie's *Ziggy Stardust*-era music and persona played in the band's output.[34] It is interesting, then, to plumb the meaning of an opening sequence that traverses so many layers of personae. Murphy, stepping into Bowie's rock star shoes, invokes glamorous, dangerous screen star Bela Lugosi, as Bowie seemingly steps into that role. As Carpenter sees it, "Murphy becomes Bowie's simulacrum in this scene, and the vampire/rock star paradigm is neatly and definitively forged: rock star Bowie plays the role of vampire, while vampiric Bowieboy Murphy ('The Count') plays the role of rock star."[35] The sequence itself is as fraught as the translation of Bowie's rock stardom to the silver screen.

Beyond its opening, *The Hunger* continues to trouble the audience's understanding of Bowie. The film's plot sounds, on the surface, like a continuation of the otherworldly personae with which Bowie has flirted since the beginning of his career. In its emphasis on the image over coherent plot, we could see a vehicle ideally suited to the gestural, visual power of Bowie. However, *The Hunger* is no

---

[34] Alexander Carpenter, "The 'Ground Zero' of Goth: Bauhaus, 'Bela Lugosi's Dead' and the Origins of Gothic Rock," *Popular Music and Society* 35, no. 1 (2012): 40–1.
[35] Carpenter, "'Ground Zero' of Goth," 39.

Man Who Fell to Earth. Bowie's character here is alluring and markedly other, but that allure is very short-lived. "Bela Lugosi's Dead" and Bowie's trajectory in the film seem to undercut the potent power of the Lugosi star role and the vampiric Other in general. Bowie's John Blaylock is, in fact, a much more identifiably human character. Rather than a hedonistic vampire, Blaylock (though he does kill and feed in the film) ultimately appears to want only to preserve a normal life. In flashback, it is revealed that he chose to become a vampire because of his love for Miriam and desire to stay with her beyond his mortal lifespan. He is shown to be a musician (playing cello in the film); his main activities, apart from spending time with Miriam, relate to this musical pursuit. He builds a relationship with a neighborhood child who visits to practice with him. Though his vampiric nature eventually forces him to attack the child for sustenance, the act is shown to be difficult for him. Blaylock is, throughout the film, shown not as a pleasure-seeking vampire, but as a being striving for a lasting relationship with Miriam and friendships within his community.

A disconnect between the character (as chosen and vulnerably performed by Bowie), and the way that character is marketed is particularly striking in *The Hunger*. Though Bowie receives second billing in the film and features prominently in the press materials, this is not really his film. He lacks the suave control of the sexy, predatory Dracula prototype; he is more conflicted and much less powerful. After about thirty minutes of *The Hunger*'s runtime, Blaylock has physically deteriorated to the point of plot obsolescence (see Figure 5.3). This film's alternate take on the vampire trope is at odds with the 1983 image of Bowie the rock star, as was most obviously shown in the film's opening scene.

Figure 5.3 Still from *The Hunger* (1983, dir. Scott).

1983 was the year of Bowie's hugely popular album *Let's Dance*, as well as the worldwide Serious Moonlight tour that supported it, both of which showed a departure for Bowie. Gone were the extraterrestrial trappings of the 1970s and the Pierrot costumes of "Ashes to Ashes," and in their place was a virile, boxing Bowie, outfitted in snazzy suits and the most 1980s of hairstyles. For the first time since the mid-1960s, Bowie appeared to be embracing a mainstream, masculine image that was somewhat at odds with his 1970s work. Interestingly, it was also at odds with his character and treatment within the film (as we've seen), but not with the promotional materials. Take, for example, the trailer for the film, which is clearly interested in marketing its stars *as stars*. This ad introduces each of the characters in turn, focusing first on Sarandon's doctor, then Bowie's tragic lover, then Deneuve's alluring predator. Each star's identifiable, aspirational feature is then individually highlighted: "the timeless beauty of Catherine Deneuve; the cruel elegance of David Bowie; the open sensuality of Susan Sarandon."[36] The trailer shows a carefully chosen portion of the film. The majority of the Bowie scenes in this trailer are drawn from the first fifteen minutes of *The Hunger*. He is shown in the club seduction scene, as well as a later shower scene with Deneuve (Figure 5.4). Though a few images of Bowie's aged visage do appear, the connection between Bowie as star and this decaying vampire is unclear, and the voiceover does not comment on it. Rather, we are asked to focus on the images of Bowie that align with a contemporary understanding of him: appealing, alluring leading man.

Figure 5.4 Still from *The Hunger* (1983, dir. Scott).

---

[36] "The Hunger Official Trailer #1 – Susan Sarandon Movie (1983) HD," uploaded by Movieclips Classic Trailers, October 5, 2012, https://www.youtube.com/watch?v=7a6YFwC2zKA Accessed April 14, 2020.

Marketing "the cruel elegance of David Bowie" makes sense in 1983: the Bowie of "Let's Dance" and "Modern Love" is a much more traditional, elegant heartthrob than the Bowie of a decade earlier. The trailer and the promotional materials seem to be selling David Bowie as a strictly defined star. While in accordance with Bowie's current musical persona, this approach is not quite aligned with the character as written and performed. This elegance and allure are almost absent from the character of John Blaylock, shown to be sexy and chic only in the film's first section. The disconnect highlights one of the complications of parlaying Bowie's musical stardom into film stardom: how can a film capitalize on the public's perception of Bowie when that perception is ever-changing? By seeking to sand the rough edges of Bowie's personae to fit comfortably in a film's press release, *The Hunger* helps to show just how difficult it is to cleanly define Bowie. We find a similar tension between character and promotion another of Bowie's leading man turns in the 1980s: Jim Henson's *Labyrinth*.

Magic Dance: *Labyrinth* and Star Image

1986's *Labyrinth* is a somewhat difficult film to pin down; not particularly successful on its release, the film has found a massive cult following in the intervening years. Like *The Hunger*, it also defies generic expectations. A brainchild of Muppet creator Jim Henson, the film is both childish and adult in its themes. The imaginative teenager Sarah (Jennifer Connelly), upset with her babysitting assignment, calls on the goblin king to come and take away her brother Toby. Much to her surprise, the goblin king Jareth (David Bowie) actually appears in her bedroom, ready to make good on the offer and steal the baby. The remainder of the movie is spent in the goblin king's realm, as Sarah struggles to make it through Jareth's labyrinth in time to save her brother. As was true of Henson's *The Dark Crystal*, the story is told mostly through the use of puppets, but the themes of responsibility, temptation, and power are strikingly grown-up.

Like these themes, Bowie's portrayal of Jareth the Goblin King and the promotion of his character are other aspects that complicate our understanding of *Labyrinth* as a whole. Jareth's character is not clearly defined (as generations of children can attest): he is appealing, as one half of our odd romantic pairing, but also deeply disturbing as the child-stealing, threatening antagonist who puts the heroine in mortal danger. Think pieces about Jareth's allure abound (whether tongue-in-cheek or serious).[37] Fan fiction about the character, most frequently paired romantically with protagonist Sarah or with the reader themselves, is readily available on many forums, including DeviantArt and Archive of Our Own. In fact, many attribute the film's success in recent years to the unique charisma and figure of David Bowie within it. It seems that this powerful, attractive quality was present in the character from its inception.

Jim Henson always intended to cast a rock star in the role, though many options were floated before landing on Bowie.[38] The chosen rock star, it was thought, would both act in the film and contribute songs to the film's soundtrack. Henson's affinity for musical films was already apparent in *The Muppet Movie* (1979), and the Muppet films featured cameos by famous performers from Steve Martin to Joan Rivers. The specificity of Jareth's rock star persona operates a bit differently, though. Mick Jagger, Sting, and Freddie Mercury were all considered for the role of Jareth.[39] While each of these men represented different kinds of musical stardom, they are united by an overt sexuality that permeates their work and presentation. In all cases, these men would bring not only rock star transmedial appeal, but also a focus on their bodies as sexual objects. This choice is an interesting one for a children's film. The focus on the body continued to be important to the character of Jareth as production began: we need only look to Jareth's body-conscious costuming to see that. Frequently clad in closely tailored vests or jackets paired with skintight leggings, Bowie's body is on display from his first onscreen appearance (see Figure 5.5). This is in keeping with the public image Bowie cultivated throughout the mid-1980s. Virile and traditionally attractive, 1980s Bowie showed off his body in shirtless boxing photos on the cover of *Let's Dance* and tailored suits in the "Modern Love" video. He did not, however, embrace a flamboyantly made-up face as did the goblin king. Thus, Bowie's casting in *Labyrinth* negotiates his cinematic star image in ways both troubling to and congruent with his musical stardom.

Unlike *The Hunger*, *Labyrinth* seems to want to embrace Bowie's earlier, alien period. His Jareth is a part of another world, literally invading the

---

[37] See, for example, Leonora Epstein, "For Everyone Whose Sexual Awakening Was Caused by David Bowie in 'Labyrinth,'" *Buzzfeed*, May 22, 2014, https://www.buzzfeed.com/leonoraepstein/for-everyone-whose-sexual-awakening-was-caused-by-david-bowi Accessed June 22, 2020.

[38] Liner notes for *Labyrinth: 30th Anniversary Edition*, directed by Jim Henson (1986, Culver City, CA: Sony Pictures Home Entertainment, 2016).

[39] John Earls, "Freddie Mercury and Rod Stewart Were Considered for David Bowie's Role in *Labyrinth*," *NME*, September 15, 2016, https://www.nme.com/news/film/freddie-mercury-and-rod-stewart-were-considered-fo-870963 Accessed June 23, 2020.

Figure 5.5 Still from *Labyrinth* (1986, dir. Henson).

peaceful suburban home of our protagonist Sarah. In this iteration of Bowie the actor, the musical David Bowie we know well is front and center. As his song "Underground" plays over the credits, Bowie's voice acclimates us to the film before we see any characters. Thereafter, Bowie's body is shown and displayed prominently throughout the film, featured in scenes that play like music videos. "Magic Dance" is a very good example of this: Bowie is the center of the sequence, dancing with Henson's puppetry goblins. Unlike depictions of Bowie in *The Hunger*, here the actor is displayed and celebrated for all his oddness. While Jareth is certainly an outsider character (like Bowie's Ziggy of the previous decade), his style is less rocker chic and more camp, embracing the fantastical nature of his role in the film as he cheerfully tosses goblin puppets. Bowie's performance of "Magic Dance" is diegetic within the film (it is the only such diegetic musical performance by a human character) and is given ample screen time, though his lyrics and actions do not move the plot forward, or even directly comment upon the plot.

This "Magic Dance" sequence is interesting for its balance of the narrative needs of the film and a countervailing desire to showcase Bowie as performer. "Magic Dance" unfolds on two parallel registers within the film. First, it follows Bowie in his castle as he diegetically performs the song. Second, the film intercuts segments of Sarah's journey through the labyrinth. The Bowie portions are shot in a way that is almost reminiscent of 1980s MTV music video style: there is frequent, fast editing, with some cutting to the beat of the song.[40] There is also constant movement within the frame, adding to the manic excitement of Bowie's performance. Were these segments to be edited together, they could form a believable music video. (In fact, the official music video for the song is just that: an edited version compiled of Bowie's performance in this sequence.) In contrast, Sarah's segments are shot in a way that matches the rest of the film. With stationary cameras and much longer shot lengths, Sarah's journey is documented in the way we might expect of a narrative feature. She travels through sections of the labyrinth, attempting to find her way to her brother. At each step, she is foiled: doorways close, signs are altered, and Sarah is left disoriented. Though she speaks no lines in the sequence, Sarah's story progresses. The sequence serves to heighten the desperation of her search for the center of the labyrinth and, by extension, her brother. Jareth's section of the sequence, though, shows no narrative purpose. He sings, dances, and tosses the baby, but by the end of "Magic Dance" we have learned nothing new about Jareth, nor has his situation developed. These differences in visual style serve to demarcate the sections, though the music of "Magic Dance" continues throughout the sequence and unifies the two. There is very little narrative reason for "Magic Dance" to exist as it does in the film: couldn't Sarah's journey be the focus, without Bowie's song and dance?

Indeed, although the film has been remembered by some as "101 minutes of Bowie rock opera and Hensonian spectacle," Bowie's music is truly of secondary importance.[41] Though his songs are sung diegetically, they do little to advance the plot and are not integrated in the way one might expect of a film musical. The fairytale aspect of *Labyrinth* aligns with classic film musical tropes outlined by Rick Altman and present in classics like *Brigadoon*, but the music here does not serve a specific purpose.[42] Sanna Qvick shows how *Labyrinth* fails to conform to the many expectations of the film musical genre, despite the fact that it has made-to-order music and a male lead who sings throughout.[43] The

---

[40] For more on the MTV aesthetic, see, for example, Kay Dickinson, "Pop, Speed, Teenagers, and the 'MTV Aesthetic,'" in *Movie Music: The Film Reader*, ed. Kay Dickinson (New York: Routledge, 2003), 143–52.

[41] Alison Stine, "*Labyrinth* and the Dark Heart of Childhood," *The Atlantic*, June 29, 2016, https://www.theatlantic.com/entertainment/archive/2016/06/labyrinth-captured-the-dark-heart-of-childhood/489146/ Accessed June 25, 2020.

[42] Rick Altman, *The American Film Musical* (Bloomington: Indiana University Press, 1987), 127.

[43] Sanna Qvick, "Goblin King in Labyrinth: An Audiovisual Close Reading of the Songs by David Bowie," *Widerscreen* 19, nos. 3–4 (2016). http://widerscreen.fi/numerot/2016-3-4/goblin-king-in-labyrinth-an-audio-visual-close-reading-of-the-songs-by-david-bowie/?fbclid=IwAR2_kjdwlhoIYfUI4e5yooDVcUU_SnQUjuc97l3m4kkTxhM2oxKFbyxBav8

music is secondary: the deletion of something like "Chilly Down" would not alter our understanding of or investment in the film's narrative. Neither Sarah nor Jareth sings an "I want" song to invite the audience to understand their motivation. Perhaps only "As the World Falls Down" is necessary, as it advances the relationship between Sarah and Jareth. Even here, though, the music and lyrics themselves are not of paramount importance. Rather, the visual style of the sequence communicates much more about the two characters. Framed as a fantasy to distract Sarah from her quest, the entire sequence is vaguely distorted, as though viewed through one of Jareth's crystal balls. In a crowded masquerade, only Sarah and Jareth drop their masks to dance with each other. "As the World Falls Down" sings of a devotion that we, the viewer, must imagine to be false, just as the visuals are framed as false and fantastical. Thus, this sequence helps to enliven the conflict and struggle at the heart of Sarah's journey, though that purpose is largely accomplished through the visual rather than the aural. Even here, Bowie's music is a charming selling point, not an integral aspect of the film's storytelling. It may be superfluous in function, but the music is catchy and mainstream enough to add to the film's appeal.

In this performance and throughout the film, *Labyrinth* treats Jareth and, by extension, Bowie as important, physical performers. This visual focus is so prominent that Galt identifies the cult popularity of *Labyrinth* as growing from it: she sees the appreciation as an "audience response to [Bowie's] physical embodiment" of the character.[44] It is true that the film seeks to highlight that physicality much more than might be expected of a children's film. Such an approach is congruent with other films' treatment of Bowie. *Merry Christmas, Mr. Lawrence* is a prime example. Wright highlights Bowie's embodiment and gesture in the film as among its most striking features.[45] In fact, we could trace this physical focus as far as Bowie's mime performances of the 1960s.

In emphasizing Bowie's erotic physicality within the film, then, *Labyrinth* is in keeping with both Bowie's contemporaneous star image and the most frequent approach to showcasing Bowie on film. However, the presentation of Bowie in *Labyrinth* is somewhat at odds with the film's marketing. Rather than focusing on Bowie's alluring physical presence, the film's advertising sought to capitalize on the artist's reputation for innovation. The trailer for the film highlights Bowie's

---

[44] Galt, "David Bowie's Perverse Cinematic Body," 131.
[45] Julie Lobalzo Wright, "David Bowie Is the Extraordinary Rock Star as Film Star," in *David Bowie: Critical Perspectives*, ed. Eoin Devereux, Aileen Dillane and Martin Power (New York: Routledge, 2014), 230–44.

creative input and, seemingly, its relationship to Bowie's earlier, groundbreaking work. This trailer opens by promising the collaboration of three leading creative minds: Henson, George Lucas, and Bowie, "one of the most innovative forces in modern entertainment."[46] While Bowie was an innovator throughout his career, such an appellation is perhaps less fitting in 1986 than in other eras. As discussed in relation to *The Hunger*, the Bowie of the mid-1980s was one who sought mass appeal. *Newsweek* heralded his "new look" and called him a "genial rake" making "'positive' rock music."[47] His personal presentation, music, and publicity all sought to create the image of a desirable, somewhat conventional heartthrob. The "innovative force" label is a bit out of step with a contemporaneous understanding of Bowie as an artist.

His character, styling, and performance within the film tell a different story, though. In many ways, the character Jareth is a direct callback to Bowie's earlier stage looks and performance style. Outfitted in tight leggings, prominent makeup, and an eye-catching hairstyle, Jareth could be one of Ziggy Stardust's Spiders from Mars. (In fact, his hair bears a striking resemblance to that of Spiders guitarist Mick Ronson.) As Qvick has noted, Bowie's makeup and hairstyles in the film can be seen as links to his 1972–3 Kansai Yamamoto-styled looks—one of the periods in which Bowie can certainly be seen as an "innovative force."[48] Thus, the promotion of the film and its depiction of Bowie's character seem a bit at odds with the Bowie of 1986. The most overt connective thread is, of course, the sexualization of Bowie onscreen; this aspect, however, is a uniting thread throughout Bowie's musical personae. This styling is the only version of Bowie shown in the film's press kit. Of the sixteen photos originally circulated before the film's release, Bowie appears in four. These four photos all show Bowie in costume as Jareth, though the other "innovative forces" (Henson and Lucas) are featured in behind-the-scenes stills.[49] Bowie's stills show him at important points in the film's plot; moments from both "Magic Dance" and "As the World Falls Down" are featured. We also see Bowie with the crystal balls his character manipulates throughout the film. Finally, the stills present Jareth in his last confrontation with Sarah. In each situation, Bowie is costumed in the tight

---

[46] "Labyrinth (1986) Official Trailer – David Bowie, Jennifer Connelly Movie HD," uploaded by Movieclips Classic Trailers, January 11, 2016, https://www.youtube.com/watch?v=O2yd4em1I6M Accessed December 13, 2021.
[47] Jim Miller, "David Bowie's New Look," *Newsweek*, July 18, 1983, 76.
[48] Qvick, "Goblin King."
[49] TriStar Pictures *Labyrinth* press Kit, https://www.worthpoint.com/worthopedia/labyrinth-press-kit-david-bowie-1846394066 Accessed June 29, 2020.

leggings and exuberant shoulder pads for which his character is remembered. He dominates each frame, his hair and body commanding attention. Even the language on the press photos describes him as the "ominous and compelling" ruler of the labyrinth, again highlighting the dangerous appeal of Bowie's Otherness within this filmic world.

Like *The Hunger*, *Labyrinth* appears in a much more traditional period of Bowie's output, coming between 1984's *Tonight* and 1987's *Never Let Me Down*. The first of these was a commercial success, but neither was particularly well received critically. This is not a period of Bowie's ostentatious otherness, but one of mainstream popular music. Bowie's *Labyrinth* song contributions make this fairly clear: "Magic Dance," "As the World Falls Down," and "Underground" are rather middle-of-the-road (though entirely charming) pop fare. Structurally, they are somewhat predictable. As Chris O'Leary has shown, "Underground" and Bowie's "Absolute Beginners" share a very similar form, carefully building to the release of their final choruses.[50] (Both also open the films in which they appear, serving similar narrative and musical functions.) "Magic Dance" has the added interest of a spoken word, rap-like opening, but in its form, synth-heavy instrumentation, and performance, it is typical of both Bowie and pop music more generally in the mid-1980s. In the words of *Newsweek*, this is indeed Bowie as "positive" rocker.[51]

Despite this musical fact, we have seen that publicity for the film seeks to cast Bowie as the outsider, outré figure he once was. This focus on oddness wasn't well received by Bowie's record label. EMI A&R executive Neil Portnow complained of "Magic Dance" that "the lyrics were about puppy dogs and goblins—not relevant to Bowie's career."[52] That EMI would be displeased is not surprising. Apart from the concerns about Bowie's acting potential shown in the 1978 memo, there's the disconnect in star image: much of their publicity during the mid-1980s went into shaping a more conventionally desirable David Bowie. To have a film role push against this could undermine those years of careful star image crafting.

The "Underground" video, released to coincide with the film, shows this star image confusion quite clearly. The video follows Bowie (presumably playing himself here, not a character), traveling from a performance to a literal

---

[50] Chris O'Leary, *Ashes to Ashes: The Songs of David Bowie, 1976–2016* (London: Repeater Books, 2018), 229.
[51] Miller, "Bowie's New Look," 76.
[52] O'Leary, *Ashes to Ashes*, 219.

underground, otherworldly escape. That underground world, accessed via a spiral staircase concealed in a manhole cover, is populated by characters from *Labyrinth*. Some YouTube commenters describe the video as a "back story" for Jareth, Bowie's character.[53] Within this origin story, Bowie's past and his star image loom large. In the seconds before he disappears into the magical, *Labyrinth* world, the video shuffles through a number of press photos from Bowie's career: we see Ziggy, the Thin White Duke, and more before Bowie transforms. This visual choice seems to echo those YouTube comments: Jareth's back story *is* Bowie, even if Bowie and his record company might wish for some distance between the two.

Stylistically, "Underground" differs from many other Bowie videos. This is, according to the artist, because of his distance from it and hands-off approach. In a 1987 interview, he bemoaned the final product, stating "I've found that the videos I put into other people's hands have always been a mistake … I just left it ['Underground'] up, and the result is just not my kind of video."[54] In fact, it seems much more a late 1980s MTV sort of video than most others Bowie made in that era. The transition from our world to the underground is achieve through recourse to the animation style most familiar to audiences from a-ha's "Take On Me" (1985). Like that one, this video blends drawn figures with live action, creating a liminal, unreal narrative space. Though Bowie had before created videos with an outlandish story (see "Blue Jean") or cutting-edge video techniques (see "Ashes to Ashes"), very little of his trademark visual style is present in "Underground." We might see "Underground" as a part of his screen acting output, then, rather than his music video oeuvre. By Bowie's account, this was a video for which he showed up and performed, rather than having an integral part in its planning. The end result shows this, as the video plays to the same understanding of Bowie's persona as *Labyrinth*. Both call back to the distant past of Bowie's career and use it to color the film and its meaning.

Labyrinth seeks to activate what Dyer calls the "large sign cluster" of audience foreknowledge.[55] Essentially, Henson and company count on the audience's long knowledge of Henson's creativity and David Bowie's status as innovative

---

[53] Christine Shane (2018) commenting on "David Bowie – Underground (Official Video)" uploaded by David Bowie, July 11, 2018, https://www.youtube.com/watch?v=Qga12-bAS4A Accessed February 20, 2021.

[54] "Dave In, Dave Out," *Music & Sound Output*, June 1987, https://web.archive.org/web/19990825055201/http://teenagewildlife.com/Appearances/Press/1987/0601/mso.html Accessed February 20, 2021

[55] Dyer, *Stars*, 121.

outsider to inform their understanding of Jareth. This invocation is indirect in the film: costuming and styling choices point toward Bowie of the past. However, in advertising, the activation of audience foreknowledge is much more direct. Rather than equating Bowie with his much more recent mainstream successes, the ads for *Labyrinth* ensure that the spectator approaches Bowie as Ziggy Stardust, Bowie as alien. As Dyer notes, such audience foreknowledge need not be fulfilled as promised within the film.[56] *Labyrinth* need only build a foundation for the audience's understanding of Bowie and Jareth; should the two not directly align within the film, the audience will still do much of the work of connecting them.

This chronological misalignment points to the difficulty of pinning down a Bowie star image. While his 1970s persona is a clear and easy fit for the character of Jareth and the needs of *Labyrinth*, Bowie had moved through many image permutations between 1972 and 1986. Thus, though he was a huge, commercially successful rock star at the time of the film's release, his musical star image actually complicated any studio desire to profit from his involvement, rather than facilitating it.

Conclusion

It is worth noting that publicity for both *The Hunger* and *Labyrinth* fights Bowie's contemporary personae in different ways, either fundamentally altering the nature of his performance in promotion, or amplifying the *avant garde*, extraterrestrial aspects of Bowie's then-outmoded early 1970s persona. To simplify these ideas a bit, we might think of the roles and their marketing as shown in Table 5.1. While seeking to balance these roles with Bowie's current musical work and persona, each publicity campaign draws on different parts of Bowie's public persona. Because of the careful control he exerted over that persona for years, each film has a difficult job pinning down exactly who Bowie is and which aspects of him are most fitting and important for the films themselves. Inevitably, some aspects of that image needed to be worn down or ignored in order to send a clear, identifiable message about the film and its star. Both films together show a difficulty in narrowing and solidifying Bowie's star image, and a desire to do so in order to profit from that persona.

---

[56] Ibid., 122.

Table 5.1 Comparison of acting roles versus filmic and musical star images, 1983 and 1986.

	1983	1986
Role	Vampire John Blaylock, *The Hunger*	Jareth the Goblin King, *Labyrinth*
Music Publicity	*Let's Dance* "Heartthrob," Nile Rodgers collaboration, "Cool," Boxing	*Tonight, Never Let Me Down* Mainstream, "Cool"
Film Role Traits	Weakened, Devoted, Against Vampire Type	Teasing, Seducer, Alluring, Dangerous
Film Publicity	"Cruel Elegance," Danger, Stylish, Sexy	Innovator, Bowie's History Anomic star type

If, as Dyer contends, star images are complex, polysemic constructions that encompass all public aspects of a star's person and work, it is not surprising that Bowie's filmic star image is a bit problematic. As an artist, he embraced the idea of publicly playing roles of his own devising for the majority of his musical career, and by the time he was given leading roles in film, he was well known as a rock "chameleon." Though that changeability kept musical audiences perpetually interested, it made it more difficult for major motion pictures to capitalize on the coup of presenting Bowie onscreen. Unlike the Beatles or Elvis before him, Bowie purposefully avoided a clearly defined star image, instead embracing a series of independent personae throughout his career.

It is this difficulty in defining "David Bowie" writ large that might explain that powerful "Bowieness" to which Lane referred in his assessment of Bowie's cameos. Rather than having a clearly defined and unified musical and filmic star image, Bowie worked to present an entirely different image than did his films and the studios promoting those films. This is unsurprising given the way Bowie evolved his musical star image. Even in films that would seem to align well with some aspect of Bowie's history and star image, there remained an inherent tension. It was nearly impossible to effectively market a film around Bowie as a leading man, if that leading man role involved any sort of nuanced character. His musical personae were built on easily identifiable, visually compelling foundations, described by Redmond as a "series of masks."[57] These foundations, though, did not lend themselves to the sort of knowable, relatable star personae that the most successful actors embrace. Even many of Dyer's anomic types

---

[57] Redmond, "David Bowie," 156.

embraced a stability in their public presentations; Bowie's mutability rendered him almost unknowable by film industry standards.

That unknowability was an asset to Bowie's musical stardom: it connoted constant evolution and boundless creativity. It was, however, a distinct liability in the world of movie stardom. Dyer analyzes "difficult" stars, those who needed a studio-constructed, concrete star image to be understood (Katharine Hepburn, for example). Hepburn's human complexity, which transgressed the bounds of ideal womanhood in the golden age of Hollywood, was seen as threatening and somewhat unattractive. Studio efforts sought to draw clearer, more relatable boundaries around the public's understanding of her, in order to better attract them to her films and characters. Bowie might be viewed similarly: his excess, his complexity, made for an uncomfortable fit in many screen roles. We can read—through the promotion, publicity, filmmaking choices, and the roles themselves—some very different understandings of who exactly Bowie wanted to be in the public imagination.

To return to the EMI memo from Arnold Holland that opened this chapter, we may ask if Bowie really was a "viable actor." He is certainly capable of acting, but the memo's "viable" label implies something more. For EMI Films, Bowie's viability would be related to his marketability; without this, he is not commercially viable as an investment for the company. Bowie's ability to sell, Dyer would suggest, is intimately related to his ability to be labeled as a type of star. As *The Hunger* and *Labyrinth* show, such a proposition is complicated. Galt asserts that Bowie, as an actor, does "not embody or act; he represents."[58] This conceptualization of Bowie as a signifier to which one could attach many signifieds matches the fluidity we find in this chapter's case studies. Bowie as sign is ever changing, thanks to his openness to attaching new meanings to the image he created. While versatile, this fluidity is much more difficult to commodify. The allure of creating a strong, profitable transmedial star image around Bowie, though, would attract directors, studios, and corporations in both film and advertising.

---

[58] Galt, "Perverse Cinematic Body," 137.

6

Mass Motivation: Advertising, Audience, and the Bowie Star Image

In his 1987 "Creation" advertisement for Pepsi, David Bowie appears in two guises within a minute-long spot. As a geeky scientist, Bowie designs his perfect woman, only to be transformed himself by the explosion of Pepsi-fueled energy that creates that woman: Tina Turner. The blast strips Bowie of his bowtie and glasses, fluffs his hair, and makes him a suitable dance partner for Turner, as they strut off to enjoy more Pepsi. This saga is underscored by Bowie's 1983 release "Modern Love;" however, here Bowie alters the lyrics to his hit, inserting "Now I know the choice is mine" into the chorus. The change neatly echoes Pepsi's own "Choice of a New Generation" tagline, but it also illustrates an important aspect of Bowie's more aggressive move into commercials in the mid-1980s. At this point, Bowie was wildly popular and financially successful on a scale he had never before achieved, thanks to the success of hits *Let's Dance* (1983) and *Tonight* (1984); this high-profile advertising work was a strategic *choice* rather than a strict *necessity*. Bowie was almost universally known and, before the release of *Never Let Me Down* in 1987, lauded as a worldwide artistic success who was selling out arenas on his Serious Moonlight tour and had broken artistic boundaries with his work in the 1970s. Indeed, Bethany Klein pegs this choice to partner with Pepsi as strikingly odd: "David Bowie's involvement does stand out against the usual music selection of the colas, which tends towards more 'commercial' artists, or those for whom commercial affiliation has less of a stigma attached."[1] Klein does not note, though, that Bowie had appeared in television ads from the late 1960s onward, and had embraced the "commercial"

This chapter expands on an earlier version of my research, reproduced here by permission of Oxford University Press, oup.com. Katherine Reed, "Selling 'David Bowie': Commercial Appearances and the Developing Star Image," in *The Oxford Handbook of Music and Advertising*, ed. James Deaville, Siu-Lan Tan, and Ron Rodman (New York: Oxford University Press, 2021), 474–87.

[1] Bethany Klein, *As Heard on TV: Popular Music in Advertising* (Burlington, VT: Ashgate, 2009), 87.

label with gusto in the mid-1980s. He was in many ways rebranding himself *as* commercial, so the stigma of commercial affiliation was almost something he sought in this redefinition of self.

This personal branding strategy becomes apparent in the connections between these ads and Bowie's use of his image in his own music videos. Commercials, like music videos, costumes, and interviews, served Bowie as a vehicle for reinforcing his star image on a very public, almost ubiquitous, stage. Only allowing the use of specific (not always brand new) songs and styling himself in specific ways, Bowie coopted advertising as another tool for the definition of his public self. Many corporations and ad campaigns were similarly only too happy to more clearly define Bowie's iconoclastic image—as a means to align themselves with it. Importantly, Bowie represented not only coolness, but a sort of self-definition that, paradoxically, aligned particularly well with advertising. "The choice is mine," he sang for Pepsi—and, in fact, his commercials capitalize on that idea. We, like Bowie, can create a "cool" version of ourselves through our choice of Pepsi or Louis Vuitton.

Bowie's involvement in advertising took many forms, from early visual work for an ad agency in the 1960s; to playing an ad man in the 1980s, singing of "mass motivation" in *Absolute Beginners* (1986, dir. Temple); to his own appearances in commercials. Of those early years in advertising, Bowie stated in a Cameron Crowe interview: "I went into advertising and it was *awful*. That was the *worst*. I got out of that and tried rock & roll because it seemed like an enjoyable way of making my money and taking four or five years to decide what I really wanted to do"[2] (emphasis original). It turns out that what he "really wanted to do" was build a long and complex musical and actorly career, which would circle back around to include advertising as one of its many prongs. In ads from 1968 to 2013, Bowie used his likeness and music as a means of dual promotion: self and product. Though this approach is not unique, Bowie's overt construction of his own star image makes his utilization of advertising particularly striking. In interviews, he is clear about his personal goals with this work, making his partnerships a bit different than the presentation of many advertising deals. Well before the ubiquity of pop star advertising, Bowie made use of the platform for his own purposes of self-definition. This chapter analyzes his 1987 Pepsi

---

[2] Cameron Crowe, "David Bowie: Ground Control to Davy Jones," *Rolling Stone*, February 12, 1976, https://www.rollingstone.com/music/music-news/david-bowie-ground-control-to-davy-jones-77059/ Accessed March 19, 2019.

spot ("Creation"), 2003 Vittel ad ("Never Get Old"), and 2013 Louis Vuitton short ("L'Invitation au Voyage") to illustrate the consistent shaping of public image Bowie executed through advertising. Bowie's iconicity as a performer is manipulated in order to effectively and immediately communicate not only Bowieness, but also the timeless coolness of each brand through the invocation of specific images.

This use of musical identity to build brand identity has reached a point of saturation in recent years, earning Meier's label of "promotional ubiquitous music."[3] By attaching a brand identity to a particular musical act, style, or work, the brand can more quickly build a relationship with the customer. This relationship feels more real and lived-in thanks to its musical backing. Meier sees music as useful in rendering authenticity for the consumer, though "authenticity" as such is anathema to much of Bowie's work. Meier writes, "not only is music useful for breaking through promotional clutter, but it can also speak to identity and signify (even if problematically) a sense of 'realness' amid experiences constructed by the brands."[4] For Bowie, any sense of realness was always already constructed, and quite consciously so. The extensive use of his constructed personae in clearly unreal environments is at the center of each of the ads analyzed here. In contrast to the "typical" artist/brand relationship, Bowie's advertising forays show a concept of personal identity that is not inherent, but chosen. Bowie himself *chose* a variety of different identities throughout his public career, many of which are referenced in these three commercials. Perhaps, then, Bowie's value to these brands lies not only in his ability to create a more "real," personal connection with the audience, but also in his ability to show the power of choice in self-definition through the invocation of his own iconic iterations. The Pepsi, Vittel, and Louis Vuitton spots show a clear distillation of artist as image that mimics Bowie's own use of his iconicity. Beyond this, Vittel and Louis Vuitton actively invite audiences to borrow Bowie's approach, creating themselves through Bowie's image and the products it supports.

From mime to stage acting to producing others' albums to appearing in commercials, all aspects of Bowie's public persona can be analyzed as facets of this unified expression of Bowieness, tied together by the way each iteration exploits specific imagery for iconic impact. Bowie stated that he and other rock stars were really actors, drawn to the medium of rock as a point of entry,

---

[3] Leslie M. Meier, "Promotional Ubiquitous Musics: Recording Artists, Brands, and Rendering Authenticity," *Popular Music and Society* 34, no. 4 (2011): 399–415.
[4] Meier, "Promotional Ubiquitous Musics," 412.

despite working in a variety of fields.⁵ His commercials from the 1980s onward show that actorly impulse and unified multimedia approach very clearly. These commercials, of course, serve the dual branding desires of Bowie and the corporation which has hired him, but they also show a distillation of visual and musical language on an even more concentrated scale than the music video, which is ultimately instructive in studying Bowie's definition of self and persona. Each of these three commercials turns to visual strategies also present in Bowie's music videos, as discussed in Chapter 3. Specifically, the advertisements borrow Bowie's fragmentation of his image into recognizable objects—his mismatched pupils, a costume choice, a hair style. Where Bowie used this objectification to define himself more clearly, these advertisements use it for immediate recognition and relation.

As authors like Joanna Love have shown, commercials present an interesting and fruitful nexus of the many forces active in shaping a performer's public persona. As in Love's analyses of Michael Jackson and Madonna's Pepsi ads, I concentrate on two main aspects of Bowie's commercial work: the incorporation and alteration of his original music, and the relation of his styling in the commercials to his contemporaneous public persona.⁶ The eras of these commercials represent interesting moments in Bowie's evolution, when his persona was either under recent revision or out of the public eye entirely. These commercial spots shed important light on the conception of "David Bowie" in these particular historical moments and the tools for altering that conception. Their use of a consistent visual language that references specific Bowie videos is instructive.

Fan Relationships and Star Image in Advertising

In addition to presenting a compendium of Bowie signs, we may also see these commercials as evidence of Bowie's role in the wider world and in fans' lives. Sean Redmond has shown the pervasive, innately personal nature of contemporary fame. Indeed, "contemporary fame speaks and is spoken about through the language of intimacy: it is a word, concept, practice, sellable commodity

---

[5] Crowe, "David Bowie: Ground Control to Davy Jones."
[6] Joanna Love, "From Cautionary Chart-Topper to Friendly Beverage Anthem: Michael Jackson's 'Billie Jean' and Pepsi's 'Choice of a New Generation' Television Campaign," *Journal of the Society for American Music* 9, no. 2 (2015): 178–203.

that smoulders at its very core."⁷ Bowie courted that intimacy, particularly in the age of the internet. He was an early adopter of internet technology and a believer in the possibilities of the expanded connection and creativity that the new form allowed. Founding his own website and internet service provider BowieNet in 1998, he frequently interacted with fans and posted on message boards under usernames that were an open secret. In fan communities in 2020, these BowieNet posts by "Sailor" are still shared as screenshots. The experiment was an indication of Bowie's view of art and celebrity in the internet age. As a *Guardian* retrospective piece noted in 2016, "he was envisioning something we all take for granted now—that link between popstar, Twitter, Instagram, fanbase and culture; that frisson between the artist as an aloof creator and the artist as an active participant in their own community."⁸ This interaction between artist and fanbase, first courted in the David Bowie fan clubs of the 1970s, served to break down the wall between Bowie and the average listener. Such close contact made Bowie's celebrity cachet all the more marketable: not some far-off star, Bowie was, paradoxically, both relatable and fantastical. This heady mix created even more desire to emulate and embrace Bowie, his look, and the products he endorsed. For advertisers, such an intimate relationship was a goldmine. For Bowie fans, it was the result of (in some cases) decades of fandom and interaction. In the commercials addressed here, one can see the development of this intimacy and its commercialization. These advertisers clearly understood the relationship between Bowie and his fans and, in most cases, targeted the fans with the most prolonged and close relationship to the artist. Later promotional spots traded on not only current Bowie icons, but much older ones as well. They invoke a shared history between the artist and his audience. Given this history, we can analyze these commercials, which stretch from 1987 to 2013, as targeting the same group of consumers as they mature and gain capital.

Beyond such direct, interactive contact with fans, celebrities also leverage their more staged public appearances as ways to create desire and intimacy. Redmond cites events like the Oscars as, essentially, long advertisements, both for the films on display and for the actors feted at the event. By extension, such an event also promotes the lifestyle and products with which each celebrity is aligned.⁹ Though

---

⁷ Sean Redmond, "Intimate Fame Everywhere," in *Framing Celebrity: New Directions in Celebrity Culture*, ed. Su Holmes and Sean Redmond (New York: Routledge, 2006), 36.
⁸ Keith Stuart, "BowieNet: How David Bowie's ISP Foresaw the Future of the Internet," *The Guardian*, January 11, 2016, https://www.theguardian.com/technology/2016/jan/11/david-bowie-bowienet-isp-internet Accessed October 4, 2021.
⁹ Redmond, "Intimate Fame Everywhere," 31.

Bowie was largely ignored by awards ceremonies like the Grammys and Oscars throughout his career, his public appearances on such red carpets can, nonetheless, be analyzed in a similar way. Appearing at fashion events like the Council of Fashion Designers of America awards with his wife, supermodel Iman, Bowie cultivated a public persona beyond that defined by his music or his acting. In this iteration, he was also an elder statesman of rock, married to a beautiful supermodel, who walked red carpets from Tribeca to Sundance and moved in the rarified spheres of high fashion. As Bowie himself jokingly said, "You would think that a rock star being married to a supermodel would be one of the greatest things in the world. It is."[10] He played this role in public ways from the 1990s onward, offering a different view of his rockstardom and fame. For fans who knew his musical and filmic work, this access to a different, less *overtly* constructed Bowie was exciting.

Of course, personal interest in and emulation of Bowie ran rampant from the early days of his fame. For example, in April 1974, *CREEM* ran a contest for Bowie lookalikes. Proclaiming the opportunity to "Get in David's Pants," *CREEM* and Bowie's management MainMan solicited fan photos for the chance to win a stage-worn item of Bowie's clothing. Such contests and magazine features show Bowie as a style icon. As the *CREEM* copy states, "Remember the first kid on your block who had a Davy Crockett coonskin cap? Elvis Presley sideburns? Beatles haircut? Peter Fonda sunglasses? Mick Jagger lips? Well this season it's David Bowie, and it seems that everywhere you turn there's another suburban streetcorner incarnation of that lunar prance."[11] It is notable that the emulation of Bowie here is not reduced to a single, purchasable item. Rather, "that lunar prance" evokes his essence, somehow. It would have been difficult for a 1974 fan to purchase Bowie's exact look in stores, given the artist's close relationship with designers like Kansai Yamamoto and Freddie Burretti, each of whom designed custom looks for Bowie. Instead, fans emulated makeup, hair, and performance swagger. Bowie of the 1980s and 1990s, though, was substantially more mainstream and, for lack of a better word, normal. This relative normalcy was marketed in much the same way that Redmond sees fame being sold in contemporary culture. For example, Bowie and wife Iman partnered with designer Tommy Hilfiger in an ad campaign selling Hilfiger's distinctly American sportswear. Even Bowie's

---

[10] Quoted in Olivia Blair, "David Bowie: The Iconic Singer's Most Profound Quotes," *The Independent*, January 11, 2016, https://www.independent.co.uk/news/people/david-bowie-best-quotes-starman-a6805536.html Accessed October 4, 2021.

[11] "Get in David's Pants," *CREEM*, April 1974, 33.

stagewear, designed in the 1990s by Alexander McQueen and in the early 2000s by Hedi Slimane of Dior Homme, was somewhat more accessible as it came from major fashion houses. This Bowie, shown in press photos and featured in magazines from *Entertainment Weekly* to *Vogue*, parlayed the intimacy his fans had long felt into an aspirational relationship that could be commodified.

Commodification of "David Bowie" is most frequently leveraged by his management and record company. In February 1997, though, Bowie took the unorthodox step of commodifying his own worth on the stock market. Bowie issued "Bowie bonds," an asset-backed bond that derived its value from the royalties accrued on Bowie's back catalogue. Assessed by Standard and Poor's, among others, these were the first so-called "celebrity bonds," or bonds that traded on the continued cachet of their namesake. According to the *New York Times*, "Mr. Bowie has opened what is envisioned as a new market," one that proved lucrative for him.[12] All the bonds in the initial offering were purchased by Prudential Insurance. The profits for this sale were important for Bowie: essentially, they provided an up-front lump sum of the royalties he would receive in the period of the bond's life. That up-front payment allowed him to make an even more lucrative move, and purchase the remaining share of his master recordings from former manager Tony DeFries, with whom Bowie had a famously rancorous parting.[13] Bowie then owned his master recordings, allowing for the continued shaping of his legacy in his final years and the period following his death (addressed in this book's final chapter). Though artists like James Brown and the Isley Brothers followed in Bowie's asset-backed footsteps, the success of the bonds was short-lived: the bottom was dropping out of the music market as it had formerly existed. The rise of Napster and online file sharing turned traditional music revenue streams into mere trickles. At the end of the bonds' ten-year term, their rating had been downgraded to nearly "junk" and they were not offered again. Bowie had managed, though, to leverage his public profile and celebrity innovator status in an important way in those waning years of traditional profitability. Though not a precise example of his music's use in advertising, the Bowie bonds saga does highlight the artist's financial sense and ability to leverage his public persona into a profitable venture. This recognition of self as commodity (not for nothing, the bonds were covered as "Bowie Bonds"

---

[12] Bloomberg News, "Bowie's Latest Hit: Royalty-tied Bonds," *New York Times*, February 21, 1997, https://www.nytimes.com/1997/02/21/nyregion/bowie-s-latest-hit-royalty-tied-bonds.html Accessed October 4, 2021.

[13] Tom Espiner, "'Bowie Bonds': The Singer's Financial Innovation," *BBC*, January 11, 2016, https://www.bbc.com/news/business-35280945 Accessed October 4, 2021.

extensively in the press, rather than "asset-backed bonds on future recording royalties") undergirds much of the approach behind Bowie's commercial appearances and endorsements from the 1980s onward.

The ubiquity of Bowie himself, along with this newfound accessibility and the longstanding close relationship of artist and fan, serves to heighten the effect of Bowie's commercials. The following Pepsi, Vittel, and Louis Vuitton commercials each provide a snapshot in the development of this fan-artist relationship, as well as the development of Bowie's public persona. Much like the publicity for the film roles discussed in the previous chapter, these ads track the use of Bowie's image by outside forces. Some contrast exists between these corporations' use of Bowie's image and his own shaping of that audiovisual star image (as seen in the first section of this book); those differences are instructive. While Bowie worked to create a rock star allure throughout the 1970s, that allure was frequently built on the changeable and inaccessible. Corporations, in contrast, have sought to use his inaccessible "coolness" to create a desire for accessibility and emulation among the general public.

Central to this alignment is the idea of branding. As Paul McDonald has discussed, the contemporary understanding of corporate branding could be described as "brand-as-person": a clear construction of what the product represents, its identity. Conversely, per McDonald, we might think of star image as "person-as-brand."[14] This line of thinking underlies much of the preceding study, though I have not yet directly addressed it. In creating a strong audiovisual star image, Bowie has created a strong brand. He linked easily identifiable iconic images with associated characteristics—hence the outsider star type discussed in Chapter 5. In McDonald's formulation, these star signifiers (the visual and aural markers) and star signifieds (the associated meaning or characteristic) come together to create a star sign, akin to the star image previously discussed. That star sign is linked to a product referent in order to create a star brand.[15] The main difference between my earlier usage of star image and McDonald's star brand is the concrete, monetizable product linked to it: a star brand can sell movie tickets, albums, and perfume, but it does not sell allegiance to the star.

With an eye toward the monetary, McDonald identifies two axes of differentiation for stars: vertical and horizontal, which convey quality and "flavor," respectively. In terms of stardom, this would be a vertical value that commands higher prices or salaries, with a horizontal personality or differentiation from

---

[14] Paul McDonald, *Hollywood Stardom* (Chichester, UK: Wiley Blackwell, 2013), 41.
[15] McDonald, *Hollywood Stardom*, 44.

other stars in the same category.[16] For example, Bowie and Michael Jackson both starred in Pepsi ads. Though their vertical value may have been similar, their horizontal value differed greatly. Both were popular music stars, but their genres differed, as did their marketable characteristics. These differences in horizontal value show why both would be useful partners for Pepsi.

McDonald's approach is much more commercially oriented than my preceding analysis. However, the features he addresses are fundamental to my star image focus. In the realm of advertising, they simply take on different significance. While Bowie certainly profited from the mere creation of a strong, unique star image, that image was not always concretely paired with a product referent. These connections and contrasts in the creation and use of star image reveal much about its construction. Both Bowie and the corporate partners that sought to monetize his fame and popularity used similar semiotic tools to create audience desire.

"Creation": Dancing with Bowie's Icons

With his 1987 Pepsi commercial, Bowie and the corporation sought to capitalize on the artist's hugely popular work of the early 1980s. The spot features "Modern Love," a hit single from *Let's Dance,* released in 1983. Though the choice of a four-year-old song for a new ad campaign is not in keeping with Pepsi's strategy with artists like Michael Jackson and Madonna, it makes sense for this stage of Bowie's career. *Let's Dance* and its sound were a departure for Bowie, one that paid great financial dividends. Bowie's late 1970s had been artistically successful, but commercially difficult. Following the critical acclaim of his Berlin trilogy (consisting of *Low*, *"Heroes,"* and *Lodger*) in the late 1970s, Bowie turned to a more salable sound in the mid-1980s. Working with producer and guitarist Nile Rodgers of Chic, he sought commercial success and achieved it. With hits like "Let's Dance," "China Girl," and "Modern Love," Bowie became more of a mainstream success than ever before. He had a presence in MTV's video rotation from the channel's inception and was featured in interviews there, increasing his public profile for a younger audience. His Serious Moonlight tour in support of the *Let's Dance* album was an international success, and was aired as a television special on HBO in February 1984. His subsequent albums, *Tonight* and *Never*

[16] Ibid., 47–8.

Let Me Down, sold well but did not achieve the same level of ubiquity that Let's Dance enjoyed. For Pepsi, a slightly older song with immediate recognition power seems an easy choice for an ad campaign.

At the same time, Bowie's mainstream visibility extended beyond his musical work. A serious acting career, begun in earnest with Nicolas Roeg's *The Man Who Fell to Earth* (1976), gained steam in the 1980s with roles in *The Hunger* (1983, dir. Scott); *Merry Christmas, Mr. Lawrence* (1983, dir. Ôshima); *Labyrinth* (1986, dir. Henson); and *Absolute Beginners* (1986, dir. Temple), was discussed in the previous chapter. His music was also used in high-profile movies: his Giorgio Moroder collaboration, "Cat People (Putting Out Fire)," closed the 1982 film of the same name. Featured prominently in periodicals like *People* and *Time* in 1986, Bowie was present in the average American home in a way he had never achieved before. Both magazines showed Bowie in traditionally masculine clothing (typically suits), and presented him as a middle of the road rock star for *all* audiences. Though he had achieved notoriety in the 1970s, that attention was often for his nonnormative appearance and persona, rather than for his mainstream popularity. This peak moment was ideal for his continued involvement in advertising, which moved to a more prominent level with the "Creation" Pepsi campaign. That deal involved a TV spot with Tina Turner, with whom Bowie had recently recorded, and Pepsi sponsorship of both their tours (Glass Spider and Break Every Rule, respectively).

In keeping with Pepsi's musician collaborations of the time, "Creation" tells a vignette of a story centering on Bowie and Turner's interaction. Unlike ads like Jackson's "The Concert," though, this spot is not longform, not part of a series, and was not premiered with the ballyhoo accompanying Jackson's. In the commercial, Bowie plays the role of a geek who is building his ideal woman with the help of a computer, *Weird Science*-style. He tears images from magazines and art history books and inputs them via scanner, waggling his eyebrows as he inexplicably tries to scan a sexy ankle boot. As the computer goes to work, Bowie kicks back—and knocks his Pepsi onto the computer. The creation kicks into hyperdrive and Tina Turner emerges, her appearance blasting off all vestiges of geekdom from Bowie and leading to their Pepsi-infused strut in front of the "Pepsi Diner," which features a Pepsi vending machine (lovingly caressed by Turner) near its entrance. This dance is set to the new "Modern Love" lyrics "now I know the choice is mine." This lyrical nod to the "Choice of a New Generation" tagline links Bowie and Turner's ad to earlier installments from Michael Jackson and others. The connection to Jackson is particularly telling, as Bowie's iconicity is exploited here in much the same way Jackson's was in his ads.

As Love has shown, Jackson's "The Concert" spot manages to evoke the performer without making much use of his highly recognizable face. Jackson had set limits on face time, and Pepsi was able to make that absence almost invisible, through evocation of iconic Jackson imagery. A glittery glove, white socks, and dancing feet stand in for Jackson's face.[17] In much the same way, Bowie's 1980s hits and persona are evoked. Though his face is visible throughout, it is in details and closeups that Pepsi's strategy is clear. First, during the opening "construction" section, we are given multiple closeups of Bowie's face. Importantly, these clarify his presence (despite his geeky disguise), but also draw attention to the features he had emphasized for years. For example, we're given a facial closeup shortly after Bowie scans a photo of a set of eyes, serving to highlight his own mismatched pupils, perhaps his most recognizable feature, and one that is emphasized in music videos like "Life on Mars?" (1973). After his transformation from geek to debonair dancer, Bowie and Turner strut, he wearing his "red shoes," an allusion to the lyrics of "Let's Dance." Much like Bowie's own music videos, the ad breaks him down to his visible, recognizable constituent parts. By highlighting eyes, hair, and red shoes, Pepsi links to the signs fans would already associate with Bowie. In fact, Pepsi subtly points to the height of Bowie's 1980s popularity, even though in 1987 that is not the most recent Bowie iteration. Beyond that, Bowie's dual roles as geek and sexy love interest are reminiscent of the video for "Blue Jean" (1984). In the Julien Temple-directed longform music video *Jazzin' for Blue Jean,* Bowie plays both the dashing "Screamin' Lord Byron" and a geeky, gawky audience member incapable of successfully making a move on a girl. Both directly and indirectly, "Creation" seeks to invoke the Bowie of *Let's Dance,* allowing both Pepsi and Bowie to continue to capitalize on it.

Musically, the "Creation" iteration of "Modern Love" is quite similar to the album version. Alterations are largely in the service of including Turner and adding Pepsi's tagline. Unlike in Pepsi's reworking of "Billie Jean," most musical structures remain the same. Love has pointed out that many of the songs offered for Pepsi campaigns by Jackson and Madonna were "anything but the benign pop songs that littered top 40 radio."[18] The risqué lyrical content of "Billie Jean" could have been a liability for Pepsi in their goal of near-universal appeal. In contrast, Bowie's "Modern Love" fits the bill quite nicely, veering away from more controversial topics and presenting a musically catchy and lyrically clean vehicle.

---

[17] Love, "Cautionary Chart-Topper."
[18] Joanna Love, "'Choice of a New Generation': 'Pop' Music, Advertising, and Meaning in the MTV Era and Beyond" (PhD dissertation, UCLA, 2012), 207.

Its lyrics deal with love, though not in any overtly sexual or problematic way. Bowie's lyrics here seem almost tailor-made for use in other, more commercial contexts: they are oblique enough as to avoid any potential controversy, and repetitive enough that small lyrical changes would have an outsized impact.

Musical differences in "Creation" tend to be omissions of sections to fit the time restrictions of the minute-long ad, rather than changes in harmonic function. For example, the song's guitar riff intro is omitted in "Creation," as is Bowie's spoken word section in the postchorus that follows. Verse 1 is also left out. The resulting structure is simplified from the single version: it consists of postchorus, Verse 2, prechorus, and one truncated iteration of the chorus. Apart from this, some of the ambiguous or dark aspects of this song's lyrics are changed in the duet version. For example, in Verse 2 "But I never wave bye-bye" is changed to "But I always wave goodbye." More substantially, the chorus lyrics are altered to include Turner in a sort of call and response, while also highlighting key Pepsi terms (notably, "choice" and "satisfies"). In all, the changes for the ad version are relatively minor, preserving the identifiable features of Bowie's single and distilling it into a more potent vehicle for Pepsi's "Choice of a New Generation" campaign.

Where the Michael Jackson and Madonna campaigns feature multiple installments which show a developing style, we can only speculate on the large-scale strategy that would have been employed in a long-standing Bowie partnership with Pepsi. The deal would reach a rocky end for Bowie with the emergence of sexual assault allegations in 1987. Stemming from an appearance in Dallas earlier that year, Bowie faced litigation alleging that he had sexually assaulted a fan and infected her with HIV. It does not seem that the case received particularly wide exposure for such a serious allegation (accounts appeared in the *Dallas Morning News* and *Dallas Times Herald* on October 30, with *The Washington Post* and *New York Times* running brief accounts of Bowie's agreement to an AIDS test early in November and at the conclusion of litigation), and a grand jury did not decide to indict him on the charges. The woman, Wanda Nichols, did not receive a settlement from Bowie, but the possibility of such action put an end to his endorsement deal. In similar situations, accusations of other artists' sexual violence have also effectively brought an end to their endorsement agreements.[19] In these cases, as in Bowie's, sexual conduct was an important enough aspect of

---

[19] Sean Redmond, "Intimate Fame," in *Framing Celebrity: New Directions in Celebrity Culture*, ed. Su Holmes and Sean Redmond (New York: Routledge, 2006), 30.

star image to alter that image for the general public. No version of the carefully constructed Bowie star image could have included the idea of Bowie as disease-spreading predator. Similarly, Pepsi's needs dictated a clean, relatable, desirable star. Nichols' account fundamentally changed that image.

Given this allegation, the only existing Bowie/Pepsi ad is "Creation," providing a window into the way that Pepsi's existing marketing strategies would have been tailored to their application in Bowie's case. Aaron Walton, who was present on the Glass Spider tour as Pepsi's representative, later described his approach to music and advertising as "using music, celebrity and pop-culture to amplify brand messages and connect with consumers *experientially*."[20] This experiential focus appears in the "Creation" ad through its emphasis on Bowie's construction of self through familiar, iconic images. Audiences were familiar with these symbols through their own experience of Bowie over the last decade and a half. Thus, Pepsi invokes not only Bowie as a popular star, but also Bowie as a memorable part of audiences' memories and cultural experiences. Throughout, we can see an attention to iconicity, as well as a strategy for musical alterations that refocuses the song's content for maximum positivity and Pepsi references. For what it's worth, Tina Turner's Pepsi partnership continued; in ad spots like "We've Got the Taste," a similar visual approach is used, focusing on Tina's iconic hair and legs before launching into her performance. Whether follow-up Bowie commercials would have continued to reach into the artist's back catalogue and identifiable visuals is unclear, but other later endorsement deals would certainly return to the artist's most iconic, consciously constructed moments.

"Never Get Old": History Repeating

Bowie himself once said, "I'm really just my own little corporation of characters."[21] In the two later commercials that I address, Vittel and Louis Vuitton take Bowie's character-based performance strategy and expand upon it, incorporating it into their own campaigns. Rather than pointing to a Bowie who is a few years out of date, these ads seek to invoke an entire history, and to capitalize upon that history and its scope. Each one points, visually, to many familiar iterations of Bowie's

---

[20] Emily Hope, "Aaron Walton, Founding Partner, Walton Isaacson," *ThinkLA*, July 10, 2018, https://www.thinkla.org/blogpost/1230000/305282/Aaron-Walton-Founding-Partner-Walton-Isaacson Accessed March 17, 2019. (emphasis added)

[21] Crowe, "David Bowie: Ground Control to Davy Jones."

public persona. Manipulating Bowie's iconicity, these ads link their brands, and Bowie himself, to a timelessness and pop culture currency connected to these images. Their use of current Bowie compositions helps to make those personae and images more contemporary.

Vittel's 2003 ad is a veritable iconography of David Bowie. The Ogilvy and Mather Paris spot plays on the idea of Vittel's bottled water as the source of new vitality—such a powerful source that Bowie's many personae spring to independent life and populate his house, as contemporary Bowie walks among them.[22] These personae are embodied by Bowie himself and the impersonator David Brighton. The commercial is set to "Never Get Old," a somewhat tongue-in-cheek acknowledgment of Bowie's aging rock star status. The song comes from his *Reality* album, released in 2003, the same year as the ad. Chris O'Leary sees humor in Bowie's irreverent approach to the aging rock star image in this song.[23] One of classic rock's remaining superstars, Bowie could pillory the seemingly unending energy, youth, and vitality he and his contemporaries were expected to project. Bowie, in his song, and Vittel, in this commercial, do just that. The music eschews any of the odder Bowie trappings: no literary references litter its lyrics, and the production and instrumentation are typical of guitar-driven rock. Musically, relatively little is surprising and nothing is altered from the album version, allowing the visuals to take the lead and capitalize on Bowie's iconicity and legacy.

The ad begins with the final chorus of the song. Here the lyrics almost exclusively repeat the "never ever gonna get old" refrain. However, the song's earlier lyrics (cut from this ad version) are actually more instructive for our understanding of the ad and Bowie's relationship with stardom and the past. From a practical standpoint, it is easy to see why Vittel would have chosen only this final chorus for the ad: it is the appropriate length, and it avoids any of the more questionable lyrics ("never gonna be enough sex … never gonna be enough bullets," for example). This final chorus focuses on the speaker (Bowie) and his addressee (the audience), while promising eternal life and youth. The earlier verses and their paratexts complicate the thirty-second ad, but help to illuminate our understanding of its place within the Bowie cosmology. As a sign, the music of "Never Gonna Get Old" can be understood to carry with it

---

[22] Duncan Macleod, "David Bowie Never Gets Old on Vittel," *The Inspiration Room*, August 28, 2008, http://theinspirationroom.com/daily/2007/david-bowie-never-gets-old-on-vittel/ Accessed March 30, 2019.

[23] Chris O'Leary, *Ashes to Ashes: The Songs of David Bowie 1976–2016* (London: Repeater Books, 2018), 526–8.

the connotative content of its many iterations, including the album and video versions. Paratextually, then, we might look at the official music video, which begins with snippets of Bowie addressing the camera. He speaks of memory, of condiments ("mustard or ketchup"), but most importantly, he speaks about the past and its edifices. He discusses buildings in Barcelona and the way they seem to exist outside of time. He states, "you take it for granted that those buildings are back in the time they were built in; they're not in the 21st century."[24] These visible structures, he implies, are not wholly of our time, though they are tangible within it. Like buildings in Barcelona's Barri Gótic, Bowie's own personae seem to exist out of time: present in our reality, but anchored in the past. With this paratextual framing, the uncanny nature of Vittel's commercial is even more pronounced.

Perhaps even more telling, though, is the way this music video begins, with Bowie directly addressing the camera and his audience. True to his longstanding video style, Bowie does not ignore the camera's gaze but acknowledges it, playing with the audience and their presence as spectators of his video. This gesture is echoed at the end of the commercial and is also referenced in the song's first verse. Bowie sings of thinking about "personal history" before singing of a movie star, drawing a picture of his interaction with that start that culminates in their eye contact as the star awaits a countdown.

This lyric reflects two important aspects of Bowie's presence in this ad: first, the star-audience relationship and second, his own history. Songs from "Life on Mars?" forward have foregrounded the relationship of spectator to screen star, but here we find Bowie positioning himself, paradoxically, on both sides of the exchange. His first-person lyrics paint him as the fan receiving the star's gaze, yet the final "countdown" hints at his own star image. Like Major Tom in Bowie's career-making hit "Space Oddity," here the star commences countdown. Lyrically, it seems Bowie may already be in conversation with his past and the concept of himself as star image. This invocation of his past (and the character of Major Tom in particular) is present in Bowie's work from "Ashes to Ashes" through "Blackstar," but here it is leveraged in the service of something beyond the Bowie star image. Bowie, his past, and his relationship to his fans are all invoked to create desire—desire for a specific product. While Bowie's song hints at all these relationships, Vittel's ad plays upon them in a much more overt way through its visual references.

---

[24] "David Bowie // Never Get Old (Official Video)," uploaded by Jay Parmar. August 28, 2010, https://www.youtube.com/watch?v=7NorNUMoewQ Accessed April 4, 2021.

Bowie's past is evoked with laser precision throughout. His cast of characters populates its world. It is easy to imagine such an ad playing on past Bowie roles in broad strokes, but here the man himself and seasoned impersonator David Brighton recreate specific and iconic images in great detail. The ad begins with Bowie seeing his current reflection paired with his Ziggy era visage in a mirror. This shot is a recreation of images from a 1972 Mick Rock session shot at Bowie's home, Haddon Hall, later to be featured on the cover of the retrospective collection *Nothing Has Changed* (2015). The cover images of *The Man Who Sold the World* (1970), *Diamond Dogs* (1974), *Low* (1977), and *Scary Monsters (and Super Creeps)* (1980) also make appearances. Digitally altered versions of Bowie himself, or the impersonator Brighton, act in these shots. The effect is that each is brought to life: not a stationary reproduction of the past, each looks like a recognizable Bowie moment but is shown to be living and breathing in the ad. A custom Alexander McQueen Union Jack frock coat, made for the cover of 1997's *Earthling*, hangs by the brownstone's door. Icons of David Bowie live everywhere in this house and this commercial.

Beyond these image recreations, there's the connection to Bowie's music videos. This ad, with its mirrored, younger Bowies, echoes the "Thursday's Child" (1999) video, which features Bowie watching a younger version of himself through the frame of a mirror. Much like the Vittel ad, the video's visuals play with concepts of age, persona, and continuity in interesting ways. The effect, in the video and the ad, is complicated. Comically, we see these Bowies interacting with and annoying each other (see Figure 6.1). Nostalgically, we may remember our own interactions with each iteration. However, there is something of the *unheimlich* or uncanny to these *doppelgängers*, adding the oddness and disconcerting nature that many have come to associate with Bowie himself.[25] Taken together, the ad presents a multivalent expression of Bowie's star image that is striking and interesting. That the ad ends with a single, contemporary Bowie breaking the fourth wall to show us the secret of his reincarnation (that is, Vittel) is even more comically *unheimlich*. Such a complex approach works because of the great specificity with which the ad invokes each separate Bowie persona.

This image precision is noteworthy as it shows a further step in the exploitation of Bowie's iconic past. More than the oblique references of "Creation," here the specific instance is key, and our memory of that instance aids in the efficacy of

---

[25] Here I refer to Sigmund Freud's concept of the unheimlich, or the uncanny. Freud sees the uncanny as revealing something of the self, perhaps unintentionally. See Sigmund Freud, "The Uncanny," in *The Uncanny*, trans. David McLintock (New York: Penguin Books, 2003), 123–76.

Figure 6.1 Three Bowies in Vittel ad.

the spot. One can easily watch and understand the main conceit of the ad without any specialized Bowie knowledge, but with the added specificity of the images, Vittel and Bowie play with identifiable history in a way that adds punch to that conceit. Bowie can jokingly sing that he is "never ever gonna get old," but there's a kernel of truth to that. Not, of course, because he stays hydrated with Vittel, but because we—in our memory and consumption of him—will never allow him to age. As consumers and fans, we hold these previous iterations of Bowie in our memory and in our record collections. We consume these variations on the Bowie star image long after their expiration dates, and much of the work they continue to do is in definition, of both Bowie and ourselves. Bowie long recognized the importance of image in defining "David Bowie" to the public, but in creating this character, he also created a mode for fans to do the same for themselves. Our appreciation for and celebration of various eras of Bowie's work help to show the world who we are and what we value. Similarly, access to the shibboleth of these Bowie images and personae allows the target audience to take part in the ad and see themselves within it.

Bowie closes the commercial with a literal knowing wink to his fans—in some ways, a continuation of the tenor of the ad as a whole. Once he exits his house of selves, Bowie turns to the camera and holds a finger to his lips. Directly addressing the audience, he breaks the fourth wall and asks us to join him in his secret: here, the life-giving power of Vittel (which, the narrator tells us, can "re-Vittel-ize"). More broadly, though, that moment is indicative of a self-consciousness that marks this commercial and Bowie's advertising appearances. Yes, he is literally "selling out"—selling his image to corporations for their profit. However, he shows himself to be aware of the incongruity of such a move for a rock legend, and jokingly asks us to keep his secret. For someone who once loomed large as a countercultural figure, the idea of making commercials should be anathema. Bowie manages to balance it, as he did so many persona changes, by acknowledging it and showing that he is complicit in it. Very simply, he cannot "sell out" because he has long chosen to be a commodity anyway. In his costumes, Bowie bonds, and albums, he had been bought and sold for years. This commercial, he tells us, is all of a piece with his other work. The visual language of the ad seems to tell the same story.

The target audience for this ad, with their knowledge of Bowies stretching back to 1970, is likely much the same as the audience for the 1986 Pepsi spot. This generational group, with buying power to spare, has been highlighted by Taylor and others as a variation on the "new petit bourgeoisie," who have imported their popular music into advertising not only because it is what speaks to them, but also because it represents a counter to the previous generation's focus on educated, trained classical musicians.[26] Such an impulse, Taylor argues, led to the popular music wave of the cola wars, but changes here as that same generation, now older and more established, affects advertising in different arenas and works with younger boomers. The idea of marketing as not presenting information, but "being invited to participate, to join the hip club" speaks directly to Vittel's approach to Bowie.[27] Now this group is aging, and the revitalized images of their rock icon allow them to see themselves in his past and in his healthy vigor. By directly recalling memorative images and experiences, Vittel's manipulation of the Bowie star image implicates the viewer, giving them the same potential for revitalization as Bowie: they, too, are "never ever gonna get old." That same focus on Bowie's past, and explicitly our consumption of and identification with that past, is present in his next major campaign, for Louis Vuitton in 2013.

---

[26] Timothy Taylor, *The Sounds of Capitalism: Advertising, Music, and the Conquest of Culture* (Chicago: University of Chicago Press, 2012), 233.

[27] Taylor, *Sounds of Capitalism*, 236.

Fantastic Voyage through the Past: "L'Invitation au Voyage"

Apart from "selling out" in advertisements, Bowie has long been present within commercial spaces. The fashion industry in particular has aligned itself closely with Bowie through use of his music, invocation of his personae, and more. As he spoofed in his *Zoolander* (2001, dir. Stiller) cameo, Bowie was something of a fashion icon. His likeness is invoked in runway shows such as Diane von Furstenberg's Autumn/Winter 2013 collection, among countless others. Even though Bowie did not appear in campaigns for them, his close collaboration with designers like Kansai Yamamoto, Alexander McQueen, and Dior Homme's Hedi Slimane helped to define Bowie's career as well as those of his designers. That he should align his image with fashion label Louis Vuitton in 2013 is not surprising.

"I'd Rather Be High," or "L'Invitation au Voyage," a Louis Vuitton advert from November 2013, came at a moment of resurgence for Bowie. In March of that year, he released *The Next Day* with very little advance notice: the video for the lead single, "Where Are We Now?", appeared on the internet in January, well before any news of the album had broken to the public at large. The album also came during the preparation of the *David Bowie Is* exhibition that would premiere at London's Victoria and Albert Museum. Importantly, it fits within this late-career moment wherein Bowie looked back on his career and took stock, actively shaping his own legacy.

With *The Next Day*, Bowie showed himself to be a still vital and vibrant musical force—and importantly, one concerned with his own history. The album's cover artwork plays on the artist's iconography. In March 2013, the *Evening Standard* wrote that the image "is intended to suggest that new great rock music (the white square) can obliterate the past—but not entirely (the old image is still partially visible)."[28] One can certainly read the album cover in this way, but I think the fact that the *"Heroes"* cover is still recognizably present is significant. The cover itself directly invokes the past while also recasting it. In fact, Barnbrook also designed a viral campaign that used this template as the basis for a meme, including text variants like "Your Idea of David Bowie Here." Different text insertions were used in posters, newspaper ads, and more.[29] Some directly invoked Bowie's past,

---

[28] "How David Bowie's White Square Infiltrated Our Minds," *Evening Standard*, March 12, 2013, https://www.standard.co.uk/go/london/music/how-david-bowies-white-square-infiltrated-our-minds-8530858.html Accessed October 4, 2021.

[29] See, for example, https://barnbrook.net/work/david-bowie-the-next-day-2/ Accessed July 22, 2020.

including one with his famous quote "tomorrow belongs to those who can hear it coming," and the ad copy from RCA's promotion of *"Heroes"* original release: "There's new wave. There's old wave. And there's David Bowie." Apart from such official, paid advertising, Bowie's record label also made the white square template available for social media users. Iconic in its simplicity, the white square proliferated, allowing fans to invoke Bowie and his past in their own lives. As the square spread in print ads and social media, it accumulated yet more meaning as Bowie's record company and private individuals partook in a writing and overwriting process. This rewriting of the past is a favorite gambit of Bowie's, and one that surfaces in his advertisement appearances of this era as well.

The Louis Vuitton ad's invocation of audience participation in reclaiming the past is a bit less overt than Barnbrook's campaign, but it still requires some form of audience shibboleth to fully function. Directed by Romain Gavras, the short finds model Arizona Muse arriving at a masquerade, serenaded by Bowie at the harpsichord. Guests dance around them, with costumes and masks loosely evocative of Bowie's earlier guises.[30] Muse finds her way to the harpsichord bench and listens as Bowie performs "I'd Rather Be High." The model is quite literally transported by the experience, clutching her LV bag and closing her eyes in a reverie—until she awakens again in modern day Venice, a sheet of printed music the only evidence of her voyage to this alternate world. The ad exists in multiple guises: there are 1- and 1.5-minute cuts, as well as a "making of" video released by Louis Vuitton. In addition, Bowie starred in a print campaign focused on promoting the brand's Tambour watches (print ads shot by David Sims).

Though this was hardly Bowie's first ad campaign, it received much attention within the fashion press. An October 31, 2013 feature in *Vogue UK* highlighted Bowie's participation and the brand's innovative roll-out of the campaign.[31] Behind-the-scenes photos and storyboard images introduced the campaign in *Vogue UK*, while the longform video was to be released first on the LV app, and later in shorter television spots. Interestingly, even the *Vogue UK* coverage, though brief on words, highlights the importance of the singer's past to the visuals of the campaign. Author Ella Alexander points out the similarities between the ad's costumed dance scene and the "As the World Falls Down" ballroom sequence

---

[30] Tim Nudd, "Ad of the Day: David Bowie Serenades Arizona Muse for Louis Vuitton," *Adweek*, November12, 2013, https://www.adweek.com/brand-marketing/ad-day-david-bowie-serenades-arizona-muse-louis-vuitton-153798/ Accessed March 17, 2019.

[31] Ella Alexander, "Join Bowie on His Louis Vuitton Voyage," *Vogue UK*, October 31, 2013, https://www.vogue.co.uk/gallery/david-bowie-louis-vuitton-campaign-revealed Accessed October 4, 2021.

from *Labyrinth*.³² Alexander also makes reference to Bowie's *The Next Day*, then only a few months old. In this press preview, then, both advertised product (LV watches and bags) and advertising face (Bowie's own) share focus. It is clear that the ad campaign is intended to boost both—but it is also explicitly intended to play upon our memory in a dreamlike, surreal way.

Visual references abound in the campaign. Among the most notable are those that depict the Rothschilds' Surrealist Ball of 1972, and, of course, the ballroom sequence of *Labyrinth*.³³ Attended by luminaries such as Salvador Dalí, Brigitte Bardot, and Audrey Hepburn, the Surrealist Ball was notable for its dreamlike decoration and dress code. Photographs documenting the party show guests with elaborate headdresses and face painting that mimicked famous Surrealist works. There are direct visual references to these looks in the LV ad, where we see partygoers painted entirely in gold, or painted with multiple faces. While for some, the Surrealist looks might be readily recognizable, it seems likely that the most prominent reference for viewers—and especially for Bowie fans—would be *Labyrinth* (Figure 6.2). Much like that film, again we find Bowie as the impresario of a fantastical ball, potentially engaged in an age-inappropriate flirtation with our female protagonist. He is, of course, not styled as Jareth the Goblin King, but in much more appropriate Louis Vuitton menswear and accessories. Still, the sequence is shot similarly, with swirling camera movement and Bowie as a sort of anchor in the middle of that activity. The ad also shares a dreamlike quality with the *Labyrinth* scene: both are shown to have been fantasies from which our female protagonists awaken.

It is worth noting, though, that hints of more outré Bowie incarnations pop up in shots of the masquerade guests. We find an attendee whose eye patch and bright red beard connect him to the *Diamond Dogs*-era Bowie of 1974. Later in the spot, we are given a brief shot of a reveler showing a Bowie-favored hand sign. (Originally made popular with the Junior Birdman scouts and their song, photographs of Bowie using this gesture span from 1972 to the early 2000s.) Neither of these visual references is given extended screen time, but they do not need it. The ad is saturated with such details. Indeed, the storyboards and behind-the-scenes footage show that even more references were planned. Planning materials feature shots of Bowie, clad in a trench coat, meandering

---

³² Alexander, "Join Bowie."
³³ It is this *Labyrinth* connection that is most frequently commented upon by fans. See, for example, the comments section for https://www.youtube.com/watch?v=kMswI4VCdMc

Figure 6.2 Ball scene from *Labyrinth* (1986, dir. Henson) versus "L'Invitation Au Voyage" (2013).

down misty, cobblestone streets. Though only presented in glimpses, these images seem to be a clear reference to Bowie's 1986 "Absolute Beginners" video.

In the one-and-a-half minute runtime of the extended ad, such references accumulate to form an avalanche of Bowie personae and material. In the grand scheme of things, these images do little to overtly sell LV luxury items. However, for the ad's ideal viewer (to borrow Eco's construction), these references do carry meaning.[34] They link to a long, shared history with Bowie and manage to bring the consumer closer to the product and the endorser. As in the Vittel ad, these references serve not as a vital endorsement of the advertiser's product, but as a way of creating shared experience with the viewer, calling upon their decades of interaction with Bowie. Throughout, we're reminded of Bowie's iconic, timeless

---

[34] Umberto Eco, *The Role of the Reader* (Bloomington: Indiana University Press, 1979).

rock star status—a timelessness we could partake in, the ad would have us infer, with the purchase of Louis Vuitton accessories. Indeed, such a purchase could operate in the same way that Bowie's use of iconic visuals helped to form public perception and understanding of him throughout his career.

The music seems similarly unmoored from a specific time or place. The song presented here is a dis/reassembly of "I'd Rather Be High"—but it is an altered version of an alternate mix, dubbed the "Venetian Mix" on the extended album release. Absent from the original album version, the harpsichord is featured prominently in that bonus mix, along with the traditional rock band accompaniment of bass, guitars, and drum set. The Venetian Mix moves the song's center of gravity from the bass end to the treble, expanding and enriching the song's sonic palette. In the ad, the harpsichord is isolated with the voice for the first twenty seconds, giving it much more prominence. The ad's remix removes the song's intro, instead giving a short harpsichord pickup into the first phrase of the first verse, where we hear the seemingly diegetic performance of these lines as Bowie accompanies himself on the harpsichord onscreen. From there, the second verse phrase is eliminated, taking us directly into the chorus as the (nondiegetic) backing band lushly swells, finally introducing the full orchestration of the Venetian Mix.

Though the visual and referential links may be appropriate for Louis Vuitton and their product, the lyrics of "I'd Rather Be High" are decidedly less so. Some lyrical sections are skipped, but no words are changed. Unlike in his Pepsi appearance, Bowie was not asked to reshape his original words to align with the ad campaign. Steeped in Evelyn Waugh and First World War references (not to mention a vocally reinforced shout of "teenage sex" a bit later in the song), "I'd Rather Be High" does not seem like a ready fit for luxury goods. However, the lyrics do not take a place of prominence in the ad. Given the abundance of Bowie-related visual information and the foregrounding of his face throughout the spot, we might assume that his persona, and not the music itself, are intended to be the focus and link, a strategy that differentiates LV's approach from Pepsi before them.

Though no record of the music played in Louis Vuitton brick-and-mortar stores in 2013 is currently accessible, it would not be much of a stretch to imagine Bowie's *The Next Day* having a presence there. Indeed, the synergistic use of music in commercial spaces is well documented.[35] Recently, LVMH (Louis

---

[35] See, for example, Jonathan Sterne, "Sounds Like the Mall of America: Programmed Music and the Architecture of Commercial Space," *Ethnomusicology* 41, no. 1 (1997): 22–50.

Vuitton's parent company) named a music director for its menswear division, which was at the time helmed by Virgil Abloh. Benji B (Benjamin Benstead) had a history of DJing and involvement with fashion events, but is now on the LV roster as the official creator and curator of the LV Menswear soundscape. In a recent interview, Benji referred to his work as "about understanding context and how to create moments by adding emotion and atmosphere."[36] This perspective on music's importance for the curation of a brand identity is undoubtedly at the heart of earlier LV work, as well.

By invoking Bowie in sound and image, BETC Paris's ad for Louis Vuitton invokes the "emotion and atmosphere" linked to Bowie. Its target audience would bring with that sound and image an important memorative mark, and perhaps a link to the construction of their own identities. Again, it would not be illogical to assume that the intended audience for all three of these commercials is the same: in their younger years, their interest in pop music would lead them to be prime targets for Pepsi's new strategy. As they reach middle age, those same consumers would be Vittel's audience. In their peak earning years, Louis Vuitton's handbags and luggage would appeal. Given this continuity, it is no surprise that the strategies employed by each corporation (and indeed, by Bowie himself) are so similar, and seek to capitalize on Bowie's nostalgic importance for this audience. LVHM's curation of soundscape in both runway presentation and commercial spaces shows a clear continuation of this strategy, seeking to appeal to and build community through a consistent, ubiquitous musical (and musicianly) identity for the brand.

What is equally striking about the ad is the way its visuals play into the latest Bowie guise. In press coverage and his own music videos supporting *The Next Day* as in the Louis Vuitton ad, Bowie's ghosts are never too far away. The album saw Bowie reunited with longtime friend and producer Tony Visconti, and many popular press reactions to the work explicitly tied it to their history and Bowie's past. Cast as a return to form after a long absence (and, though this remained largely unspoken, after the critically unappreciated albums of the 1990s and early 2000s), *The Next Day* was both a new start and an invocation of past work. Simon Reynolds' review touches on both points, labelling the 1990s works as "running close to empty," and *The Next Day* a "twilight masterpiece" that explores Bowie's

---

[36] Sophie Soar, "How I Became … Music Director for Louis Vuitton Menswear," *Business of Fashion*, November 12, 2018, https://www.businessoffashion.com/articles/careers/how-i-became-music-director-for-louis-vuitton-menswear Accessed March 15, 2019.

recurring themes, masks, and locales.[37] We can see an alignment of Bowie's commercial work and his own promotion via album art and music videos; both seek to capitalize on the iconicity of David Bowie. Bowie's current persona and value lies, here, in his history.

Conclusion

These commercials elucidate a common thread among Bowie's various uses of the moving image: in each medium, he seeks to foreground images both recognizable and malleable, able to be reconfigured for a new setting. This eye toward the possibilities of image was present from his earliest appearances and is deeply informed by his work on the stage and as a visual artist. In Bowie's later commercials, we can see a savvy move. The artist transplants his image campaign from the more traditional (his music videos and acting roles) into the media currently most accessible to him (commercial videos aiming to exploit his iconicity). While MTV was, in 2003, less likely to give extensive air time to the latest video from such an established and older musician, companies were still likely to want the endorsement of the rock superstar David Bowie. Indeed, he recognized this potential even earlier. During his more experimental late 1970s, Bowie's celebrated Berlin trilogy albums were a tough sell to radio stations. Undeterred, Bowie appeared in a number of ads for Crystal Jun Rock, which he admitted were useful for the paycheck as well as the increased exposure, hard to come by after his less mainstream experiments with Brian Eno.[38] By aligning his goals with those of corporations eager to cash in on his fame, Bowie employed another prong in his strategy of self-promotion and definition.

While his appearances share much in common with, for example, Michael Jackson's groundbreaking Pepsi spots of the 1980s, Bowie's engagement with advertising was both more complete and, in some ways, less guarded. Like Jackson and Madonna, Bowie capitalized on the iconic aspects of his performance persona, but unlike the others, he used advertisements not only for increased exposure of new works and a paycheck, but also to refine and represent his public construction of self. While Jackson in particular is depicted through his

---

[37] Simon Reynolds, "The Singer Who Fell to Earth," *The New York Times*, March 10, 2013.
[38] Chris O'Leary, "Crystal Japan," *Pushing Ahead of the Dame*, September 1, 2011, https://bowiesongs.wordpress.com/2011/09/01/crystal-japan/ Accessed March 20, 2019.

current iconic attributes, Bowie's strategy relies on a consciously anachronistic use of iconic imagery. He is not reflecting the present, but reshaping himself through the past. Cycling through collective memory's iconography of David Bowie served both the corporation doing the advertising and Bowie himself. More than marketing a single, contemporary idea of Bowie, both parties in these advertisements seek to capitalize on the entire history he shared with worldwide audiences. The Bowie of *Diamond Dogs* was just as useful to Vittel (and indeed Bowie himself) as was the Bowie of *Reality*. His later ads show this potential even more clearly, perhaps reflecting the increased cultural capital and power that Bowie held. As an elder statesman of rock, he did not retreat from advertising as some indication of "selling out," but rather embraced its potential in the sphere of public opinion.

Bowie's entrance into the advertising arena coincided with his rise to greater acting acclaim. In both, we can see the myriad forces at play in the manipulation of his star image. While both endeavors were ultimately helpful in promoting Bowie's brand on a worldwide stage, they also show the ambivalent side of such image usage. In each of the ads and films Bowie appeared in, the star image of "David Bowie" is, in some way, complicated or diluted. The coopting of Bowie as sign is helpful to both parties involved, but fundamentally alters the meaning of that carefully constructed sign. Depictions of Bowie onscreen continue this trend, acting as, in some cases, copies of copies that further hone the meaning of Bowie as sign.

7

Who Can I Be Now?: Fannish Creation and Depictions of Bowie on Film

"What are you? Where are you from? Bowie taught me that when they demanded your identity papers, you didn't have to comply. Or if you wanted, you could invent your own papers, tell whatever damn story you pleased."
—Hari Kunzru, emphasis added[1]

"That door. He unlocked it. For me, for you. For us. He gave us everything. He gave us ideas, ideas above our station. All THE ideas and a specific one. Of life. The stellar idea that we can create ourselves whoever we are. He let us be more than we ever knew possible."
—Suzanne Moore, emphasis added[2]

Following David Bowie's death in January 2016, tributes poured in from all sides. Fans, critics, and fellow musicians shared their memories, highlighting what Bowie meant in their lives and careers. One notable common thread among these tributes was the sense of possibility presented by Bowie. Indeed, this aspect of Bowie's career eclipsed most others in these press tributes. While specific albums or characters were mentioned, many column inches were devoted to the example Bowie set for his audience. As both Hari Kunzru and Suzanne Moore wrote, Bowie showed a new sort of self-determination. It seems that Bowie's freedom in forming and reforming himself, all while in the public eye, gave his fans permission to do the same. This fluidity was communicated most

---

This chapter is derived in part from an article published in *Popular Music and Society* vol. 41, no. 5 (2018) <copyright Taylor & Francis>, available online: https://www.tandfonline.com/doi/abs/10.10 80/03007766.2017.1390436

[1] Hari Kunzru, "For Those of Us Whose Identity Is Fluid, David Bowie Was a Secular Saint," *The Guardian*, January 12, 2016, http://www.theguardian.com/commentisfree/2016/jan/12/david-bowie-was-a-secular-saint-hari-kunzru Accessed March 15, 2016.

[2] Suzanne Moore, "My David Bowie, Alive Forever," *The Guardian*, January 11, 2016, http://www.theguardian.com/commentisfree/2016/jan/11/my-david-bowie-alive-forever Accessed March 15, 2016.

obviously through the *dramatis personae* of Bowie's career, but is also present in his music. Howard Goodall labels Bowie as one of the "'second wave' absorbers who synthesize pioneer developments," or who create culturally important works not by being the first to use a particular musical language, but by using others' advances in an effortless way.[3] By incorporating and recombining pre-existing innovations, Bowie is able to form a powerful expression of self through musical language first created by others. This tactic of radical reformation is most clear in Bowie's glam rock period of the early 1970s. His glam rock shows a semiotic system that provides for reinvention and reinvigoration, particularly reinvention of the self. This is Bowie's lasting cinematic legacy, the scope of which extends far beyond his own film roles. In works by and for fans that focus on Bowie's creative impulse rather than the particulars of his life and career, this legacy lives on. By examining *Velvet Goldmine*'s Bowie-inspired creative process and, to a lesser extent, *Flight of the Conchords'* "Bowie" episode, this chapter highlights the success of adaptations that focus on Bowie's *modus operandi* of borrowing and reworking, rather than the more traditional biopic formulation that aims to recreate historical fact. To examine these approaches, I return to the semiotic play that marked Bowie's glam years, tracing the influence of that approach on the filmmakers and fans who sought to continue his legacy.

Many scholars have commented on this sort of modeling in Bowie's work. P. David Marshall discusses "productive consumption" as an aspect of Bowie's creative process, an idea that certainly translates to fan responses.[4] Beyond this, Amadeo D'Adamo writes of Bowie's modeling of existential navigation in his work. In D'Adamo's formulation, Bowie's career "offers fans not simply forms of identity to be imitated but rather different strategies of meaning-creation for the fan to apply to her own experiences."[5] For many, this role as guide for existential navigation seems to be central to their understanding of Bowie and to their own engagement with his works and life. More than a static idolized figure, Bowie was an active agent of identity creation. To truly tell Bowie's story in any artform would be to translate that function, not just to communicate the details of his life. If we accept such a focus, the challenges inherent in bringing Bowie to the screen in a believable, effective way are many.

[3] Howard Goodall, "Bowie | Music," in *David Bowie Is Inside*, ed. Victoria Broackes and Geoffrey Marsh (London: V&A Publishing, 2013), 165.
[4] P. David Marshall, "Productive Consumption: Agency, Appropriation, and Value in the Creative Consuming of David Bowie," *Continuum* 31, no. 4 (2017): 564–73.
[5] Amadeo D'Adamo, "Is Bowie Our Kierkegaard?: A Theory of Agency in Fandom," in *David Bowie and Transmedia Stardom*, ed. Ana Cristina Mendes and Lisa Perrott (New York: Routledge, 2020), 60.

Adapting Bowie: The Biopic Challenge

Despite Bowie's fame and continued popularity, the film industry has yet to produce a successful Bowie biopic. Even in the era of such biographical hits as *Bohemian Rhapsody* (2018, dir. Bryan Singer) and *Rocketman* (2019, dir. Dexter Fletcher), Bowie's filmic legacy remains elusive. Why is it so hard to capture the essence of the Starman for the silver screen? It may well be because, for fans, his ability to form and re-form himself was more important than the very facts of his life.

Recent attempts to adapt Bowie's story for the screen highlight the difficulty of translating this self-determination in any compelling way. In 2020, news began to circulate of the imminent release of one such film project based on David Bowie's career. From the first, *Stardust* (2020, dir. Gabriel Range) was received among Bowie fans with some skepticism. Press accounts of the film posted to Bowie-centric Facebook groups were met with two typical responses: that it looked like an abomination of Bowie's memory, and that fans would likely still watch it. Such interest is a typical response to Bowie-related media. Even projects that do not have the estate's blessing or clearance to use the artist's music are still often the subject of much discourse and fan attention. In the case of *Stardust*, fans' skepticism was aided by Duncan Jones's early tweets about the film. On January 19, 2019, Bowie's son tweeted, "Im [*sic*] not saying this movie is not happening. I honestly wouldn't know. Im [*sic*] saying that as it stands, this movie won't have any of dads [*sic*] music in it, & I can't imagine that changing. If you want to see a biopic without his music or the families [*sic*] blessing, thats [*sic*] up to the audience."[6] As he noted, the Bowie estate and family had at that point denied music rights for the film; in the end, it included none of Bowie's music in original recording or new interpretation. Musically, *Stardust* was a far cry from Bowie's luminous 1971 sound, instead featuring covers of other artists' work.

As for the film itself, *Stardust* is a rather dreary adaptation of an important epoch in Bowie's career. The film finds him on the cusp of his glam period, striving to find his next sound and persona. *Stardust*'s thesis, explicitly stated by characters in the film, is simple: "Who are you?", manager Tony DeFries

---

[6] Duncan Jones, @ManMadeMoon, Twitter post, January 31, 2019, 12:06 pm, https://twitter.com/ManMadeMoon/status/1091065215842570240?ref_src=twsrc%5Etfw%7Ctwcamp%5Etweetembed%7Ctwterm%5E1091065215842570240%7Ctwgr%5E%7Ctwcon%5Es1_&ref_url=https%3A%2F%2Fconsequenceofsound.net%2F2019%2F02%2Fdavid-bowie-duncan-son-stardust-biopic%2F

asks a young Bowie. "I need to have a person I can sell." The idea of personal identity and its role in art or music is a fitting one for a Bowie biopic. Positing a fear of inherited schizophrenic tendencies, *Stardust* sees Bowie's personae as an extended exercise in drama therapy, a working out of his demons through the characters he inhabited on stage. Such a hypothesis makes sense: Bowie's brother Terry Burns did indeed deal with mental health issues throughout his life, and much of Bowie's work touches on these themes, implicitly or explicitly. However, to tell Bowie's story through such a lens ultimately proves unsuccessful. *Stardust* wishes to explain Bowie on the cusp, to find the facts of his development and illuminate his later work through them. In doing so, it misses the point of Bowie's career and public life: such authentic insight into the artist was never really important. Instead, the process of creation and self-determination held the most appeal for fans.

Interestingly, Duncan Jones's commentary on the idea of a Bowie biopic did not end with his disavowal of *Stardust*. He went on to tweet about the creatives whose involvement he *would* approve of for a filmic handling of his father's legacy. Jones floated the idea of an animated film, to be helmed by author Neil Gaiman and director Peter Ramsay, and featuring "dad's characters."[7] Jones's statement makes two things clear: first, that he sees it as difficult for any live actor to step into Bowie's shoes and, second, that it is Bowie's *characters*, not necessarily Bowie himself, who could best be brought to the silver screen in a new film. These characters, presumably Major Tom, Halloween Jack, the Thin White Duke, *1. Outside*'s Nathan Adler, and more, would be the stand-ins for the artist David Jones, much as they were in his own creative endeavors as David Bowie. The suggestion clarifies some of the pitfalls of *Stardust* and hearkens back to Bowie's *Diamond Dogs* and *Major Tom* filmmaking attempts, discussed in Chapter 4. In these projects, as in many of his others, Bowie used the moving image to capture his characters and more fully explore and expand on his musical works. The idea of creating a character as a representative of Bowie's ideas followed him throughout his lifetime and, it seems, struck his son as the most appropriate way to memorialize Bowie. As such, this rogues' gallery of characters points to an important idea: that Bowie's legacy could be best continued not by recreating him, but by stepping into his creative process and using the same tools and ideas

---

[7] Duncan Jones, @ManMadeMoon, Twitter post, January 31, 2019, 3:01 pm, https://twitter.com/ManMadeMoon/status/1091109163600568320?ref_src=twsrc%5Etfw%7Ctwcamp%5Etweetembed%7Ctwterm%5E1091109163600568320%7Ctwgr%5E%7Ctwcon%5Es1_&ref_url=https%3A%2F%2Fconsequenceofsound.net%2F2019%2F02%2Fdavid-bowie-duncan-son-stardust-biopic%2F

he explored. Essentially, a successful biopic would not be a biopic at all, but a sort of fan fiction exercise building on Bowie's own work of persona creation.

In fact, Gaiman (one of Jones's suggested collaborators) had been down this fan fiction path before. With his short story "The Return of the Thin White Duke," Gaiman builds a world around Bowie's 1976 persona. In this telling, an all-powerful Duke leaves his homeland in search of something more. Gaiman makes many oblique references to *Station to Station*, the album and eponymous song, from which he takes the story's title. He also weaves in details of Bowie's real biography, pointing to a long-lost home in Beckenham by the story's end that seems to echo Bowie's roots in the Beckenham Arts Lab community. The ethereal Thin White Duke becomes the earthly Bowie in a neat move of reverse engineering. In doing so, Gaiman not only creates a fictional backstory for Bowie, but also engages with the postmodern *bricolage* that so defines Bowie's own output. Gaiman calls this story "unabashedly fan fiction,"[8] and viewing it through this lens can give us insight into the ways Bowie's legacy has been understood and expanded on by fans.

While Gaiman's story is generally well received, the depiction of Bowie onscreen is fraught territory for fans. Holding their idol aloft, it is both tantalizing and somewhat blasphemous to think of him being embodied by anyone else. In film and television, though, depictions of Bowie continue. It seems that filmmakers, much like the fans themselves, remain fascinated with Bowie as a figure and as a cultural icon. However, Bowie's estate and archive have remained relatively closed to outside projects, forcing a level of distance and creativity in any planned onscreen iterations of Bowie. In films like *Bohemian Rhapsody* (2018), this meant elusive glimpses of Bowie onscreen, without any extended narrative presence. In *Stardust*, it seems to mean a focus on the circumstances of Bowie's origins and rise rather than on the cultural figure or the music itself. For all, the challenge remains: what does it take to embody Bowie, his creative impulse, and his legacy on screen? How can a work depict Bowie in a way that transcends mere imitation? In examples ranging from television's *Flight of the Conchords* to *Velvet Goldmine* (1998, dir. Todd Haynes), we find varied approaches. Of course, less high-profile fan-made works have undertaken this same labor for decades, whether in videos, fanfic sites, or social media groups. In general, the most successful depictions of Bowie in the moving image are not

---

[8] Neil Gaiman, "The Return of the Thin White Duke," *neilgaiman.com* Accessed January 19, 2021, https://www.neilgaiman.com/Cool_Stuff/Short_Stories/The_Return_of_the_Thin_White_Duke?fbclid=IwAR1UsKqp5VK3SPK7y0Hvgp6l__i8ODMQMJ6fLNHUUERzMkmvubFqf4wIx58

those that seek to adapt the ineffable quality of Bowie as a cultural figure, but, as Duncan Jones suggested, those that follow his creative mode of operation.

Though I argue for the success of loose adaptations like *Velvet Goldmine*, I should note that fan and critical reactions remain mixed. Notably, critic Roger Ebert wrote of *Velvet Goldmine* that, "David Bowie (if Slade [the film's rock star] is indeed meant to be Bowie) deserves better than this."[9] While I agree that the film's alien glam rocker is neither as creative nor as charismatic as Bowie, I think Ebert misses part of the film's point: it is not about its Bowie character. Much like Bowie's own career, the film is concerned with other personae and other modes of expression. Indeed, the film succeeds because it is a film about Bowie's process and, even more, about his fans. Similarly, the *Conchords*' "Bowie" episode is nominally about the man himself—but in fact, its focus is the character Bret, a stand-in for Bowie fans. In the way these projects translated Bowie's long career through others' experience of it, we find some of the most successful depictions of Bowie onscreen.

Bowie, on Screen but Absent

While his acting career is long and quite varied, depictions of Bowie himself onscreen tend toward a consistent image: Bowie as iconic innovator, breaking ground for other, unique artists to come. That guru aspect is central to Bowie's specter throughout and cameo in *Bandslam* (2009, dir. Todd Graff). Here, the artist acts as an aspirational imaginary pen pal to the film's main character—until Bowie actually sees and responds to the boy's band video online, providing the boy's big break. In appearances like *Bandslam*, Bowie is a kind of patron saint of the struggling creative mind. His image or his influence shows a path forward for younger artists searching for their way.

Despite his pop cultural longevity, such depictions of Bowie did not begin in earnest until the mid-1990s. At this point, Bowie's career stretched into four separate decades, and his successes included a variety of musical genres. The timing of this shift to elder statesman seems fitting, given the public perception of Bowie's star image. As the preceding chapters show, many of the artist's career moves were complicated by his careful consideration of the public's perception of him. In the height of his 1980s pop stardom, he continued to take roles like

---

[9] Roger Ebert, "Velvet Goldmine," *RogerEbert.com*, November 6, 1998, https://www.rogerebert.com/reviews/velvet-goldmine-1998 Accessed March 5, 2021.

Jareth in *Labyrinth*, which changed and challenged that public perception. By the 1990s, though, Bowie had settled into a personal and professional stage that allowed for the smooth integration of many of his previous star images. With his 1992 marriage to supermodel Iman and his latest collaboration with Brian Eno on *1. Outside* (1995), Bowie rejuvenated his fashion and *avant garde bona fides*. The Bowie star image of the late 1990s was thus one of a legendary iconoclast, somehow reconciling his pop hits with his experimental music and styling. From this vantage point of history, filmic depictions of Bowie took a similar form.

While many films celebrate Bowie's iconoclasm, few attempt to formally mimic his process of meaning-making. As a "second-wave innovator," we can see Bowie forming his own works through the cultural touchstones he inherited. He links himself with postmodernism and a type of *bricolage* in interviews, and the well-trod description of Bowie as photostat machine also hammers the point home. Bowie as "creative genius" hinges on the idea of Bowie as "cultural magpie." His greatest innovations come from his reuse and subversion of the cultural legacy he inherited. In order to understand Bowie's semiotics, we must examine his borrowing and reshaping.

The pastiche of Bowie's particular brand of glam provided a mode of meaning-making for his fans. Like T. Rex and Roxy Music, Bowie incorporated a variety of different musical and lyrical references from the building blocks of popular culture. It is not breaking new analytical ground to address the variety of stylistic influences on glam rock, but these influences alone are not my focus. The style's referentiality lent Bowie its power: calling on well-known and commonly understood cultural signs, Bowie and his confederates were actively reshaping not only their own identities, but also the pop cultural world as it was known, bringing those signs into new and often odd relation to each other. This ultimate subversive act empowered Bowie's fans—if he could mash Judy Garland, the Rolling Stones, Jacques Brel, and more into an intergalactic, gender-bending experiment, any new expression seemed achievable. Bowie's music taught his audiences to use the signs they were given in a new and different way.

Both *Flight of the Conchords*'s "Bowie" episode, and *Velvet Goldmine* focus on rock musicians and use Bowie's mode of creation either explicitly or implicitly. In *Conchords*, one half of the show's title duo deals with a crisis of confidence and is coached through it by apparitions taking the form of various Bowie personae. In *Velvet Goldmine*, director Haynes tells the tale of a Bowie-like glam rocker and his impact on the lives of his fans. In each, Bowie's "photostat machine" approach is evident. This is occasionally played for laughs, as in *Conchords*. That

Bowie would feature in a musical comedy show is not surprising; indeed, he embraced the comedic within his own film and TV cameo appearances, as in *Zoolander* (2001, dir. Ben Stiller) and the television show *Extras* (2006). What is striking, though, is that Bowie's importance for fans is clear even in this joking *Conchords* episode, as he guides Bret (Bret Mckenzie) through a difficult time. Played by Jemaine Clement, *Conchords*'s Bowie appears in a variety of guises, introducing himself by his era and costume. He doles out advice, such as "it never hurts to do something absolutely outrageous;" he advocates wearing an eyepatch. Though clearly intended to be comical, the episode distills the relationship between Bowie and his fans to its essential parts: the artist is depicted as an almost omniscient presence, appearing to the fan in moments of need and providing iconoclastic guidance through his unique approach to self-curation. The *Flight of the Conchords* episode mimics this on a small scale: in the song "Bowie's in Space," Mckenzie and Clement make musical reference to several Bowie songs, altering their voices much as Bowie himself did to fit different musical styles. Visually, the sequence also borrows from Bowie's work, invoking specific images from the original "Space Oddity" promotional video, as well as costuming from 1974 performances of "Rebel Rebel." Clement and Mckenzie are using Bowie's own referential, reformational mode of construction here, but to very different, parodic ends. This sort of fannish creation sets Bowie fandom apart in both commercial and personal works created by fans. Nowhere is this as clear as in Todd Haynes's 1998 paean to the power of glam rock, *Velvet Goldmine*. Through Haynes's play with visual and musical signs within the film, Bowie's glam semiotics comes to vivid, Technicolor life, and inspires another generation to adopt its method.

Many fan responses to Bowie's glam era exist, but few explore the genre's power and semiotic complexity as deeply as does *Velvet Goldmine*. Taking its title from an unreleased *Ziggy Stardust* era song, the film was intended as a sort of reflection on Bowie's glam persona. In fact, this title is the only concrete mark of Bowie left on the film—Haynes was denied life rights and music rights (for the *Ziggy* material) and so abandoned the idea of telling Bowie's story directly.[10] Instead, Haynes's film becomes the ultimate glam rock statement. An amalgam of visual references to Bowie, literary allusions, and musical quotations, *Velvet Goldmine* is, in film form, a reflection of Bowie's ethos of pop culture conglomeration. It tells the story of a glam rock fan who undergoes the same

---

[10] Todd Haynes, *Velvet Goldmine* (New York: Hyperion, 1998), xv.

sort of process, finding and creating himself out of fragments of his glam heroes' creations. For this analysis, then, *Velvet Goldmine* provides a real-world case study for the hypothesis that Bowie's free-wheeling semiotic play provides an ideal template for adapting Bowie on film.

Velvet Goldmine makes frequent use of pre-existing glam rock songs (by artists other than Bowie) and newly composed songs aping that style. These musical moments provide the stage for Haynes's reshaping of history. The film's rewriting depends on the nature of its media: exploiting film's indexical power, *Velvet Goldmine* makes convincing and confusing use of visual references in order to jumble and rewrite the historical events it represents, drawing most heavily on Bowie's life. The music it uses is equally important, acting as an immediate memorative hook for the audience. Rather than taking the rock star's perspective as its focus, *Velvet Goldmine* instead deals mostly with the *fan* experience through the character Arthur Stuart (played by Christian Bale). This fan-centered approach to pop culture historiography leads *Velvet Goldmine* into a rich exploration of the role music and memory play in identity formation, a role emphasized most often through the film's musical montages.

Glam rock has long served as a site for transgressive reinvention, most famously through Bowie. In *Velvet Goldmine*, Haynes capitalizes on this transformative impulse in glam and the way it energized its fans. The film weaves together far-flung cultural progenitors to create an artistic, queer lineage stretching from Bowie back to Oscar Wilde, through the fans themselves. With original recordings and faithful cover versions of glam classics, the film's soundtrack holds together its alternative historical narrative. Cover songs here act as sites of personal and historical imagining, through which Haynes's film incorporates audience memory and prompts creative engagement with an existing musical archive. *Velvet Goldmine*'s audience is encouraged to act as their own human photostat machines, creating themselves and their histories anew through the film's music.

Velvet Goldmine's musical appropriation prompts a very active and explicitly creative form of audience engagement with history, reflected in the websites and fanfic inspired by the film. Haynes identifies the efficacy of this approach: "I've always felt that when you see material through a frame—and for me that period or that historical setting is a frame—it allows a viewer to make their own connections to why it's relevant."[11] By providing a separate temporal frame for

---

[11] Kate Winslet, "Interview: Todd Haynes," *Interview*, February 22, 2011 http://www.interviewmagazine.com/film/todd-haynes/#_ Accessed December 13, 2021.

his subjects, Haynes gives his audience the distance to reinterpret and reassess the familiar. In *Velvet Goldmine,* these reassessments typically form a sort of reclamation project, bringing disparate past events and creations into alignment with an idea of gay community and heritage. Haynes himself explicitly links *Velvet Goldmine* to such an approach, calling it a part of a "long tradition of gay reading(s) of the world."[12] That freedom to re-read and re-evaluate is itself built into glam rock.

I am not alone in pointing to the centrality of pastiche to Bowie's persona, nor am I the only scholar to see this power reflected in his onscreen depictions. In particular, Glenn D'Cruz has written on the hauntology of Bowie's onscreen depictions: the unmooring of a singular "truth" or "authenticity" in Bowie's own presentation provides some of the impetus and power of *Velvet Goldmine*, in his reading. D'Cruz and I differ in our understanding of that film's ultimate meaning for fans, though. In the film's bleak depiction of the year 1984 and Brian Slade's latest guise, Tommy Stone, D'Cruz reads a kind of ambivalence about the potential of this radical definition of self. He sees that "the space of experimentation and play opened up by the spectres of Bowie are exorcised from the Orwellian world that constitutes the 'present' of the film's complex temporal scheme."[13] Indeed, the dystopian "present" of the film's timeline does not seem to offer much respite or glam excess. However, I read the film as not seeking to pass judgement on this miscarriage of glam reinvention. Instead, I see a celebration of fan response as the center of the film's meaning: a fan response that includes the film itself, which can be read as an exercise in the same glam semiotics practiced by Bowie. In the fan creation that is *Velvet Goldmine* and in self-published responses to it, we can see the continuing promise of glam self-definition.

Velvet Goldmine serves as a lens through which to reconsider the work of glam rock, focusing on music's role in memory and the formation of identity. To better understand this, I address three central aspects of this rewriting: glam rock's own semiotic system, the film's manipulation of historical signs (both musical and visual), and finally the fans' engagement, both onscreen and off. Through the case study of *Velvet Goldmine*, we will approach the semiotic freedom and continued resonance of Bowie's career and use of the moving image.

---

[12] Petra Dierkres-Thurn, *Salome's Modernity: Oscar Wilde and the Aesthetics of Transgression* (Ann Arbor: University of Michigan Press, 2011), 182.

[13] Glenn D'Cruz, "He's Not There: *Velvet Goldmine* and the Spectres of David Bowie," in *Enchanting David Bowie: Space, Time Body, Memory*, ed. Toija Cinque, Christopher Moore, and Sean Redmond (New York: Bloomsbury Academic, 2015), 271.

Semiotics of Glam

Glam rock is particularly well suited to Haynes's project of reinterpretation and identity formation. The fluid sexual identities of performers like Bowie, Jobriath, and T. Rex's Marc Bolan play into the themes of *Velvet Goldmine*, but the music offers even more than do the performer's images. Semiotically, glam rock is a complex system in its own right. Its musical style can be seen as an amalgam of many earlier idioms, including music hall song, folk styles, and harder rock influences. Shelton Waldrep singles out this era as a time of particular artistic success for Bowie, highlighting his "melding of music with various visual media" as carrying new power.[14] It is this melding that would later be taken up by fans like Haynes in their own creations. Barish Ali and Heidi Wallace even argue for a much more complex reading of Bowie's authorship, in part because of this distinctly postmodern approach to creation.[15] Taking cues from Barthes and Foucault, Ali and Wallace read "David Bowie" the author as a sort of construct created by the art itself.[16] Rather than focusing on the figure of Bowie and his role as author, though, this chapter is concerned with the system of signs that allowed for his creation, and the way that system empowered fans to create themselves wholecloth in much the same way Bowie did.

In contemporaneous criticism, glam was often seen as the antithesis of this sort of powerful and transgressive invention. Dick Hebdige describes Bowie and his contemporaries disparagingly: "Left to its own devices, pop tended to atrophy into vacuous disco-bounce and sugary ballads, while 'glam' rock, representing a synthesis of two dead or dying subcultures—the Underground and the skinheads—began to pursue an exclusively white line away from soul and reggae."[17] Hebdige sees Bowie as partaking "in a game of make-believe which has embarrassed and appalled some commentators on the rock scene who are concerned for the 'authenticity' and oppositional content of youth culture."[18] For Hebdige writing in 1979, the visual trace of glam rock was likely much stronger than any remaining aural memory. Popular music media made much of glam rockers' flaunting of gendered norms in dress and styling, an aspect on which

---

[14] Shelton Waldrep, *Future Nostalgia: Performing David Bowie* (New York: Bloomsbury, 2016), 7.
[15] Barish Ali and Heidi Wallace, "Out of This World: Ziggy Stardust and the Spatial Interplay of Lyrics, Vocals, and Performance," in *David Bowie: Critical Approaches*, ed. Eoin Devereux, Aileen Dillane, and Martin J. Power (New York: Routledge, 2015), 265.
[16] Ali and Wallace, "Out of This World," 266.
[17] Dick Hebdige, *Subculture: The Meaning of Style* (New York: Routledge, 1979), 60.
[18] Hebdige, *Subculture*, 60.

Hebdige focuses. Beyond this, seeing the way that bands like the Clash freely borrowed from other, more diverse idioms with clearly political end-goals likely also shaped his view of Bowie's musical eclecticism as somewhat superficial. It is important to remember, though, that the power of Bowie's glam rock comes not from its overtly political content, but the subversive way in which it engages with existing cultural objects and norms.

Hebdige dings Bowie for being "patently uninterested either in contemporary political and social issues or in working-class life in general ... his entire aesthetic was predicated upon a deliberate avoidance of the 'real' world and the prosaic language in which that world was habitually described, experienced and reproduced."[19] On the contrary, the glam rock of *Ziggy Stardust* is deeply concerned with the idioms that "described, experienced and reproduced" the real world—but Bowie uses that "prosaic language" in unexpected and unconventional ways. That defamiliarization of common symbols is, in large part, the point of the *Ziggy* music and lyrics. Again, though, we might see Hebdige's criticism as coming from a rock- and punk-centric attitude that may have seen glam as a pop foray without the substance or "authenticity" of groups like the Clash. Ironically, the criticism of glam as a constructed and superficial form can also be leveled against punk groups, most notably in the creation and curation of the Sex Pistols.

Bowie had always been open about the artistic agenda of his brand of glam rock and the way he consciously played with meaning and cultural objects. In a 2002 interview, he stated of his contemporaries: "some of us, I think, us small, pompous arty ones ... Probably read too much George Steiner and kind of got the idea that we were entering to this kind of post-culture age and that we'd better do something postmodernist—quickly, before somebody else did."[20] He and others like Bryan Ferry and Marc Bolan certainly did seem to know their postmodern theorists. In Steiner's work, we can find the view of splintered, reformed twentieth-century society that permeates the work of Roxy Music and Bowie. Glam, in these hands, can operate as an utterance of the culture and concerns of the general public, built from their own familiar materials. Glam rockers' embrace of a fractured, eclectic postmodern world took the form of wide musical and lyrical borrowing. Contrary to Hebdige's assertions, Bowie and

---

[19] Ibid., 61.
[20] "David Bowie on the Ziggy Stardust Years: 'We Were Creating the 21st Century in 1971,'" *NPR*, January 11, 2016 http://www.npr.org/2016/01/11/462653510/david-bowie-on-the-ziggy-stardust-years-we-were-creating-the-21st-century-in-197 Accessed December 13, 2021.

company obliquely addressed class, sexuality, and political issues of a wide variety long before Johnny Rotten and Joe Strummer found their respective bands.

We can take as an example of this semiotic play Bowie's *The Rise and Fall of Ziggy Stardust and the Spiders from Mars* (1972). The loose narrative of the songs shows the influence of the late 1960s concept album, including *Sgt. Pepper's Lonely Hearts Club Band* (1967) and *In the Court of the Crimson King* (1969), among others. Within the album's tracks, styles as diverse as music hall sing-alongs ("Lady Stardust"), jangly driving rock á la the Rolling Stones ("Suffragette City"), and Jacques Brel-style ballads ("Rock and Roll Suicide") make sometimes awkward bedfellows. This wide variety of styles was seen by some critics as musical dilettante-ism. Lester Bangs in particular hammered Bowie for a lack of authenticity, arguing that the performer put on a mantle of another style whenever it suited him, rather than seeking a truly personal expression. In one review, Bangs called Bowie "as accomplished an eclectician (aka thief) as Elton John."[21] Bangs was certainly not wrong: much of Bowie's music was stylistic imitation, but that was largely the point. By drawing on so many immediately familiar styles, Bowie was able to communicate his personae and ideas to his audience. Styles and genres served as conduits that took the listener to a certain idea or atmosphere immediately.

Like most subgenres, though, glam's music required a knowledge of these styles and an understanding of the artist's unique form of play in order to make sense of something like *Ziggy Stardust* or the earlier *The Man Who Sold the World* (1970). Bowie's ideal audience shared this social treasury or encyclopedia of knowledge and, through their understanding and enjoyment of the music, could revel in their community. In keeping with the common interpretation of glam rock as a camp form, Doris Leibetseder sees the genre as one that "makes use of the relationship with the readers and of the projecting imagination, in that the object becomes a screen or an indirect mirror through which the viewer can simultaneously see the author and the like-minded viewers," after Eve Sedgwick.[22] Bowie's manipulation of familiar signs fits within this interpretation by constructing a clear relationship among creator, audience, and common cultural knowledge. As Chris O'Leary states, "Ziggy is fluid and unknowable, a pictograph whose meaning alters depending on who looks at it. His existence

---

[21] Lester Bangs, *Psychotic Reactions and Carburetor Dung*, ed. Greil Marcus (New York: Anchor, 2003), 163.

[22] Doris Leitbetseder, *Queer Tracks: Subversive Strategies in Rock and Pop Music* (Burlington, VT: Ashgate, 2012), 62.

depends on his audience. ... taking from listeners' collective memories."[23] These familiar musical styles and lyrical allusions facilitate Bowie's play.

The example of a few *Ziggy* songs, such as "Starman" and "Lady Stardust," can be taken as indicative of the whole album. The album itself shows a wide diversity of styles; as such, no sample of songs can encompass its entirety. "Lady Stardust" is an exemplary case study, though, in its varied influences and method of recombination. I will identify uses of particular musemes, or common musical semantic units that recur in a variety of works and genres, identifying their referents in order to examine the complexity of Bowie's semiotic play.[24] In addition, lyrical analysis pinpoints yet more specific references. Analyzing these layers of meaning provides a clearer understanding of the way that Bowie's music during this era served to empower its listeners to move toward freer self-definition through the recombination of common cultural symbols in their own lives.

"Lady Stardust" is perhaps best known as an ode to Bowie's contemporary, T. Rex frontman Marc Bolan, but the song's musical content is much less clear than its lyrics. Though ostensibly pointing to Bolan, Bowie uses much older and more established musical signs. The opening piano figure provides the first of these (Figure 7.1). Museme 1 (hereafter M1) is identifiable by light piano syncopation. Stylistically, M1 acts as a genre synecdoche for the British music hall style. Variations on this museme can be heard in many popular recordings of the late 1960s and 1970s. M1 variants tend to feature the strong driving rhythm, emphasis on eighth notes and syncopation, and repetitious quality found in the *Ziggy* song's opening. The Beatles and the Kinks in particular provide many examples: M1 is present in parts of the Kinks' *Village Green Preservation Society* (as in "Do You Remember Walter?") and the Beatles' *Magical Mystery Tour* ("Your Mother Should Know") and myriad other McCartney songs in the band's oeuvre.[25] This museme's prevalence in popular music of the time could alone justify its inclusion, but Bowie's own history makes it yet more relevant. His training in mime and interest in British stage traditions is well documented through his involvement with Lindsay Kemp. Given his own connection to music hall style

---

[23] Chris O'Leary, "Ziggy Stardust," *Pushing Ahead of the Dame*, April 26, 2010, https://bowiesongs.wordpress.com/2010/04/26/ziggy-stardust/ Accessed December 13, 2021.

[24] For more on this mode of analysis, see Philip Tagg, *Fernando the Flute: Analysis of Musical Meaning in an ABBA Mega-hit* (Liverpool: University of Liverpool Institute of Popular Music, 1991).

[25] For a full explanation of the music hall style and its popularity in rock music of this period, see Barry Faulk, *British Rock Modernism, 1967–1977: The Story of Music Hall in Rock* (Burlington, VT: Ashgate, 2010).

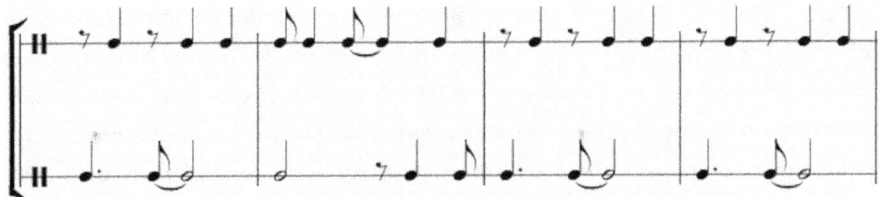

Figure 7.1 Museme 1: piano rhythm, mm. 1–4 (author's transcription).

and its 1960s cultural renaissance, Bowie's simple piano introduction becomes a multivalent sign function, especially for contemporary British audiences for whom the music hall style would have particular resonance.

Museme 2, in the chorus of "Lady Stardust," is closely related to M1, and points directly to the same musical tradition. The chorus' sing-along quality, amplified by its repetitive phrasing and sighing motives, forms the basis for this museme. Like M1, M2 finds many realizations in popular rock songs of the era, which serve as interobjective comparison material (IOCM) for this museme.[26] The Beatles and the Kinks again provide clear examples ("When I'm 64" and "Sunny Afternoon," respectively), but more contemporaneous performers like Elton John use it as well. The clearest examples of M2, though, come from the work of Marc Bolan. Many of T. Rex's hits share this anthemic quality (see, for example, the codas of "Metal Guru," "Hot Love," and more). Through these two musemes, then, Bowie appears to be creating a rock song that ties directly to contemporary and historical British pop antecedents. It is in the combination of these musemes with the song's lyrical content that Bowie manages to turn innocuous common tropes into a more subversive utterance by using these tropes in new and different ways.

"Lady Stardust" overtly invokes gender-obscuring lyrical turns, but also engages with the more metaphorical "alien" themes of the album, and Bowie's glam personae as a whole. First and most obviously, the song titled "*Lady Stardust*" is intended as an ode to a man; this gender fluidity is notable in the chorus, which refers to the title character with male pronouns. The intermingling of gendered pronouns and titles continues throughout, with no apparent desire to pin down Stardust's identity any more specifically. Beyond this, though, Bowie invokes the "others" to which his alien characters relate. In the song's verses, other characters leave their hiding places in order to get a closer experience

---

[26] Philip Tagg, "Analysing Popular Music: Theory, Method and Practice," *Popular Music* 2 (1982): 46.

of Lady Stardust, described alternately in human and animalistic terms. This otherworldliness is also highlighted by the change in Bowie's vocal quality for this song. With each song on *Ziggy*, Bowie's singing voice takes on a slightly new and different timbre, donning mantles for each new role in the context of a song; in fact, one could track the artist's musical references and genre mixing solely through vocal timbre. Each song represents a character or facet of a character, bolstering the idea that we are not hearing an "authentic" David Bowie on the album. Here in "Lady Stardust," Bowie's voice is higher and more nasal than elsewhere on the album. It bears a strong resemblance to Marc Bolan's tone; Bowie had mimicked his friend before, as on the *Man Who Sold the World* song "Black Country Rock."[27] The juxtaposition is particularly striking in the album's context, as he changes from the more belting voice of "It Ain't Easy" and "Star," which bookend "Lady Stardust," to this nasal vocal persona.

These same musemes appear throughout the album, as do many others. In fact, Bowie's direct stylistic reuse is so ubiquitous as to be overwhelming. Why view him as an important innovator if his biggest hits are merely built from the work of others? It is in the recombination of these familiar musical puzzle pieces, though, that Bowie truly creates new work. On *The Rise and Fall of Ziggy Stardust and the Spiders from Mars*, Bowie embraces a new, postmodern way of engaging with common musical language, using seemingly static signs to create a new, ever-changing musical utterance.

We can analyze the power of Bowie's music for young audiences as stemming from the complexity of the compositions' semiotic play. A typical *Ziggy Stardust* song shows effective blending of the three semiotic levels discussed by Charles Sanders Peirce: firstness, secondness, and thirdness.[28] Though Peirce does not do so explicitly, many have described these levels as relating to chronological experience, a useful lens for this musical situation.[29] In this formulation, firstness refers to the in-the-moment, lived experience of listening. This level, not referring to anything outside itself, is of course present in all musical listening. On the

---

[27] Philip Auslander explores this concept of using others' voices in much greater depth. See, for example, *Performing Glam Rock: Gender and Theatricality in Popular Music* (Ann Arbor: University of Michigan Press, 2006), 109–10.

[28] These labels and their meanings can be somewhat confusing, due to Peirce's reliance on a variety of triads to explain his theory of signs. For more explanation, see Charles Sanders Peirce, *The Collected Papers of C. S. Peirce*, Vols. 1–6, ed. Charles Hartshorne and Paul Weiss; Vols. 7–8, ed. A. W. Burks. (Cambridge: Harvard University Press, 1931–58).

[29] Floyd Merrell, "Peirce's Concept of the Sign," in *Routledge Companion to Semiotics and Linguistics*, ed. Paul Cobley (New York: Routledge, 2001), 32.

level of secondness, Bowie's *Ziggy Stardust* songs achieve astonishing saturation. This level relates to the past, and indexically refers to a meaning outside of the song itself. We might see the stylistic references and direct musical quotations as operating on this level of secondness. The level of thirdness, or symbolic meaning, is perhaps the most important for this examination of Bowie's glam rock work. If the previous two levels dealt with the present and past, thirdness comes closest to pointing toward the future, and dealing explicitly with mediation, a function of Bowie's reuse of commonly understood signs.[30]

Bowie's play with thirdness shows exactly why his music was so subversive and liberating. In Peirce's theory, thirdness relates to the symbolic, or the creation of meaning without direct recourse to the thing itself, rather giving more agency to the part of the interpreter and the interpreter's broader cultural milieu. In this way, we can see Bowie's invocation of commonly recognized cultural signs, used to project a new and different meaning, as operating on this third semiotic level. It is here that the interpreter or audience is relied upon to construct their own meaning and own personae. While the meanings created are new, they are being built through the use of a common cultural vocabulary. Bowie models this mode of operation in his eclectic and free use of commonly understood musical signs or musemes. With the example of this free semiotic play, many listeners took up the challenge themselves, taking an active role in their curation of common signs to define themselves, as shown in the fan responses to Bowie's life and work cited at this chapter's opening.

The same holds true for *Velvet Goldmine*: the film operates on all of Peirce's semiotic levels simultaneously, and makes very clear its creative use of thirdness. Copped costuming similarities and stage antics throughout the film are glaringly obvious if you love Bowie and the world of glam rock, but don't serve quite the same purpose for the uninitiated—the film as a whole alters depending on who looks at and listens to it. This is not to say that the film is only enjoyable for some sort of "insider" clique of viewers. Rather, I would argue that Haynes is speaking to a community through their curated and remembered signs, playing on the level of thirdness that Bowie's music so richly exploits. Much like Bowie's *Ziggy Stardust* fan group, Haynes's viewers can get a different, perhaps more

---

[30] Ben Curry posits a theory of musical valency which applies these trichotomies differently. Using his concept of valency to analyze musical form, Curry's approach provides an alternate application of Peirce's theory which is also relevant to the questions of self-determination discussed here. See pages 419–20 in particular. Ben Curry, "Valency – Actuality – Meaning: A Peircian Semiotic Approach to Music," *Journal of the Royal Musical Association* 142, no. 2 (2017): 401–43.

thorough, idea of *Velvet Goldmine* because of their recognition of a common history within its characters, sounds, and images. The fandom that recognizes the visual and musical signs of glam is in some ways more receptive to the sort of historiography Haynes is constructing because of their recognition of themselves within its lexicon.

Manipulating History: Invoking Bowie's Encyclopedia

Like Bowie himself, fans of glam rock made free use of a wide variety of cultural signs, often recombining those signs to create new and personalized meaning. Bowie's commercials of the 1980s and 2000s banked on this exact relationship between artist and fan: a shared sort of self-definition. We see this in both the *Flight of the Conchords* episode "Bowie" and in Haynes's *Velvet Goldmine*. Both focus on the fan and their struggle with defining themselves, while also seeking to evoke Bowie through semiotic play with a shared encyclopedia of Bowie-related signs. Despite their similarities, these two projects differ in their approach to adapting Bowie and the level of semiosis on which their depictions rely. While *Velvet Goldmine* operates on the level of thirdness, the *Conchords* episode hews more closely to secondness. The final result is a difference in semiotic openness and, consequently, a difference in how directly each is able to ape Bowie's own mode of expression.

In interpreting both *Velvet Goldmine* and the *Conchords* "Bowie" episode, it is useful to consider how we might make sense of their differing approaches to adaptation. Linda Hutcheon describes the lure of adaptation as the pleasure of return with the potential for alteration, "the revisiting of a theme with variations."[31] Indeed, we might separate these two works by the way they approach that repetition. In *Conchords*, these variations are obvious in their antecedents. They exist in order to be recognized and visual references are highlighted and identified via dialogue. Introducing himself, for example, Clement states, "It's not Jemaine, it's 1972 David Bowie from the Ziggy Stardust tour." The mimicry is broad and obvious; its recognition is guaranteed, as is the pleasure that comes from that recognition. In *Velvet Goldmine*, the revisiting is not so much a straight reference to a single work, but rather a cooption of Bowie's working process. The recognition here comes through the mode of creation, rather than the creative objects themselves.

---

[31] Linda Hutcheon, *A Theory of Adaptation* (New York: Routledge, 2006), 115.

The Conchords give to their adaptation a sense of overdetermination. Fan and musician Bret is having a crisis of confidence, and Bowie appears to him several times throughout the episode with advice, culminating in the song "Bowie's in Space." *Conchords*, as a television comedy show, grew out of the musical comedy performances of Mckenzie and Clement, so the insertion of song is in keeping with the show's format. This particular song points to Bowie's works very clearly, mimicking lyrics and costume. In "Bowie," the overt, acknowledged return to the familiar is part of the joke: we are able to laugh at the ridiculousness of 1972 David Bowie appearing to a struggling musician in his bed, in part *because* he announces himself as 1972 David Bowie. *Conchords*'s variation is very carefully controlled. It happens very explicitly on screen and, though the fan experience is central to the pastiche, it does not require of us any special knowledge or any fannish creation of our own. They are not so much playing with signs that Bowie created as they are inserting them wholecloth into their narrative. The *Conchords* jokes work because we cannot change them, cannot misinterpret them, cannot see them as too much of a variation on a theme. The careful costume and makeup design throughout are integral to this process. Though actor and creator Jemaine Clement does not physically resemble a young Bowie, we are never in doubt about who and what he represents. *Conchords*'s "Bowie" is a direct revisitation of a familiar theme—to extend the musical metaphor, the variation here occurs only in the accompaniment, while the theme itself is inserted in its original form. It differs from the semiotic play present in Bowie songs like "Lady Stardust."

The song "Bowie's in Space" is essentially a mashup: Clement and Mckenzie borrow specific sonic aspects of Bowie's work, combine them with visual recreations of iconic videos, and add new comedic lyrics to them. The song features four main sections, largely avoiding the verse/chorus structure we might expect. In its introduction, "Bowie's in Space" borrows the soundscape of "Space Oddity." The acoustic guitar is at the fore, a mellotron-like instrument is present, and the vocals follow a dialogue pattern much like the Bowie original. (Of course, being a comedy show, *Conchords* inserts its own humor into the lyrics, focusing on the possibility of cosmic chilliness causing telescopic antennae nipples.) Visually, too, this first section has a clear antecedent: its costuming and camera point of view are modelled on the video for "Space Oddity" included in *Love You till Tuesday*. Beyond this, Clement even inserts a moment of mime, an early Bowie hallmark. The section ends with a transition reminiscent of the original song's transitions in timbral buildup.

The song's second section jumps forward in Bowie's career. A descending bassline echoes "Jean Genie" and takes the song into a more uptempo section featuring a video transmission from Bowie himself (this time played by Mckenzie). Here, Bowie is costumed as he was in another, real-life broadcast: his TV performance of "Rebel Rebel" from 1974. Clad in an eyepatch and red pants with suspenders, Mckenzie does his best Bowie swagger as this section unfolds. As in the opening, visuals and sound align to point to a specific moment in Bowie's performance history.

A short return to "Space Oddity" follows, bringing with it the visuals of the opening. A final tip of the hat to early 1970s Bowie comes in the form of a lingering piano line in the fade out, pointing to the ending of "Life on Mars?". The final section of "Bowie's in Space," a coda, differs in style and points to one last Bowie era: 1983's *Let's Dance*. With a bassline full of syncopation and a groovy saxophone solo, this coda makes its references clear. Should the spectator happen to miss the musical parody, though, Clement and Mckenzie provide a clear visual connection. The two are outfitted in oversized suits and dance as though marching in place—both clear recreations of Bowie in his "Modern Love" video. Though this sequence references a different era than the rest of the song, it, too, takes very recognizable sounds and images, recreating them in clear and comical ways.

"Bowie's in Space" references Bowie songs so directly that it is almost impossible to spin out new meanings from their presentation. We are meant to identify and experience the pleasure of recognition, but are not asked to go beyond that in our engagement with the text. In contrast, *Velvet Goldmine*'s songs tap into musematic materials common to Bowie songs. This difference may seem small; after all, aren't both tapping into the same sort of play that Bowie valued? Their approaches are certainly similar. However, the direct and overdetermined referentiality of the Conchords's "Bowie's in Space" shuts down audience interpretation, whereas *Velvet Goldmine*'s new songs practically require it. They are, respectively, what Roland Barthes might call readerly and writerly texts.[32] Such a difference is striking and gets to the heart of the differences in these two texts' approaches. Much like Bowie and his own musical and visual work, *Velvet Goldmine* taps into a history of semiotic play that differs from *Flight of the Conchords*'s loving parody. While both are clearly linked to Bowie's working procedure, *Velvet Goldmine* works to revive Bowie's language rather than simply borrowing words from it.

---

[32] Roland Barthes, *S/Z: An Essay*, trans Richard Miller (New York: Hill and Wang, 1974), 5.

Capitalizing on the thirdness of these pilfered expressions allows Haynes to do precisely this in *Velvet Goldmine*; his subject is glam rock, but he approaches it as glam denizens would, refracting and recombining the style and its images. The film's semiotic play matches Bowie's: *Velvet Goldmine* could be viewed as a hodgepodge of referential images, styles, and songs, but I argue instead that it shows the influence of Bowie's uniquely postmodern mode of expression. In doing so, Haynes crafts a creative lineage for himself and his community by reshaping historical events and figures. As such, the film requires a more nuanced analysis than does a text like "Bowie's in Space." To address Haynes's manipulation of history, I examine just a few instances from the film, as the character Brian Slade's movements and performance intentionally play with the emblems of glam throughout.

As a film about a Bowie-like glam star, *Velvet Goldmine* uses the musical, stylistic, and visual language of the era. More than that, though, the film employs the same strategies of reuse discussed above in *The Rise and Fall of Ziggy Stardust and the Spiders from Mars*. Like Bowie, Haynes borrows freely from common cultural signs, in order to reshape our understanding of glam, its music, and its uses for audiences. Bowie provides both subject and mode of operation for the film: Haynes models the glam fan's individualized use of common signs, aping Bowie's own reuse. The film's musical moments show this most clearly.

Newly Composed *Velvet Goldmine* Songs

Since Haynes was denied Bowie's music and life rights, *Velvet Goldmine*'s soundtrack consists of a number of 1970s songs from contemporaneous bands as well as newly composed songs in the glam style. These new songs are the compositional work of musicians in Placebo, Shudder to Think, and more, and each of them betrays the influence of Bowie's mode of composition. The clearest examples of this influence come in "The Whole Shebang," by Grant Lee Buffalo, and "Ballad of Maxwell Demon," by Shudder to Think. While both are clearly evocative of the glam style, "The Whole Shebang" takes a specific Bowie work as its formal template: "Oh! You Pretty Things." This song, on the album *Hunky Dory* (1971), serves as a youth anthem and draws on existing musemes in much the same manner as "Lady Stardust." Grant Lee Buffalo does the same, structuring "The Whole Shebang" around the central musemes of Bowie's song. The two songs share not only formal structure (unsurprising for songs in this idiom), but also musical and lyrical material within each of these formal divisions.

"The Whole Shebang" does eliminate some of the formal ambiguity of Bowie's original, which elides two verses, but otherwise the two share many similarities.

"Oh! You Pretty Things" was an early Bowie hit, and fits comfortably within the same compositional style period as the *Ziggy Stardust* material. It is notable for its foregrounding of the piano and vocalist in the introduction. It is this prominent piano that then presents the first important museme, a music hall synecdoche related to M1 above. Both "Pretty Things" and "Whole Shebang" use this museme to transition into the chorus. In the chorus, Grant Lee Phillips (lead singer of Grant Lee Buffalo) alters his vocal timbre, much as Bowie did when assuming others' voices. Phillips assumes a much more clearly British accent (particularly in the chorus), an obvious interpretive choice for the American artist. This actorly presentation, particularly in the emulation of another's voice, aligns with the theatrical aspects of Bowie's performance highlighted by Auslander and others.

Beyond these musematic and formal similarities, the newly composed songs share lyrical connections to Bowie originals. In "The Whole Shebang," this occurs most obviously in the introduction and chorus. Just like "Oh! You Pretty Things," in this new song our speaker addresses the audience directly, invoking both fate and a change, either coming or already present. (In typical Bowie fashion, though, these lyrics are more complex than they first seem: Bowie hides Nietzschean references alongside allusions to Aleister Crowley and the occult.) "Pretty Things" operated as just such an anthem of change. It literally calls on a young generation to awaken, and in its echoing vocals in the chorus, seems to imply a gathering crowd, brought together by our narrator's exhortation. In the context of *Velvet Goldmine*, "The Whole Shebang" is shown to be much the same. These songs act as mission statements for the glam era: both convey the newness, rebellion, and pastiche-like mode of composition that were at the heart of the musical movement.

Lyrical connections are even clearer in "The Ballad of Maxwell Demon." Shudder to Think's composition blends some of Bowie's less sensical lyrics with the variety of literary allusions he frequently employed. Lyricist Craig Wedren incorporates pictorially vivid but nonsensical phrases into the song's chorus, deftly mimicking the cut-up lyrics of songs like "Moonage Daydream." Wedren also taps into Bowie's penchant for dystopian literature. Where Bowie invokes works like *1984* (through the *Diamond Dogs* album), Wedren opts instead for *Fahrenheit 451* references (the "vicious metal hounds" of the first verse, for example). While none of these lyrical moments are enough to stop the listener in their tracks and disrupt the musical moment, their totality evokes Bowie's method of composition in a powerful way. Rather than quoting directly, Wedren and Shudder to Think instead emulate Bowie's mode of meaning-creation. This tack brings the new composition much closer to the original composer's style than would any mimicry.

Beyond the lyrical, "Ballad of Maxwell Demon" also trades in musical Bowieisms. An invocation of "All the Young Dudes" is apparent in the chorus of "Ballad," as the descending bass line drives to the chorus's completion just as in the Bowie original. Shudder to Think continue to musically reference Bowie, too, as in the opening interval of the song's verse. The octave leap mirrors Bowie's famous use of the "Over the Rainbow" interval in both "Starman" and "Life on Mars?", where it appears in the singing of each song's title phrase. Interestingly, none of these musical or lyrical moments point directly to what should be obvious templates: the songs introducing Ziggy Stardust, like "Five Years" (which opens that album) and, of course, "Ziggy Stardust." In fact, Haynes's screenplay implies that "The Ballad of Maxwell Demon" would operate as these songs do, introducing it as "the first song to tell the story of the tragic space hero named Maxwell Demon."[33] It seems that Wedren and Shudder to Think have taken Haynes's direction down a less literal path, mirroring Bowie in process rather than in content directly.

Visual Traces in *Velvet Goldmine*

Haynes's filmmaking decisions are also evocative of the film's unnamed subject, as are costume designer Sandy Powell's sartorial choices. Brian Slade's appearance, movements, and performance intentionally invoke Bowie throughout the film. For example, in the film's first unveiling of Slade in performance singing "Hot One," we see him, dressed in a one-armed purple Lycra jumpsuit, draping his arm seductively over the shoulders of his guitarist, Trevor. This image clearly calls back to the first appearance of Ziggy Stardust on the BBC's *Top of the Pops* in July 1972. Singing "Starman," Bowie (who had recently declared himself bisexual) similarly draped his arm around guitarist Mick Ronson's shoulders. This move was widely viewed as Bowie's coming on to a man, a watershed expression of non-normative sexuality on national television. Joe Moran describes the moment: "Dressed in a multicoloured lycra [*sic*] jumpsuit, he

---

[33] Haynes, *Velvet Goldmine*, 44.

put his arm languidly round his guitarist Mick Ronson and looked seductively into his eyes."³⁴ Artists like Morrissey and Boy George cite this performance as influential for them. In his *Autobiography*, Morrissey states of Bowie's "Starman": "The vision is profound—a sanity heralding the coming of consciousness from someone who—at last!—transcends our gloomy coal-fire existence."³⁵ Brian Slade invokes that subtle subversion, amplifying its provocative power. Like much of *Velvet Goldmine*, the moment takes Bowie's original allusions in a much more overt direction.

The "Hot One" sequence in *Velvet Goldmine* buries its "Starman" image allusion along with many others, including a visual quotation of Bowie's "Jean Genie" video (Figure 7.2). Haynes, without needing to state the history he is referencing, brings in an iconic and groundbreaking television experience, drawing connections to Bowie even though he was denied both life and music rights for the film. The title is the only remaining clear textual marker of the project's origin as an explicitly Bowie-centered film. Haynes's various other references are essentially a cultural shorthand, evoking Bowie though not directly.

Figure 7.2 Still from *Velvet Goldmine* (1998, dir. Haynes).

---

³⁴ Joe Moran, "David Bowie Misremembered: When Ziggy Stardust Played with Our Minds," *The Guardian*, July 6, 2012, https://www.theguardian.com/commentisfree/2012/jul/06/david-bowie-ziggy-starman Accessed December 10, 2021.
³⁵ Morrissey, *Autobiography* (New York: Putnam and Sons, 2013), 62.

Semiotically, these Bowie-inspired moments operate as signs with, on some level, an undefined referent. For the model viewer of the film, they have a very specific referent in Bowie; the actions themselves, however, once divorced from their original context, are no longer unambiguous. Here Haynes actively plays with the indexical nature of film. The potential of film to convey realness has been a defining feature since the medium's inception, but in this case that potential is used to create an alternate reality. Presenting an image of a "real" thing, in general the filmic image acts as an index for that thing, a "pure assurance of existence": it is a sign that, on its most obvious level, conveys that "real" object.[36]

In *Velvet Goldmine*, however, the real object that the film seeks to communicate is not the thing that it shows. The image is, in fact, an index of Jonathan Rhys Meyers as Maxwell Demon, since it has a direct, physical, and causal relationship to the actor and the film. It is also carefully constructed as an icon conveying Bowie. Haynes goes to great lengths to seem to communicate an authenticity to the era through the fabricated images of glam rock performers (most often Bowie, though also Jobriath and Bryan Ferry of Roxy Music), through costume, voice, and gesture. There is a false firstness to Haynes's film, one that is constructed mainly through its faux documentary aspects. This is conveyed through changes in film quality—the "newsreel" footage, the concert videos, and the Super 8 quality home movie moments. The film is crafted to act as a multilayered sign that conveys "glamness" and frequently "Bowieness."[37] In reality, though, Haynes is manipulating the sign system by intermingling and confusing these two semiotic levels with the intention of reshaping the archive and, with it, collective memory.

Haynes strives to foreground and take advantage of the indexical nature of film. Various sequences are presented in the manner of archival footage: after the title sequence, Brian Slade is introduced in a faux BBC News segment. In addition to the news announcer's voice-over, this section is delineated from the surrounding footage by a change in image quality (from film to video), meant to root the segment in a different, more realistic style. In fact, the dialogue itself is gleaned from 1970s news footage about the glam rock phenomenon. Curt Wild's brief comments come from an interview with Lou Reed during his *Transformer*-era engagement with glam. In this and other sequences in the film,

---

[36] Mary Ann Doane, *The Emergence of Cinematic Time: Modernity, Contingency, the Archive* (Cambridge: Harvard University Press, 2002), 16.

[37] Here, the image acts as a dicisign, in Peirce's terminology. It is asserting the relationship of its interpretant to something real, though not necessarily grounding this in fact or actual physical relation.

Haynes's filmmaking decisions bring *Velvet Goldmine* into a confusing space between fictional film and historical document. As Robynn Stilwell has written, different media construct and negotiate space and modes of communication differently;[38] Haynes manipulates those differences. Playing on our shared cultural understanding of the way that news segments communicate and construct the world they purport to show, these sections of *Velvet Goldmine* purposefully manipulate our perception of the type of story it tells. These decisions, coupled with the careful recreation of Bowie in the figure of Slade, serve to purposefully manipulate the power of cinema to act as "assurance of existence" by assuring the existence of a fabricated historical "reality."

For all of the film's careful play with semiotically charged images, sounds, and filmic techniques, Haynes's creation is not groundbreaking: rather, it goes over exactly the same ground that Bowie himself did with *Ziggy*. We might see the film's project as an outgrowth of glam's manipulation of meaning. Like Bowie before him, Haynes takes clearly defined cultural signs, recombines them in new and innovative ways, and creates for himself and his cohort a new identity out of these established meanings. In this way, Haynes can be seen as committing the ultimate act of glam rock fan creation. Though *Velvet Goldmine* is a very public and clear example of such fan authorship inspired by Bowie, countless other examples exist. One notable group comes from second-generation fans: *Velvet Goldmine*'s own audience. In the fan response to glam rock in the context of that film, a sophisticated semiotic play is readily visible.

"That's Me!": Personal Reinvention through Public Performances

Haynes's film empowers fans not only through its semiotic play, but also through its depiction of fandom. In particular, says Haynes, the film is "about the Arthur Stuart character, the Christian Bale character who is basically interpreting and traversing through this history."[39] In the character of Arthur, *Velvet Goldmine*

---

[38] Robynn J. Stilwell, "Audiovisual Space in an Era of Technological Convergence," in *The Oxford Handbook of New Audiovisual Aesthetics*, ed. John Richardson, Claudia Gorbman, and Carol Vernallis (New York: Oxford University Press, 2013), 125–45.

[39] Todd Gilchrist, "Todd Haynes Thanks the Fans for Helping Him Remember the Details and Backstory of 'Velvet Goldmine,'" *Indiewire*, December 16, 2011, https://www.indiewire.com/2011/12/todd-haynes-thanks-the-fans-for-helping-him-remember-the-details-backstories-of-velvet-goldmine-254993/ Accessed December 10, 2021.

shows the potential of stars and their star images to empower the fan. Arthur's intense identification with Slade is externalized as he shouts, "That's ... that is me, that!," while watching a televised Slade press conference that discusses the singer's sexual orientation (Figure 7.3). For Arthur, Slade's pronouncements about his bisexuality not only resonate, but also provide Arthur with a way to shape and express his own nascent sexual discovery.[40]

By consuming and manipulating the mediated star image he receives, Arthur expresses himself more fully, in much the same way the Haynes's film encourages its fans to respond. As Cornel Sandvoss states, "fan consumption thus becomes a generally understood language through which one's identity is communicated and assessed."[41] Arthur's engagement with Slade fandom allows him to examine an aspect of his identity with which he is struggling and, through his role as fan, find a similar social group that reflects his new identity. We first meet Arthur as an unhappy teen in suburban Manchester, dressing and acting like his peers. Through his interest in Slade, though, Arthur is able to explore aspects of his personality for which he had never had a clear expression. Reformulating Slade's style, persona, and music in his own way, Arthur performs the semiotic act shown by Bowie in his *Ziggy* compositions and by Haynes throughout the film.

Figure 7.3 Still from *Velvet Goldmine* (1998, dir. Haynes).

---

[40] Philip Auslander also highlights this scene, and indeed Haynes's depiction of fandom, as particularly evocative of the power of glam performance. See, for example, *Performing Glam Rock*, 234.
[41] Cornel Sandvoss, *Fans: The Mirror of Consumption* (Malden, MA: Polity Press, 2005), 3.

Haynes's film clearly depicts the power of the fan relationship to develop and express identity; through this focus and its semiotic openness, *Velvet Goldmine* encourages a particularly free fandom that has flourished in online forums.

Two main threads of online fandom define the *Velvet Goldmine* fan community. The slash fanfic groups, like listservs vglist and Gliterrati (both now inactive), involve a group of fans invested in making alternative, explicitly sexual narratives involving the film's characters in a wide variety of scenarios, ranging from BDSM to holiday themes. *Velvet Goldmine* fan writing illustrates the agency the film affords to its spectators. As Henry Jenkins writes, fans act as "important theorists of their own practice," here showing their understanding of and engagement with Haynes's film through their own creations.[42] It is another concrete manifestation of the active role demanded of the audience in *Velvet Goldmine*, both during viewing and after. This sort of fandom is, unsurprisingly, a clear analogue for the Bowie fan communities that flourished on BowieNet and other corners of the internet.

From its earliest days, Bowie fandom has been a tight-knit community. The first American Bowie fan club was formed in Cleveland by Brian Sands in the early 1970s; official fan clubs followed with mailing lists and newsletters.[43] As with many fandoms, the arrival of the internet was transformative, not least because Bowie himself was an ardent believer in the new medium's powers. In 1998, he founded BowieNet: more than an artist website, BowieNet was an internet service provider (ISP) that allowed fans to have a davidbowie.com website and exclusive, seemingly unfiltered access to the artist. Posting under the username Sailor, Bowie interacted with fans and seemed to see this experiment as an important outgrowth of his more traditional work. Nicolas Pegg describes Bowie as "reveling in the delights of chat rooms," with Bowie stating "I like the idea of a network community."[44] This attitude toward fan involvement and creation is in accord with Bowie's own fannish work: throughout his early career, he very clearly drew from inspirational artists and sought to create his own work out of the materials they provided. In a similar way, Bowie's embrace of the internet and its possibilities seems to have offered up the same opportunity for his own fans.

---

[42] Henry Jenkins, *Fans, Bloggers, and Gamers: Exploring Participatory Culture* (New York: New York University Press, 2006), 62.

[43] "Brian Sands and David Bowie," *The Ziggy Stardust Companion*, last modified December 12, 2018, http://www.5years.com/briansands.htm Accessed April 7, 2021.

[44] Nicolas Pegg, *The Complete David Bowie (Revised and Updated 2016 Edition)* (London: Titan Books, 2016), 585.

BowieNet and *Velvet Goldmine* entered the world in the same year, and the responses they inspired share many similarities. Fan fiction and slash fic are not creations of the *Velvet Goldmine* fandom, of course, but in the context of this film and its antecedents, the mode of construction for these stories becomes yet more interesting. Responding to the practice of vidding (fan videos created using actual pieces of the original text—a practice common to *Velvet Goldmine* fandom but not discussed here), Alexis Lothian asks "will transformation be the new originality?"[45] This question could easily have been posed in response to Bowie's mode of creation—and frequently was. What makes the *Velvet Goldmine* fan creations unique among fanfic and vidding is the conscious way with which they are engaging with their predecessors' compositional tools. Ross Hagen has analyzed "real person fan fiction" as rehabilitating or reclaiming some of the artifice present in pop musicians' public personae.[46] This *Velvet Goldmine* community is engaging in yet another way: by coopting Bowie's artifice and reuse for their own creations, these fans are not just legitimizing a constructed persona, but showing the value of that type of construction. *Velvet Goldmine* slash fic is not the beginning of this practice, but it is a different *use* of it, purposefully connecting to an artistic lineage that stretches back to Bowie and beyond.[47]

The largest currently accessible online repository of *Velvet Goldmine* slash is at the site Satellite of Love. This website archived many examples of fanfic from the most active period of fan writing; no new work has been added since 2005. Many of the stories concentrate on pairings introduced or hinted at within the film. The Brian/Curt and Arthur/Curt pairings (hereafter B/C and A/C) are the most popular, with eighty-nine and thirty-seven stories, respectively. In keeping with the film and its couples, very few of these stories center on heterosexual pairings, though some Brian/Mandy fic exists. For my purposes, I concentrated on the two most active pairings, B/C and A/C. The fan writing found in these communities is particularly interesting for the way that it engages with the mode of composition and meaning-making discussed above.

---

[45] Alexis Lothian, "Living in a Den of Thieves: Fan Video and Digital Challenges to Ownership," *Cinema Journal* 48, no. 4 (Summer 2009): 133.

[46] Ross Hagen, "'Bandom Ate My Face': The Collapse of the Fourth Wall in Online Fan Fiction," *Popular Music and Society* 38, no. 1 (2015): 49.

[47] It's worth noting that Haynes's films generally seem to spark this sort of engagement–this is true of his latest, *Carol* (2015), as well. See Angela Wattercutter, "Inside the Cult of *Carol*, the Internet's Most Unlikely Fandom," *WIRED*, May 16, 2017, https://www.wired.com/2017/05/carol-modern-cult-movie-fandom/?mbid=social_fb Accessed December 13, 2021.

Each of these stories not only takes from the characters and the world created by Haynes, but also adds to it more cultural landmarks associated with the glam rock scene, rock bands which would follow, classic literature, and more. There are encounters between Curt Wild and Kurt Cobain, invocations of Orwell's *1984*, and explicit quotations of and references to David Bowie's own songs. The authors of these stories act out the glam semiotics Bowie first showed, taking freely from the cultural products presented to them and recombining them to create something that communicates differently and carries more meaning for them. Take, for example, "Different Colors Made of Tears," an A/C pairing written by the user kimberlite.[48] The plot of this slash fic follows Curt and Arthur in the years after the film, as they, now lovers, are attacked by an obsessed fan. As the title suggests, the story takes a BDSM turn. That title is a quotation of the Velvet Underground song "Venus in Furs," which is itself a reference to the Sacher-Masoch novel of the same name. (This chain of references is also invoked in the film, as Maxwell Demon's backing band is called the Venus in Furs.)

Much of the story focuses on that attacker and the sado-masochistic sex he forces our main characters into, but a large section also deals with the relationships between those characters, and the community they have created through their love and art. In one section, kimberlite refers to the triadic relationship of Arthur, Curt, and Mandy (Brian Slade's ex-wife) as "an odd, but wonderful family."[49] The phrasing is important—it points to the idea of self-determination and definition that many have discussed in the wake of Bowie's death, and that Haynes himself explicitly explores in *Velvet Goldmine*. Here that sort of self-made community is accessible to fans through the glam semiotics shown by Bowie, aped by Haynes, and taken up by fans in these slash fic communities. More than exploring the ideas of different or forbidden sexual relationships, these stories flesh out the ties that bind these characters into a community, and they use the language of glam to do so.

In his audio commentary for the recent Blu-ray release of the film, Haynes mentions a second type of fan sites, those exploring the film's allusions, naming Varda the Message in particular.[50] Active from 2004 to 2005, this Livejournal site posted daily trivia unpacking the images, words, and sounds of *Velvet Goldmine*. Its name is itself a reference: it quotes a line from the film that uses Polari, the

---

[48] Kimberlite, "Different Colors Made of Tears," *Satellite of Love* Accessed January 11, 2021. http://satellite.shriftweb.org/archive/stories/differentcolors.shtml

[49] Ibid.

[50] *Varda the Message* Accessed January 11, 2021, http://vardathemessage.livejournal.com

coded language prevalent in Britain's gay community in the twentieth century. In fact, the site (now inactive but still searchable) is so exhaustive that Haynes himself used its archives to refresh his memory and prepare himself to record this new audio commentary. Created at a time when attention to the glam rock era and its stars was only recently revived, sites like Varda the Message required massive amounts of work in order to cull pertinent information and compile it in a way that made sense and was relevant. Presumably, a shared interest in constructing a history for their community (in the film, online, and perhaps in their everyday lives) prompted the undertaking of such time-consuming research.

The importance of *Velvet Goldmine*'s online afterlife through such sites is twofold. First, through meticulous chronicling of the film's many allusions, it points to the sort of semiotic openness that allows for a more active audience engagement.[51] This is the same semiotic play shown by Bowie's own glam music. Second and perhaps more importantly, though, Varda the Message, Satellite of Love, and their contemporaries show the true potential of such appropriation: by tapping into audience memory and fostering a new work/spectator relationship, these musical moments have the potential to mobilize audiences in the real world, away from the relatively isolated experience of viewing a film. These sites' authors and visitors are actually building a community, brought together by the ideas Haynes explores in *Velvet Goldmine*, the same ideas originated by Bowie in his Ziggy era.

Some recent authors have pegged Varda the Message and its ilk as little more than adoring fandom—Rob White, for example, describes the site as approaching the film "as if with valentine hearts in its field of vision."[52] Though White dismisses these sites as overly admiring, noncritical responses, Varda the Message shows the way that the spectator constantly returns to *Velvet Goldmine* as a means to "rewrite history." Empowered through the film's own reimagining, *Velvet Goldmine*'s audience is similarly pushed to explore how the spectator can become an active creator. The film's use of a semiotically loaded musical language shows the potential of popular music as a tool for historiography and definition of self, drawing on the pastiche that is so audible in the original music of the era.

---

[51] We might also file the podcast "The Whole Shebang" under this type of fannish creation. See, for example, https://wholeshebangpod.libsyn.com/ Accessed December 13, 2021.

[52] Rob White, *Todd Haynes* (Champaign: University of Illinois Press, 2013), 57.

Conclusion

Velvet Goldmine highlights the powerful nature of David Bowie (during his *Ziggy Stardust* era) and his continuing film image in particular. No scene conveys this more vividly than the film's second montage set to "Hot One." Arthur purchases *The Ballad of Maxwell Demon* LP and takes it home to begin the ritual of exploration that defines one's first experience with a new record. He carefully spreads out the gatefold to show Brian Slade's full, reclining, partially nude body (a visual reference to the self-titled *Jobriath* album, and to Bowie's *Diamond Dogs* cover) and peruses *NME*-style articles about the fictitious pop star. Finally, he uses the new-found freedom afforded him by this *Maxwell Demon* experience and takes tentative steps into his Manchester neighborhood—glammed up and dressed as *himself*, appropriating the style and symbols shown by his new idol (Figure 7.4).

This simple moment conveys the power of glam process as Bowie practiced and wore it: teaching his fans by example, Bowie empowered multiple generations to act as their own manipulators of culture, in order to more fully express themselves. For Arthur in *Velvet Goldmine*, this meant altering his own previously existing clothing to show his difference from his Mancunian peers and surroundings. For fans of *Velvet Goldmine*, this new form of expression manifested itself in their online activity, continuing the film's glam reclamation

Figure 7.4 Still from *Velvet Goldmine* (1998, dir. Haynes).

project. For these fans, though, the important aspect of glam rock was not its outré fashion or scandalizing stage antics. It is for this reason that so many deeply personal responses surfaced following Bowie's passing: for many, he was not only a favorite musician, but also a guide in the ways of navigating public expression. Henry Jenkins has called fan creation a new form of folk art, "reaffirming the right of everyday people to actively contribute to their culture."[53] For these glam fans, though, the point is not so much contributing to broader culture, but instead shaping a highly individualized and personal expression from common popular culture. As a performer and persona, Bowie displayed a shocking use of common forms of expression that provided many with a way to express themselves through the materials they had inherited. Just as fictional Bowie exhorted Bret in *Conchords*, Bowie's work encouraged fans to "do something absolutely outrageous."

The complex semiotic play of Bowie's early 1970s albums was criticized as lacking in originality, but that was largely the point. Rather than creating something new, Bowie instead borrowed familiar tropes in order to rework a musical language that did not, in its original form, open itself to his particular alien expression. As shown above, many of the musemes incorporated in *The Rise and Fall of Ziggy Stardust and the Spiders from Mars* are not only very common, but also quite traditional. The power of Bowie's work, then, came not from creating something that was literally alien to contemporary audiences, but from the incorporation of familiar, ordinary signs to make a new and different meaning. This radical reworking of the everyday resonated for a wide audience; in Bowie's music, they heard an openness of expression that allowed its author to be himself (or any chosen incarnation of himself) even within a traditional system of music- and meaning-making. Through the artifice and camp of glam rock, David Bowie's music served as a means to inch closer to glittering, free self-expression. In interpreting that freedom on film, *Velvet Goldmine* stands as a quintessential depiction of Bowie's legacy.

In depicting Bowie *the man*, though, *Velvet Goldmine* and so many other projects fall short. For many critics and fans, this is the ultimate failing; even a nuanced work like *Velvet Goldmine* is written off as a loss for its inability to

---

[53] Henry Jenkins, *Convergence Culture: Where Old and New Media Collide* (New York: New York University Press, 2006), 132.

capture Bowie's essence. Indeed, as Duncan Jones hinted, such an approach to adaptation is doomed to fail, existing as it would as a copy of a copy. Rather, the most successful translation of Bowie is a continuation of his work. In a world without Bowie himself, this route is particularly tantalizing. What could it mean to take Bowie's work as starting point rather than a finish line? In the creations of fans, we find some possibilities.

8

Conclusion: Living On

In the years since Bowie's death, he has remained oddly present. Much as he promised in 1971's "Quicksand," he, though mortal, is still living on. Such an afterlife seemed all but promised by his approach to his art. Self-referential and multimedia in realization, Bowie's output welcomes continued engagement and animates his past in ways that are conducive to repeated listenings and analyses. (This book alone serves as proof of the way Bowie's fifty-year-old works continue to fascinate.) With such a history, we should perhaps not be surprised that Bowie lives on, strutting across our screens in performance and revived in interviews that continue to go viral, speaking on prescient subjects like the role of the internet in contemporary culture or pernicious racism in the music industry. His very *modus operandi* set him up for such an animated afterlife.

As the preceding chapters have shown, Bowie's art gains some of its vitality through its rich engagement with other works from across different media. From video references to *The Quartermass Experiment*, to lyrical allusions to *1984*, to invocations of the voices of Judy Garland and Marc Bolan, Bowie's works were always nexuses of meaning that asked to be expanded outward. The use of his person in advertising and film acting showed much the same tendency. In fact, Bowie fans have been so steeped in this approach that it is second nature for them to engage with his works in this way. Their own continued listening and creation is a testament to the power of Bowie's semiotic play as a fan tool.

Indeed, Bowie's continued artistic presence is in many ways facilitated by the sort of community he fostered among fans during his lifetime. In online groups that mimic the halcyon days of BowieNet, contemporary fans daily share favorite clips, album rankings, and Bowie jokes. In this constant representation and reframing of Bowie's career, he remains a vital force in their fan practices and lives. Far from shrinking in the years after his death, these groups have continued to grow and add new members, some of whom are discovering Bowie and his oeuvre for the first time. Beyond this fan-directed engagement with existing works, the steady release of new Bowie material also drives his afterlife.

The Bowie estate continues to provide new fan fodder, focusing on remasters, previously unreleased live recordings, documentary partnerships, and more. The year 2020 saw the release of new editions of live shows from the 1990s, expanding the repository of recordings to which fans have easy access. There are still some works, long hoped for by fans, that have failed to receive an official release, among them a video recording of the Diamond Dogs tour or the demo of the *Ernie Johnson* opera. With the estate's slow opening of their vaults, our Bowie encyclopedia promises continued growth in the coming years. Though the artist himself is no longer with us, there has rarely been a better time to be a Bowie completionist: we now have much more material with which to engage.

Beyond all this, Bowie's lasting influence on other artists is also clear, particularly in the use of the moving image, as a main component of his afterlife. Long gone are the days when Bowie planned but could not fund films based on his albums; today, such projects proliferate. Most artists release videos with their singles, while some push the video idea to the conclusion Bowie foresaw. In album-length audiovisual works, we can see echoes of Bowie's plans for the moving image. Beyond these extended works, contemporary popular music holds many examples of the kind of polysemic, rich approach that Bowie championed from the 1960s onward.

We might see, then, two main areas of Bowie's afterlife in the moving image: the estate-approved legacy releases, and his influence on fans and working artists today. These two areas intertwine many of the same connective threads explored in the preceding chapters of this study. Bowie's approach to a construction of self and music worked through the integration of music and the moving image; this formula remains as vital today as it was in Bowie's lifetime.

Bowie's Afterlife in His Own Works

One prime example of the Bowie estate's shaping of his legacy is the "David Bowie Is" augmented reality app launched in January 2019. The AR experience promised to bring the *David Bowie Is* exhibition, which had traveled the world for six years, to the user's own home.

As a visitor to the *David Bowie Is* exhibition, a fan of Bowie, and an academic, I confess to quite a bit of anticipation on the launch of the app. The fan communities I participate in were excited, sharing information on the operating system updates that everyone would need in order to access the app as well as news on the different devices with which it was compatible. In fact, the AR app provided the closest thing to an anticipatory fan community experience I had felt since the show itself closed in Brooklyn. The app, narrated by the artist's friend Gary Oldman, took audiences through each era of Bowie's career. It showed photos, images of sketches and lyrics, and video, some of which had not been released before. Through the app's augmented reality technology, users were able to see these objects within their own spaces: a Bowie costume could seem to stand on your kitchen table. It was, in some ways, the closest a fan could come to virtual contact with their idol since the launch of BowieWorld, a Sims-like platform in which one could build an avatar and a three-dimensional world around Bowie fandom.[1] Always forward-looking and technologically savvy, Bowie's team built one final, inhabitable virtual space for fans to experience Bowie's art. Drawing together a variety of pieces from the David Bowie archive, the app is a savvy piece of legacy shaping. Wandering through its virtual galleries, one is presented with an image of Bowie as multimedia artist. It is a culmination of the ideas explored throughout this book, blending Bowie's music videos, stage performances, screen performances, and more into a unique experience. Interestingly, the app's creation seems to question some of the main divisions of this study. In a platform like this, Bowie is always already sign and auteur.

Beyond the latest technology, Bowie's star image continues to be carefully controlled. We might look, for example, to the box set series released from 2015 onward. Beginning with *Five Years*, released months before his death, this series charts the development of Bowie's style. More than this, it also provides explicit framing for his career. Each set is lovingly crafted, with new mixes, previously unreleased tracks, and beautiful packaging. The CD sets include a book of images, essays, and interviews. Apart from its status as a collector's item, *Five Years* is an act of hagiography. It covers the years 1969 to 1973 even though, as a *Pitchfork* review notes, this is not the beginning of Bowie's career. Douglas Wolk writes, "In fact, there could theoretically be a *Five Years 1964–1968*, tracing his evolution from rock 'n' roll wannabe to fussy vaudevillean, although it would mostly be kind of awful."[2] While the quality of such a first *Five Years* is debatable, Wolk's point stands: even in the framing of the first box set's release, there is an inherent historiographic judgment. Certain albums (and legendary

---

[1] BowieWorld's website is still active, though the platform itself may not be. Accessed March 3, 2021 http://www-static.us.worlds.net/cgi-bin/download.cgi?action=full&bundle=BowieNMCurrentVer

[2] Douglas Wolk, "David Bowie: Five Years," *Pitchfork* October 1, 2015, https://pitchfork.com/reviews/albums/21066-five-years-1969-1973/ Accessed March 2, 2021.

single releases and rarities) are given space within this high-end, retrospective framing. Notably, works like "The Laughing Gnome" are not. That same bent toward personal historiography has continued in the releases that followed, including those that were released posthumously. The Bowie estate has curated video and audio of many live performances since his death, in addition to their involvement in the augmented reality app and the broader release of Bowie's final stage work, *Lazarus*, streamed online in January 2021. In all this, Bowie's audiovisual presence remains, and is as strictly controlled as it was during his lifetime.

That said, the import and impact of that presence have been altered. In the way that Lisa Perrott identifies throughout his career, a certain hauntological aspect permeates Bowie's posthumous releases and appearances. The "No Plan" video, released almost a year after the artist's death, shows this most clearly. The video opens on a bank of televisions, displayed in the window of a Newton Electrical store. Before the music even enters, Bowie's ghost is present: this image speaks to his role as Thomas Jerome Newton in *The Man Who Fell to Earth* and, even more directly, to the image from that film that graces the cover of this volume. Such visual references abound, as YouTube commenters on the video document. It is worth noting that the video plays not only on well-known Bowie references, but also on the imagery of *Lazarus*, a musical which had, at the time, only been seen by live audiences in New York and London. Audiovisual elements from the song's staging in the musical are echoed here, including the play with doubles and reflection in the glass of the store window, as well as the reuse of video footage played onstage during this number. "While we know this video was not devised by Bowie," Leah Kardos writes, "its existence speaks to the continuing entanglements of Newton, Major Tom, and other Bowie myths in popular consciousness."[3] As with most Bowie videos, "No Plan" presents a number of possible interpretations, playing on the shared encyclopedia of signs among his fans.

There is, however, one notable absence: Bowie's visage does not appear in the video, though his voice and words are present. The lyrics of the song are presented on the onscreen televisions, directing the ear and eye to Bowie's corporeal absence. Commenter Olivia Pete speaks to this directly, stating, "Haunting. This video is arguably more powerful than Lazarus just for the fact

---

[3] Leah Kardos, *Blackstar Theory: The Last Works of David Bowie* (New York: Bloomsbury Academic, 2021), 129.

that he's never seen. You really get the sense that it's his spirit speaking to us from beyond the grave. He's not dead he's just in a different place."[4] ("Lazarus," the video Pete refers to in her comment, was the final video Bowie shot during his lifetime. It was released on January 7, 2016—mere days before Bowie's death—and is typically seen as a swan song.) Such a reading is in keeping with the hauntological understanding many fans have of Bowie's *Blackstar* and subsequent releases. In addition to feeling both his presence and absence, fans tend to make note of the way that absence is handled, explicitly speaking to their relationship to this departed creator through his work.

This kind of hauntology differs from that present throughout much of Bowie's work. Where he once borrowed from others as a "human photostat machine," here he instead pursues his practice of self-referential work. That work is tinged, however, by the future nostalgia noted by Shelton Waldrep and others. Sharing a nostalgia for an alternate, lost world, these works seem to communicate the possibilities lost by Bowie's untimely death, the albums and performances we will never see. That sense of loss is not unique to Bowie's passing; indeed, on the death of Prince a month later, similar tributes were released and celebrated. Bowie's posthumous releases, though, play on the long history of his own audiovisual style and, through that mechanism, create a multivalent personal requiem. In his audiovisual works throughout his career, Bowie showed his fans how to remember and mourn him, but also how to continue on in their own creative consumption.

All the Young Dudes: Bowie's Afterlife in Audiovisual Influence

We can also see the lasting influence of Bowie in the work of other musicians. The creation of a clear public persona through music video is now, of course, common practice. We might look to various eras of Madonna and Lady Gaga's careers as prime examples of the weaponization of the moving image as an integral part in pop stardom. Both show a canny ability to craft and communicate a clear star image, even through various transformations, which directly reflects Bowie's

---

[4] Olivia Pete, 2017, comment on "David Bowie – No Plan (Video)," uploaded by David Bowie, January 7, 2017, https://www.youtube.com/watch?v=xIgdid8dsC8 UghPt_IFkbl6M3gCoAEC Accessed March 2, 2021.

work. (So, too, could their film stardom.) In larger-scale projects, we find others following the path presented by Bowie's unrealized film plans. Landon Palmer points to the emotion pictures and visual albums of Janelle Monáe and Beyoncé as a sort of hybrid of the music video and film stardom he studies in earlier artists.[5] In fact, I would argue that Bowie presaged this development decades earlier. In his planned *Diamond Dogs* film, Bowie intended to bring together his music, myriad visual and literary references, and more to expand and give nuance to the world of his album. Similarly, *Lemonade* and *Dirty Computer* both create visual worlds to narrativize and contextualize the songs of the audio album. In each, the artist expands our understanding of the content of their work, creating more extended and complex forms of meaning-making than would be possible with music alone. Beyoncé's *Lemonade* in particular was immediately understood as a rich and multivalent text. The "*Lemonade* Syllabus," created by Candace Benbow, was published online in May 2016 and points to the many ideas and traditions Beyoncé incorporated into her visual album. Benbow's work foreshadowed the wider academic interest *Lemonade* would spark: courses and conferences proliferated, all of which hinted at the richness and importance of the visual album as a multimedia text.[6] Of course, Beyoncé's album draws on and depicts the Black American experience and systemic racism in a way none of Bowie's works could. In content, the albums could not be more different. Still, it is worth noting that Bowie worked toward the same sort of multimedia, multivalent expression, both in his audiovisual touring stage shows and in his planned film projects. In Knowles' and Monáe's visual corollaries to their albums, we can see the evolution of that concept.

Bowie's planned *Diamond Dogs* film is similar to what we find in Monáe's work in particular. Conceived as a unified artwork, Bowie's film and its narrative grew at the same time as the album itself, in much the way that Monáe's *Dirty Computer* album and emotion picture did. It is worth noting that Bowie may be seen as a direct influence, at least in Monáe's case. The centrality of character and narrative to her career mirrors Bowie's approach, as does her consistency of image. Whether playing Cindi Mayweather or Jane 57821, Monáe recognizes

---

[5] Landon Palmer, *Rock Star/Movie Star* (New York: Oxford University Press, 2020), 216–17.
[6] Candace Benbow, *Lemonade Syllabus*, May 6, 2016, https://issuu.com/candicebenbow/docs/lemonade_syllabus_2016 Accessed April 10, 2021.

the power of multimedia narrative in her work.[7] Her film acting seems a clear extension of this interest. She also, like Bowie, is clearly taken with the science fiction worlds of the past, particularly *Metropolis*. Her first albums together constitute her *Metropolis Suite*, and point to a future where humans and technology are in conflict. More specifically, she also makes reference to "the Dogs," in the title sequence for her "Tightrope" video, set at "the Palace of the Dogs." Within that video, Monáe and her friends evade guards while illicitly dancing to "the funkiest horn section in Metropolis," as her lyrics testify. While I have no proof that this reference (at the opening of her "Tightrope" video) is in any way related to Bowie's *Diamond Dogs*, she is still incorporating a broader narrative, communicated through the moving image, in her work, much as Bowie did throughout his decades-long career.

Monáe herself has pointed to this connection, stating, "Bowie has been a huge inspiration to me with regard to creating concept albums, new worlds, and alter egos."[8] This connection should not diminish the creative achievement of Monáe's emotion film and blending of music and the moving image. Monáe's work is very clearly her own, and centers the perspective of a twenty-first-century American who is Black and queer. Like Bowie's work, Monáe's is highly referential, engaging in complex semiotic play that her fans delight in teasing out. As analyses of Monáe's work have shown, she taps into long histories of semiotic play within Black culture; Arns, Chilla, Karjalainen, Lilja, Mairhofer-Lischka, and Valnes see Monáe's work as connected to Gates's concept of signifyin(g).[9]

It seems clear that, regardless of source of inspiration, Monáe values many of the same ideas that were central to Bowie's work. In a 2013 interview (in which the interviewer accompanied Monáe to the *David Bowie Is* exhibition), she herself quotes Bowie. She highlights his idea that "all art is unstable. Its meaning is not necessarily that implied by the author. There is no authoritative

---

[7] In fact, Monáe adds the written word to her creative universe: in 2022, she released *The Memory Librarian: And Other Stories of Dirty Computer* (New York: Harper Voyager, 2022), which expands on the story introduced by the album and emotion picture.

[8] Florian Obkircher, "Four Songs That Fueled Janelle Monáe's Creativity," *The Red Bulletin*, June 21, 2018, https://www.redbull.com/us-en/theredbulletin/janelle-monae-top-4-songs Accessed March 31, 2021.

[9] Frederike Arns, Mark Chilla, Mikko Karjalainen, Esa Lilja, Theresa Mairhofer-Lischka, and Matthew Valnes, "Interpreting Meaning in/of Janelle Monáe's 'Tightrope': Style, Groove, and Production Considered," in *Song Interpretation in 21st Century Pop Music*, ed. Ralf von Appen, André Doehring, Dietrich Helms, and Allan F. Moore (Burlington, VT: Ashgate, 2015), 198.

voice. There are only multiple readings. I am a messenger, and once it's out there it is no longer about me."[10] Monáe invokes Bowie's approach of semiotic play, of fannish creation, of community in this reference. It is perhaps in these ways that we can see Bowie most clearly since his passing. In the ongoing creation of new, playful works; in the expansion of the idea of what a musical work should be; in the freedom of self-definition through art and style. Here, Bowie is living on.

---

[10] Quoted in Kate Mossman, "Janelle Monáe: 'I'm a Time Traveller. I Have Been to Lots of Different Places." *The Guardian*, June 30, 2013, https://www.theguardian.com/music/2013/jun/30/janelle-monae-electric-lady-album-interview Accessed April 10, 2021.

Bibliography

Agawu, Kofi. "Theory and Practice in the Analysis of the Nineteenth-Century 'Lied.'" *Music Analysis* 11, no. 1 (March 1992): 3–36.

Ali, Barish and Heidi Wallace. "Out of This World: Ziggy Stardust and the Spatial Interplay of Lyrics, Vocals, and Performance." In *David Bowie: Critical Perspectives*, edited by Eoin Devereux, Aileen Dillane, and Martin J. Power, 263–79. New York: Routledge, 2015.

Altman, Rick. *The American Film Musical*. Bloomington: Indiana University Press, 1987.

Arns, Frederike, Mark Chilla, Mikko Karjalainen, Esa Lilja, Theresa Mairhofer-Lischka, and Matthew Valnes. "Interpreting Meaning in/of Janelle Monáe's 'Tightrope': Style, Groove, and Production Considered." In *Song Interpretation in 21st Century Pop Music*, edited by Ralf von Appen, André Doehring, Dietrich Helms, and Allan F. Moore, 197–212. Burlington, VT: Ashgate, 2015.

Auslander, Philip. *Performing Glam Rock: Gender and Theatricality in Popular Music*. Ann Arbor: University of Michigan Press, 2006.

Bangs, Lester. *Psychotic Reactions and Carburetor Dung*. Ed. Greil Marcus. New York: Anchor, 2003.

Barthes, Roland. *Mythologies*. Translated by Annette Lavers. New York: Hill and Wang, 1972.

Barthes, Roland. *S/Z: An Essay*. Translated by Richard Miller. New York: Hill and Wang, 1974.

Barthes, Roland. *Image-Music-Text*. Selected and translated by Stephen Heath. New York: Hill and Wang, 1977.

Bazin, Andre. "On the *politique des auteurs*." In *Cahiers du Cinéma: the 1950s: Realism, Hollywood, New Wave*, edited by Jim Hillier, 248–59. London: BFI, 1985.

Benbow, Candace. *Lemonade Syllabus*. May 6, 2016. https://issuu.com/candicebenbow/docs/lemonade_syllabus_2016 Accessed April 10, 2021.

Berger, John. *Ways of Seeing*. New York: Penguin, 1972.

Bonde Korsgaard, Mathias. *Music Video after MTV: Audiovisual Studies, New Media, and Popular Music*. New York: Routledge, 2017.

Bowie, David and Enda Walsh. *Lazarus: The Complete Book and Lyrics*. London: Nick Hern Books, 2016.

Broackes, Victoria. "Putting out Fire with Gasoline: Designing David Bowie." In *David Bowie Is Inside*, edited by Victoria Broackes and Geoffrey Marsh, 117–62. London: V&A Publishing, 2013.

Buckley, David. *Strange Fascination: The Definitive Story*. London: Virgin Books, 2005.

Buckley, David. "Revisiting Bowie's Berlin." In *David Bowie: Critical Perspectives*, edited by Eoin Devereux, Aileen Dillane, and Martin J. Power, 215–29. New York: Routledge, 2015.

Burroughs, William S. and Brion Gysin. *The Third Mind*. New York: Viking Books, 1978.

Canby, Vincent. "Film: John Landis' *Into the Night*." *New York Times*, C8. February 22, 1985.

Cann, Kevin. *Any Day Now: The London Years 1947–1974*. London: Adelita, 2011.

Carpenter, Alexander. "'Give a Man a Mask and He'll Tell You the Truth': Arnold Schoenberg, David Bowie, and the Mask of Pierrot." *Intersections* 30, no. 2 (2010): 5–24.

Carpenter, Alexander. "The 'Ground Zero' of Goth: Bauhaus, 'Bela Lugosi's Dead' and the Origins of Gothic Rock." *Popular Music and Society* 35, no. 1 (2012): 25–52.

Cave, Dylan. "British Landmark Music Videos and the BFI National Archive." *Music, Sound, and the Moving Image* 11, no. 1 (2017): 79–98.

Chinen, Nate. "David Bowie, Master of the Music Video." *New York Times*. January 11, 2016. https://www.nytimes.com/2016/01/12/arts/music/david-bowie-master-of-the-music-video.html Accessed October 4, 2021.

Chion, Michel. *Audio-Vision: Sound on Screen*. Edited and translated by Claudia Gorbman. New York: Columbia University Press, 1994.

Coates, Norma. "*Hullabaloo*: Rocking the Variety Show in the Mid-1960." In *The Bloomsbury Handbook of Popular Music Video Analysis*, edited by Lori A. Burns and Stan Hawkins, 11–128. New York: Bloomsbury Academic, 2019.

Copetas, Craig. "Beat Godfather Meets Glitter MainMan: William Burroughs Interviews David Bowie." *Rolling Stone*. February 28, 1974. https://www.rollingstone.com/music/music-news/beat-godfather-meets-glitter-mainman-william-burroughs-interviews-david-bowie-92508/.

Crowe, Cameron. "David Bowie: Ground Control to Davy Jones." *Rolling Stone*. February 12, 1976. https://www.rollingstone.com/music/music-news/david-bowie-ground-control-to-davy-jones-77059/.

Curry, Ben. "Valency – Actuality – Meaning: A Peircian Semiotic Approach to Music." *Journal of the Royal Musical Association* 142, no. 2 (2017): 401–43.

Daniels, Florence S. "Jules Fisher: Oral History Memoir." William E. Wiener Oral History Library of the American Jewish Committee at New York Public Library. February 1993.

D'Adamo, Amedeo. "Is Bowie Our Kierkegaard?: A Theory of Agency in Fandom." In *David Bowie and Transmedia Stardom*, edited by Ana Cristina Mendes and Lisa Perrott, 57–71. New York: Routledge, 2020.

"David Bowie on the Ziggy Stardust Years: 'We Were Creating the 21st Century in 1971.'" *NPR*. March 15, 2016. http://www.npr.org/2016/01/11/462653510/david-bowie-on-the-ziggy-stardust-years-we-were-creating-the-21st-century-in-1971.

D'Cruz, Glenn. "He's Not There: *Velvet Goldmine* and the Spectres of David Bowie." In *Enchanting David Bowie: Space, Time Body, Memory*, edited by Toija Cinque, Christopher Moore, and Sean Redmond, 259–74. New York: Bloomsbury Academic, 2015.

Denisoff, R. Serge, and George Plasketes. "Synergy in 1980s Film and Music: Formula for Success or Industry Mythology?." *Film History* 4, no. 3 (1990): 257–76.

Denisoff, Serge, and William Romanowski. *Risky Business: Rock in Film*. New Brunswick: Transaction Publishers 2016.

Devereux, Eoin, Aileen Dillane, and Martin J. Power. "Say Hello to the Lunatic Men: A Critical Reading of 'Love Is Lost'." *Contemporary Music Review* 37, no. 3 (2018): 257–71.

Dickinson, Kay. "Pop, Speed, Teenagers, and the 'MTV Aesthetic'." In *Movie Music: The Film Reader*, edited by Kay Dickinson, 143–52. New York: Routledge, 2003.

Dierkres-Thurn, Petra. *Salome's Modernity: Oscar Wilde and the Aesthetics of Transgression*. Ann Arbor: University of Michigan Press, 2011.

Dillane, Aileen, Eoin Devereux, and Martin J. Power. "Culminating Sounds and (En)visions: *Ashes to Ashes* and the Case for Pierrot." In *David Bowie: Critical Perspectives*, edited by Aileen Dillane, Eoin Devereux, and Martin J. Power, 35–55. New York: Routledge, 2015.

Dimery, Robert. "'By the Age of 14, He Was Already a Cult Figure': How David Bowie's Formative Years Shaped His Art." *GQ UK*. February 5, 2021. https://www.gq-magazine.co.uk/culture/article/david-bowie-childhood Accessed March 17, 2021.

Doane, Mary Ann. *The Emergence of Cinematic Time: Modernity, Contingency, the Archive*. Cambridge: Harvard University Press, 2002.

Doggett, Peter. "David Bowie's Lost Rock Opera." *Record Collector*. June 1995. 92.

Dombal, Ryan. "David Bowie: The Next Day." *Pitchfork*. March 11, 2013. https://pitchfork.com/reviews/albums/17855-david-bowie-the-next-day/ Accessed March 19, 2021.

Doyle, Sean. "Video Essay: The Soundtracks of the Man Who Fell to Earth." *Film Comment*. https://www.filmcomment.com/video-essay-the-soundtracks-of-the-man-who-fell-to-earth/ Accessed March 22, 2021.

du Noyer, Paul. "Contact." In *Bowie on Bowie: Interviews and Encounters with David Bowie*, edited by Sean Egan, 365–76. Chicago: Chicago Review Press, 2015.

Dyer, Richard. *Stars*. London: BFI, 1979.

Earls, John. "Freddie Mercury and Rod Stewart Were Considered for David Bowie's Role in *Labyrinth*." *NME*. September 15, 2016. https://www.nme.com/news/film/freddie-mercury-and-rod-stewart-were-considered-fo-870963.

Ebert, Roger. "The Hunger (1983)." *RogerEbert.com*. May 3, 1983. https://www.rogerebert.com/reviews/the-hunger-1983.

Eco, Umberto. *Theory of Semiotics*. Bloomington: Indiana University Press, 1975.

Eco, Umberto. *The Role of the Reader*. Bloomington: Indiana University Press, 1979.

Egan, Sean, editor. *Bowie on Bowie: Interviews and Encounters with David Bowie*. Chicago: Chicago Review Press, 2015.

Eggar, Robin. "Tin Machine II Interview." In *Bowie on Bowie: Interviews and Encounters with David Bowie*, edited by Sean Egan, 192–206. Chicago: Chicago Review Press, 2015.

Eisner, Lotte H. *The Haunted Screen: Expressionism in German Cinema and the Influence of Max Reinhardt*. Translated by Roger Greaves. Berkeley: University of California Press, 1973.

Elsaesser, Thomas. "Germany: The Weimar Years." In *The Oxford History of World Cinema*, edited by Geoffrey Nowell-Smith, 136–50. New York: Oxford University Press, 1996.

Epstein, Leonora. "For Everyone Whose Sexual Awakening Was Caused by David Bowie in 'Labyrinth.'" *Buzzfeed*. May 22, 2014. https://www.buzzfeed.com/leonoraepstein/for-everyone-whose-sexual-awakening-was-caused-by-david-bowi.

Fast, Susan. *In the Houses of the Holy: Led Zeppelin and the Power of Rock Music*. New York: Oxford University Press, 2001.

Faulk, Barry. *British Rock Modernism, 1967–1977: The Story of Music Hall in Rock*. Burlington, VT: Ashgate, 2010.

Fisher, Jules. Interview with the Author. August 11, 2020.

Fisher, Jules Papers. Rock and Roll Hall of Fame Library and Archives. Cleveland, Ohio.

Fisher, Lucy. "The Image of Woman as Image: The Optical Politics of *Dames*." *Film Quarterly* 30, no. 1 (Autumn 1976): 2–11.

Fisher, Lucy. "Greta Garbo: Fashioning a Star Image." In *Idols of Modernity: Movie Stars of the 1920s*, edited by Patrice Petro, 137–58. New Brunswick: Rutgers University Press, 2010.

Frith, Simon. *Performing Rites: On the Value of Popular Music*. Cambridge: Harvard University Press, 1996.

Gallagher, Paul. "Tony Oursler: David Bowie's Latest Work Is Astounding. There's a Level of Detail and Variety in It with the Highest Level of Production." *Independent*. January 13, 2013. https://www.independent.co.uk/news/people/profiles/tony-oursler-david-bowie-s-latest-work-astounding-there-s-level-detail-and-variety-it-highest-level-production-8449414.html Accessed October 4, 2021.

Galt, Rosalind. "David Bowie's Perverse Cinematic Body." *Cinema Journal* 57, no. 3 (Spring 2018): 131–8.

Gamson, Joshua. *Claims to Fame: Celebrity in Contemporary America*. Berkeley: University of California Press, 1994.

Gilchrist, Todd. "Todd Haynes Thanks the Fans for Helping Him Remember the Details and Backstory of 'Velvet Goldmine.'" *Indiewire*. December 16, 2011. http://blogs.indiewire.com/theplaylist/todd-haynes-talks-velvet-goldmine-blu-ray-re-release.

Gold, Jeff Collection. ARC-0037 Rock and Roll Hall of Fame Library and Archives. Cleveland, Ohio.

Goodall, Howard. "Bowie | Music: Lucky Old Sun Is in My Sky." In *David Bowie Is Inside*, edited by Victoria Broackes and Geoffrey Marsh, 163–92. London: V&A Publishing, 2013.

Goodwin, Andrew. *Dancing in the Distraction Factory: Music Television and Popular Culture*. Minneapolis: University of Minnesota Press, 1992.

Gross, Terry. "David Bowie on the Ziggy Stardust Years: 'We Were Creating the 21st Century in 1971.'" *NPR*. https://www.npr.org/2016/01/11/462653510/david-bowie-on-the-ziggy-stardust-years-we-were-creating-the-21st-century-in-197 Accessed March 20, 2019.

Hagen, Ross. "'Bandom Ate My Face': The Collapse of the Fourth Wall in Online Fan Fiction." *Popular Music and Society* 38, no. 1 (2015): 44–59.

Hann, Michael. "Watch the Reworked Video for David Bowie's Life on Mars." *The Guardian*. November 4, 2016. https://www.theguardian.com/music/musicblog/2016/nov/04/david-bowie-life-on-mars-watch-reworked-video-mick-rock Accessed February 19, 2021.

Harrington, Roger. "Gone Glam Digging." *Washington Post*. November 6, 1998.

Haynes, Todd. "Interview: Todd Haynes." *Interview*. http://www.interviewmagazine.com/film/todd-haynes/#_. Accessed May 17, 2017.

Haynes, Todd. *Velvet Goldmine: A Screenplay*. New York: Hyperion, 1998.

Hawking, Tom. "'The Next Day': Meet David Bowie's Final Incarnation, Meta-Bowie." *Flavorwire*. March 11, 2013. https://www.flavorwire.com/376749/the-next-day-meet-david-bowies-final-incarnation-meta-bowie Accessed February 10, 2021.

Hawkins, Stan. *The British Dandy: Masculinity, Popular Music and Culture*. New York: Routledge, 2009.

Hebdige, Dick. *Subculture: The Meaning of Style*. New York: Routledge, 1979.

Hegarty, Paul and Martin Halliwell. *Beyond and before: Progressive Rock since the 1960s*. New York: Bloomsbury Academic, 2011.

Hendler, Glenn. *Diamond Dogs*. New York: Bloomsbury Academic, 2020.

Hertzberg, Hendrick. "Three Musical Situations." *The New Yorker*. June 30, 1975. https://www.newyorker.com/magazine/1975/07/07/three-musical-situations Accessed November 30, 2021.

Holm-Hudson, Kevin. *Genesis and the Lamb Lies Down on Broadway*. New York: Ashgate, 2008.

Holm-Hudson, Kevin. "'Who Can I Be Now?': David Bowie's Vocal Personae." *Contemporary Music Review* 37, no. 3 (2018): 214–34.

Holmes, Su. "'Starring … Dyer?': Re-Visiting Star Studies and Contemporary Celebrity Culture." *Westminster Papers in Communication and Culture* 2, no. 2 (2005): 6–21.

Hope, Emily. "Aaron Walton, Founding Partner, Walton Isaacson." *ThinkLA*. July 10, 2018. https://www.thinkla.org/blogpost/1230000/305282/Aaron-Walton-Founding-Partner-Walton-Isaacson.

Hutcheon, Linda. *A Theory of Adaptation*. New York: Routledge, 2006.

Ingram, Susan. "Constellating Stardom, Berlin Style: Bowie, Christiane F., Hedi Slimane." In *David Bowie and Transmedia Stardom*, edited by Ana Cristina Mendes and Lisa Perrott, 11–21. New York: Routledge, 2020.

Insdorff, Annette. "A Silent Classic Gets Some 80's Music." *New York Times*. August 15, 1984. https://www.nytimes.com/1984/08/05/movies/a-silent-classic-gets-some-80-s-music.html Accessed March 15, 2021.

Jenkins, Henry. *Fans, Bloggers, and Gamers: Exploring Participatory Culture*. New York: New York University Press, 2006.

Jenkins, Henry. *Convergence Culture: Where Old and New Media Collide*. New York: New York University Press, 2006.

Jones, Dylan. "Bowie: Most Stylish Man." In *Bowie on Bowie: Interviews and Encounters with David Bowie*, edited by Sean Egan, 350–5. Chicago: Chicago Review Press, 2015.

Kachka, Boris. "Bowie Collaborator Tony Oursler on the Icon's Art-World Ties, Generosity, and Final Years." *Vulture*. February 1, 2016. https://www.vulture.com/2016/02/tony-oursler-on-david-bowies-art-world-ties.html Accessed October 4, 2021.

Kardos, Leah. "Bowie Musicology: Mapping Bowie's Sound and Music Language across the Catalogue." *Continuum: Journal of Media and Cultural Studies* 31, no. 4 (2017): 552–63.

Kardos, Leah. *Blackstar Theory: The Last Works of David Bowie*. New York: Bloomsbury Academic, 2021.

Keathley, Christian. *Cinephilia and History, or the Wind in the Trees*. Bloomington: Indiana University Press, 2006.

Kimberlite. "Different Colors Made of Tears." *Satellite of Love*. http://satellite.shriftweb.org/archive/stories/differentcolors.shtml Accessed May 17, 2017.

Klein, Bethany. *As Heard on TV: Popular Music in Advertising*. Burlington, VT: Ashgate, 2009.

Kracauer, Siegfried. *From Caligari to Hitler: A Psychological History of German Film*. Princeton Classics Edition. Princeton: Princeton University Press, 2019.

Kunzru, Hari. "For Those of Us Whose Identity Is Fluid, David Bowie Was a Secular Saint." *The Guardian*. January 12, 2016. http://www.theguardian.com/commentisfree/2016/jan/12/david-bowie-was-a-secular-saint-hari-kunzru.

Lane, Anthony. "David Bowie in the Movies." *The New Yorker*. January 13, 2016. https://www.newyorker.com/culture/cultural-comment/david-bowie-in-the-movies.

Leitbetseder, Doris. *Queer Tracks: Subversive Strategies in Rock and Pop Music*. Burlington: Ashgate, 2012.

Loder, Kurt. "Stardust Memories." *Rolling Stone*. April 23, 1987. https://www.rollingstone.com/music/news/david-bowie-the-rolling-stone-interview-19870423 Accessed May 17, 2018.

Lothian, Alexis. "Living in a Den of Thieves: Fan Video and Digital Challenges to Ownership." *Cinema Journal* 48, no. 4 (Summer 2009): 130–6.

Love, Joanna. "'Choice of a New Generation': 'Pop' Music, Advertising, and Meaning in the MTV Era and Beyond." PhD dissertation, UCLA, 2012.

Love, Joanna. "From Cautionary Chart-Topper to Friendly Beverage Anthem: Michael Jackson's 'Billie Jean' and Pepsi's 'Choice of a New Generation' Television Campaign." *Journal of the Society for American Music* 9, no. 2 (2015): 178–203.

MacKinnon, Angus. "The Future Isn't What It Used to Be." In *Bowie on Bowie: Interviews and Encounters with David Bowie*, edited by Sean Egan, 102–39. Chicago: Chicago Review Press, 2015.

Macleod, Duncan. "David Bowie Never Gets Old on Vittel." *The Inspiration Room*. August 28, 2008. http://theinspirationroom.com/daily/2007/david-bowie-never-gets-old-on-vittel/.

Manghani, Sunil. "The Pleasures of (Music) Video." In *Music/Video: Histories, Aesthetics, Media*, edited by Gina Arnold, Daniel Cookney, Kirsty Fairclough, and Michael Goddard, 21–40. New York: Bloomsbury, 2017.

Marshall, P. David. "Productive Consumption: Agency, Appropriation, and Value in the Creative Consuming of David Bowie." *Continuum* 31, no. 4 (2017): 564–73.

Meier, Leslie M. "Promotional Ubiquitous Musics: Recording Artists, Brands, and Rendering Authenticity." *Popular Music and Society* 34, no. 4 (2011): 399–415.

Merrell, Floyd. "Peirce's Concept of the Sign." In *Routledge Companion to Semiotics and Linguistics*, edited by Paul Cobley, 28–39. New York: Routledge, 2001.

Miller, Jim. "David Bowie's New Look." *Newsweek*. July 18, 1983, 76.

Monáe, Janelle. *The Memory Librarian: And Other Stories of Dirty Computer*. New York: Harper Voyager, 2022.

Moore, Allan, and Ruth Dockwray. "The Establishment of the Virtual Performance Space in Rock." *Twentieth-Century Music* 5, no. 2 (2008): 219–41.

Moore, Suzanne. "My David Bowie, Alive Forever." *The Guardian*. January 11, 2016. http://www.theguardian.com/commentisfree/2016/jan/11/my-david-bowie-alive-forever.

Moran, Joe. "David Bowie Misremembered: When Ziggy Stardust Played with Our Minds." *The Guardian*. July 6, 2012. http://www.theguardian.com/commentisfree/2012/jul/06/david-bowie-ziggy-starman.

Morrissey. *Autobiography*. New York: Putnam and Sons, 2013.

Mossman, Kate. "Janelle Monáe: 'I'm a Time Traveller. I Have Been to Lots of Different Places.'" *The Guardian*, June 30, 2013. https://www.theguardian.com/music/2013/jun/30/janelle-monae-electric-lady-album-interview Accessed April 10, 2021.

Mulvey, Laura. "Visual Pleasure and Narrative Cinema." In *Film Theory and Criticism: Introductory Readings*, edited by Leo Braudy and Marshall Cohen, 833–44. New York: Oxford University Press, 1999.

Murray, Charles Shaar. "Sermon from the Savoy." In *Bowie on Bowie: Interviews and Encounters with David Bowie*, edited by Sean Egan, 159–74. Chicago: Chicago Review Press, 2015.

"The New Bowie." *Melody Maker*. October 12, 1974. 39.

Nudd, Tim. "Ad of the Day: David Bowie Serenades Arizona Muse for Louis Vuitton." *Adweek*. November 12, 2013. https://www.adweek.com/brand-marketing/ad-day-david-bowie-serenades-arizona-muse-louis-vuitton-153798/.

Obkircher, Florian. "Four Songs the Fueled Janelle Monaé's Creativity." *The Red Bulletin*. June 21, 2018. https://www.redbull.com/us-en/theredbulletin/janelle-monae-top-4-songs Accessed March 31, 2021.

Ochs, Michael Collection. Rock and Roll Hall of Fame Library and Archives. Cleveland, Ohio.

O'Connell, John. *Bowie's Bookshelf: The Hundred Books That Changed David Bowie's Life*. New York: Gallery Books, 2019.

O'Leary, Chris. "Ziggy Stardust." *Pushing Ahead of the Dame*. April 26, 2010. https://bowiesongs.wordpress.com/2010/04/26/ziggy-stardust/.

O'Leary, Chris. "Crystal Japan." *Pushing Ahead of the Dame*. September 1, 2011. https://bowiesongs.wordpress.com/2011/09/01/crystal-japan/.

O'Leary, Chris. *Ashes to Ashes: The Songs of David Bowie 1976–2016*. London: Repeater Books, 2018.

Paglia, Camille. "Theater of Gender." In *David Bowie Is Inside*, edited by Victoria Broackes and Geoffrey Marsh, 69–98. London: V&A Publishing, 2013.

Palmer, Landon. "'And Introducing Elvis Presley': Industrial Convergence and Trans Media Stardom in the Rock'n'Roll Movie." *Music, Sound, and the Moving Image* 9, no. 2 (Autumn 2015): 177–90.

Palmer, Landon. *Rock Star/Movie Star: Power and Performance in Cinematic Rock Stardom*. New York: Oxford University Press, 2020.

Pegg, Nicolas. *The Complete David Bowie*. Revised and Updated Edition. London: Titan Books, 2016.

Peirce, Charles Sanders. *The Collected Papers of C. S. Peirce*. Vols. 1–6. Ed. Charles Hartshorne and Paul Weiss; Vols. 7–8, ed. A. W. Burks. Cambridge: Harvard University Press, 1931–58.

Peraino, Judith. "Plumbing the Surface of Sound and Vision: David Bowie, Andy Warhol, and the Art of Posing." *Qui Parle* 21, no. 1 (Fall/Winter 2012): 151–84.

Perone, James. *Listen to Pop! Exploring a Musical Genre*. Santa Barbara, CA: ABC-CLIO, 2018.

Perrins, Darryl. "'You Never Knew That, That I Could Do That': Bowie, Video Art, and the Search for Potsdamer Platz." In *Enchanting David Bowie: Space/Time/Body/Memory*, edited by Toija Cinque, Christopher Moore, and Sean Redmond, 323–36. New York: Bloomsbury Academic, 2015.

Perrott, Lisa. "Time Is Out of Joint: The Transmedial Hauntology of David Bowie." In *David Bowie and Transmedia Stardom*, edited by Ana Cristina Mendes and Lisa Perrott, 116–36. New York: Routledge, 2020.

Pettigrew, Jason. "Goth Inventors Bauhaus Recall the Night They Met David Bowie." *Altpress.* January 23, 2018. https://www.altpress.com/features/bauhaus_undead_met_david_bowie_the_hunger/.

Qvick, Sanna. "Goblin King in Labyrinth: An Audiovisual Close Reading of the Songs by David Bowie." *Widerscreen* 19, nos. 3–4 (2016). http://widerscreen.fi/numerot/2016-3-4/goblin-king-in-labyrinth-an-audio-visual-close-reading-of-the-songs-by-david-bowie/?fbclid=IwAR2_kjdwlhoIYfUI4e5yooDVcUU_SnQUjuc97l3m4kkTxhM2oxKFbyxBav8

Ravitz, Mark. Conversation with the Author. October 18, 2019.

Ravitz, Mark. Personal Email Communication with the Author. November 3, 2019.

Redmond, Sean. "Intimate Fame Everywhere." In *Framing Celebrity: New Directions in Celebrity Culture*, edited by Su Holmes and Sean Redmond, 27–44. New York: Routledge, 2006.

Redmond, Sean. "David Bowie: In Cameo." *Cinema Journal* 57, no. 3 (Spring 2018): 150–7.

Reynolds, Simon. "The Singer Who Fell to Earth." *The New York Times.* March 10, 2013.

Richardson, John. *An Eye for Music: Popular Music and the Audiovisual Surreal.* New York: Oxford University Press, 2012.

Rockwell, John. "Pop Music: Bowie Puts on Lavish Show at the Garden." *The New York Times.* July 21, 1974.

Sandvoss, Cornel. *Fans: The Mirror of Consumption.* Malden, MA: Polity Press, 2005.

Scott, Jane Papers. ARC-0370 Rock and Roll Hall of Fame Library and Archives. Cleveland, Ohio.

Scrudato, Ken. "David Bowie: Life on Earth." In *Bowie on Bowie: Interviews and Encounters with David Bowie*, edited by Sean Egan, 365–76. Chicago: Chicago Review Press, 2015.

Sexton, Jamie. "Prisoner of Cool: Chloë Sevigny, Stardom, and Image Management." In *Cult Film Stardom: Offbeat Attractions and Processes of Cultification*, edited by Kate Egan and Sarah Thomas, 73–89. New York: Palgrave Macmillan, 2012.

Soar, Sophie. "How I Became … Music Director for Louis Vuitton Menswear." *Business of Fashion.* November 12, 2018. https://www.businessoffashion.com/articles/careers/how-i-became-music-director-for-louis-vuitton-menswear.

Sounes, Howard. *Down the Highway: The Life of Bob Dylan.* New Updated Edition. New York: Grove Press, 2021.

Spata, Christopher. "Bowie's Stripped Down Tampa Tour Stop in 1974 Still Resonates." *Tampa Bay Online.* http://www.tbo.com/events-tampa-bay/bowies-stripped-down-tampa-tour-stop-in-1974-still-resonates-20160111/ Accessed May 17, 2018.

Sterne, Jonathan. "Sounds Like the Mall of America: Programmed Music and the Architecture of Commercial Space." *Ethnomusicology* 41, no. 1 (1997): 22–50.

Stevenson, Nick. "David Bowie Now and then: Questions of Fandom and Late Style." In *David Bowie: Critical Perspectives*, edited by Eoin Devereux, Aileen Dillane, and Martin J. Power, 280–94. New York: Routledge, 2015.

Stilwell, Robynn J. "Audiovisual Space in an Era of Technological Convergence." In *The Oxford Handbook of New Audiovisual Aesthetics*, edited by John Richardson, Claudia Gorbman, and Carol Vernallis, 125–45. New York: Oxford University Press, 2013.

Stine, Alison. "*Labyrinth* and the Dark Heart of Childhood." *The Atlantic*. June 29, 2016. https://www.theatlantic.com/entertainment/archive/2016/06/labyrinth-captured-the-dark-heart-of-childhood/489146/.

Tagg, Philip. "Analysing Popular Music: Theory, Method and Practice." *Popular Music* 2 (1982): 37–65.

Tagg, Philip. *Fernando the Flute: Analysis of Musical Meaning in an ABBA Mega-hit*. Liverpool: University of Liverpool Institute of Popular Music, 1991.

Taylor, Timothy. *The Sounds of Capitalism: Advertising, Music, and the Conquest of Culture*. Chicago: University of Chicago Press, 2012.

Tevis, Walter. *The Man Who Fell to Earth*. London: Pan, 1976.

Truffaut, Francois. "A Certain Tendency of the French Cinema." In *Movies and Methods*, edited by Bill Nichols, 224–37. Berkeley: University of California Press, 1976.

Turner, Steve. "How to Become a Cult Figure in Only Two Years: The Making of David Bowie." In *The Sound and the Fury: Rock's Back Pages Reader*, edited by Barney Hoskyns, 17–26. London: Bloomsbury, 2003.

Varda the Message. http://vardathemessage.livejournal.com Accessed May 15, 2017.

Velvet Goldmine. Directed by Todd Haynes. 1998; Los Angeles: Miramax Lionsgate, Blu-ray, 2011.

Vernallis, Carol. *Experiencing Music Video: Aesthetics and Cultural Context*. New York: Columbia University Press, 2004.

Vernallis, Carol. *Unruly Media: YouTube, Music Video, and the New Digital Cinema*. New York: Oxford University Press, 2013.

Vernallis, Carol and Hannah Ueno. "Interview with Music Video Director and Auteur Floria Sigismondi." *Music, Sound, and the Moving Image* 7, no. 2 (Autumn 2013): 167–94.

Vernallis, Carol, Holly Rogers, and Lisa Perrott, editors. *Transmedia Directors: Artistry, Industry, and New Audiovisual Aesthetics*. New York: Bloomsbury Academic, 2020.

Viertel, Jack. *The Secret Life of the American Musical: How Broadway Shows Are Built*. New York: Sarah Crichton Books, 2016.

Waksman, Steve. "The Road to Altamont: The Rolling Stones on Tour, 1969." In *Beggars Banquet and the Rolling Stones' Rock and Roll Revolution: "They Call My Name Disturbance"*, edited by Russell Reising, 167–82. New York: Routledge, 2020.

Waldrep, Shelton. *The Aesthetics of Self-Invention: Oscar Wilde to David Bowie*. Minneapolis: University of Minnesota Press, 2004.

Waldrep, Shelton. *Future Nostalgia: Performing David Bowie*. New York: Bloomsbury Academic, 2016.

Walker, Michael. *What You Want Is in the Limo*. New York: Spiegel and Grau, 2013.

"Watch David Bowie's $12.99 Love Is Lost Video Here Now." *DavidBowie.Com*. October 31, 2013. https://web.archive.org/web/20131105001515/http://www.davidbowie.com/news/watch-bowie-s-1299-love-lost-video-here-now-52201 Accessed March 13, 2021.

Wattercutter, Angela. "Inside the Cult of *Carol*, the Internet's Most Unlikely Fandom." *WIRED*. https://www.wired.com/2017/05/carol-modern-cult-movie-fandom/?mbid=social_fb Accessed May 17, 2017.

Watts, Michael. "Oh You Pretty Thing." *Melody Maker*. January 22, 1972.

Watts, Michael. "Confessions of an Elitist." In *Bowie on Bowie: Interviews and Encounters with David Bowie*, edited by Sean Egan, 77–101. Chicago: Chicago Review Press, 2015.

White, Rob. *Todd Haynes*. Champaign: University of Illinois Press, 2013.

Willis, Ellen. "Records: Rock, Etc." *New Yorker*. July 6, 1968. 56.

Wolk, Douglas. "David Bowie: Five Years." *Pitchfork*. October 1, 2015. https://pitchfork.com/reviews/albums/21066-five-years-1969-1973/ Accessed March 2, 2021.

Wright, Julie Lobalzo. "David Bowie: The Extraordinary Rock Star as Film Star." In *David Bowie: Critical Perspectives*, edited by Eoin Devereux, Aileen Dillane, and Martin J. Power, 230–44. New York: Routledge, 2015.

Wright, Julie Lobalzo. "The Boy Kept Swinging: David Bowie, Music Video, and the Star Image." In *Music/Video: Histories, Aesthetics, Media*, edited by Gina Arnold, Daniel Cookney, Kirsty Fairclough, and Michael Goddard, 67–78. New York: Bloomsbury Academic, 2017.

Media Bibliography

Film and Television

2001: A Space Odyssey. Directed by Stanley Kubrick, 1968.
Bandslam. Directed by Todd Graff, 2009.
The Cabinet of Dr. Caligari. Directed by Robert Wiene, 1920.
A Clockwork Orange. Directed by Stanley Kubrick, 1971.
Cracked Actor. Directed by Alan Yentob, 1975.
David Bowie: Five Years. Directed by Francis Whatley, 2013.
David Bowie: The Last Five Years. Directed by Francis Whatley, 2017.
Flight of the Conchords. "Bowie." Directed by Troy Miller, 2007.
The Hunger. Directed by Tony Scott, 1983.
The Image. Directed by Michael Armstrong, 1969.
Into the Night. Directed by John Landis, 1985.
Just a Gigolo. Directed by David Hemmings, 1978.
Labyrinth. Directed by Jim Henson, 1986.

The Last Temptation of Christ. Directed by Martin Scorsese, 1988.
The Linguini Incident. Directed by Richard Shepard, 1991.
The Man Who Fell to Earth. Directed by Nicolas Roeg, 1976.
Merry Christmas, Mr. Lawrence. Directed by Nagisa Ōshima, 1983.
Metropolis. Directed by Fritz Lang, 1927.
Midnight Special. "1980 Floor Show." Directed by Stan Harris, 1973.
Performance. Directed by Nicolas Roeg, 1970.
The Prestige. Directed by Christopher Nolan, 2006.
Stardust. Directed by Gabriel Range, 2020.
Velvet Goldmine. Directed by Todd Haynes, 1998.
The Wild One. Directed by Laslo Benedek, 1953.
Ziggy Stardust and the Spiders from Mars: The Motion Picture. Directed by D.A. Pennebaker, 1983.
Zoolander. Directed by Ben Stiller, 2001.

Albums

Bowie, David. *1. Outside*. Arista/BMG, 1995.
Bowie, David. *Blackstar*. Sony Legacy, 2016.
Bowie, David. *Cracked Actor*. Rhino, 2017.
Bowie, David. *David Bowie*. Deram, 1967.
Bowie, David. *Diamond Dogs*. RCA, 1974.
Bowie, David. *Five Years*. Rhino/Parlophone, 2015.
Bowie, David. *"Heroes."* RCA, 1978.
Bowie, David. *… hours*. Virgin, 1999.
Bowie, David. *Hunky Dory*. RCA, 1971.
Bowie, David. *Let's Dance*. EMI, 1983.
Bowie, David. *Live at Santa Monica 1972*. RCA, 1972.
Bowie, David. *Low*. RCA, 1977.
Bowie, David. *Nothing Has Changed*. Sony Legacy, 2014.
Bowie, David. *Never Let Me Down*. EMI, 1987.
Bowie, David. *A New Career in a New Town*. Rhino/Parlophone, 2017.
Bowie, David. *The Next Day*. Virgin/ISO, 2013.
Bowie, David. *Reality*. ISO, 2003.
Bowie, David. *The Rise and Fall of Ziggy Stardust and the Spiders from Mars*. RCA, 1972.
Bowie, David. *Scary Monsters (And Super Creeps)*. RCA, 1980.
Bowie, David. *Space Oddity*. Phillips, 1969.
Bowie, David. *Station to Station*. RCA, 1976.
Bowie, David. *Tonight*. EMI, 1984.

Bowie, David. *Who Can I Be Now*. Rhino/Parlophone, 2016.
Bowie, David. *Young Americans*. RCA, 1975.
Jobriath. *Jobriath*. Elektra, 1973.
Knowles, Beyoncé. *Lemonade*. Legacy, 2016.
Monáe, Janelle. *The ArchAndroid*. Atlantic, 2010.
Monáe, Janelle. *Dirty Computer*. Bad Boy Records, 2018.
Monáe, Janelle. *Electric Lady*. Bad Boy Records, 2013.
Pop, Iggy. *The Idiot*. RCA, 1977.

Acknowledgments

This book's long journey into being would not have been possible without the support of many people. First, my thanks to my family, who have always been willing to lend an ear to my musings and worries. I would not have been able to complete this book's images without the help and film expertise of my husband, Greg Brown. Most especially, thanks to my mother Michele Reed, my first and most exacting editor, who would never let me put a comma out of place. To my brother and father, Mike and Bill, many thanks for their support throughout this process. I owe my officemate and constant companion Maxwell many treats for his patience while I wrote.

Bowie's many collaborators were central to the works I discuss here, and many of them shared their insight with me. My thanks to Jules Fisher, Mark Ravitz, and Mick Rock for sharing their creative work and memories of these projects.

The classroom can be a great incubator for research projects. Nowhere was this more clear than in my Spring 2017 course on David Bowie, taught at Utah Valley University. I owe a debt of gratitude to my students for their enthusiasm, thoughtful questions, and fascinating creative projects. You helped me to see Bowie's works through different eyes. Thanks also to my colleagues, both at California State University, Fullerton and elsewhere, for their stimulating conversations and expert advice. I am grateful for the formative guidance of Silvio dos Santos, Jennifer Thomas, S. Alexander Reed, Marsha Bryant, and Robert Ray during my studies. My thanks to Robynn Stilwell for her guidance and support. I am grateful to John Koegel for his mentorship and feedback. I thank Morgan Rich for her unfailing insight, humor, and friendship.

This project was supported by two grants, one from my institution—California State University, Fullerton—and one from Case Western Reserve University and the Rock and Roll Hall of Fame Library and Archives. These grants allowed me to travel and complete my research at the Rock Hall. CSUF's grant also helped me to secure the rights for some of the images that bring this book to life. Many thanks to Jennie Thomas, librarian and archivist extraordinaire, and everyone else at the Rock Hall who helped me delve into their wonderful holdings.

Portions of this book have been presented at various conferences, including the 2016 Bowie Interart | Text | Media conference, Music and the Moving

Image, and the American Musicological Society's annual meeting. My thanks to conference coordinators and attendees for their comments, most especially Bowie experts Leah Kardos, John Richardson, Glenn Hendler, and Chris Carter. Thanks also to the organizers and participants in the AMS Popular Music Junior Faculty Symposium in 2014 and 2016, especially Joanna Love, Kate Galloway, Eric Hung, Fred Maus, Robynn Stilwell, and Daniel Goldmark, among many others. Their feedback and insight into the publishing process shaped this project. Two chapters have also appeared elsewhere in shorter versions. Chapter 7 expands on the research in "Singing the Alien: Velvet Goldmine and David Bowie's Glam Semiotics," *Popular Music and Society* vol. 41, no. 5 (2018) <copyright Taylor & Francis>, available online: https://www.tandfonline.com/doi/abs/10.1080/03007766.2017.1390436

Chapter 6 expands on an earlier version of my research, reproduced here by permission of Oxford University Press, oup.com: Katherine Reed, "Selling 'David Bowie': Commercial Appearances and the Developing Star Image," in *The Oxford Handbook of Music and Advertising*, ed. James Deaville, Siu-Lan Tan, and Ron Rodman (New York: Oxford University Press, 2021), 474–487. My thanks to the editors and publishers of both pieces.

Finally, thanks to Leah Babb-Rosenfeld and Rachel Moore of Bloomsbury Academic, who guided this project through the publication process during a most difficult pandemic year. Their kindness and care were instrumental in its completion.

Index

Locators followed by "n." indicate endnotes

ABBA band 5–6
   "Fernando" 30
   Mamma Mia! 5–6
Abloh, Virgil 166
Absolute Beginners (Temple) 61, 124, 152
   "Absolute Beginners" 137, 164
   mass motivation 144
advertising/advertisements
   "The Concert" (Jackson) 152–3
   Crystal Jun Rock 167
   fan relationships and star image 146–51
   Louis Vuitton short ("L'Invitation au Voyage") 145, 155, 161–7
   Ogilvy and Mather Paris spot 156
   "Pepsi Diner" 152
   Pepsi spot ("Creation") 143, 145, 151–5, 158
   Vittel ad ("Never Get Old") 145, 155–60, 164
Agawu, Kofi 30
a-ha, "Take On Me" 138
Aladdin Sane (Bowie) 33, 56, 72, 78, 88, 91
   "Jean Genie" 48, 48 n.10, 52, 99, 188, 192
Alexander, Ella 162–3
Ali, Barish 179
Alice Cooper (rock band) 74, 93, 98
"All the Young Dudes" (Bowie) 191, 207–10
Alomar, Carlos 91
Altman, Rick 134
Anderson, Laurie 9
archival materials 14, 60, 72–3, 75, 78, 86, 96, 103
Armstrong, Michael, *The Image* 2, 114
"Ashes to Ashes" (Bowie) 3, 14, 45, 47, 57–64, 66–70, 69 n.55, 109, 130, 157
Astronettes 80

audio-visual legacy/work 2, 5, 14–15, 36, 77, 95, 150, 208
augmented reality (AR) app 73, 79, 101, 204–6. *See also* David Bowie Is app
Auslander, Philip 20, 98, 98 n.65, 115–16, 184 n.27, 190, 195 n.40
avant garde art world 35, 45, 139, 175

Bale, Christian 194
Bangs, Lester 50, 181
Bardot, Brigitte 163
Barnbrook, Jonathan 32
Barthes, Roland 29 n.23, 60, 65, 179, 188
Basil, Toni 74, 81, 97
Bauhaus, "Bela Lugosi's Dead" 125–9
The Beatles (rock band) 1, 22, 36, 39, 182–3
   Help! 39
   Magical Mystery Tour ("Your Mother Should Know") 182
Beckenham Arts Lab 9, 173
Beethoven, Ludwig van, "Ode to Joy" 2, 10, 96 n.62
"Be My Wife" (Bowie) 54
Benbow, Candace, *Lemonade Syllabus* 208
Benedek, Laslo, *The Wild One* 119
Benji B (Benjamin Benstead) 166
Berger, John, *Ways of Seeing* 39, 48–9
Berkeley, Busby 53
Berlin trilogy 65, 151, 167
Beyoncé, *Lemonade* 75, 208
Blackstar (Bowie) 4, 32, 46, 61, 207
   "Blackstar" 61, 157
   "Lazarus" 2, 4–7, 5 n.16, 33 n.33, 44, 61, 206
Black Tie White Noise (Bowie) 122
"Blue Jean" (Bowie) 61, 153
Bolan, Marc 20, 116, 179–80, 182–4, 203. *See also* T. Rex (rock band)

Bolder, Trevor 99
Bonde Korsgaard, Mathias 46
Bowie, David (David Robert Jones) 1, 19, 27, 37, 38, 42–3, 71, 94, 113–14, 117–18, 136, 140, 143, 146, 149, 151, 159, 167, 179, 187. *See also specific works of Bowie*
   afterlife in audiovisual influence 207–10
   audiovisual media, self and use 34
   Berlin footage 65–7, 76
   biopic challenge 171–4
   Bowieness 58, 120–1, 140, 145, 193
   career as experimenting 2 (*see also* lives and careers (Bowie))
   as cinephile 9–12, 21, 70, 118
   as creative genius 175
   as disease-spreading predator 154–5
   in film 114–18 (*see also specific films*)
   as iconic innovator 174
   as junior visualizer 8
   live musical performance 8
   masks 20, 22–8
   modus operandi 19, 64, 103, 170, 203
   as multimedia artist 44, 75, 205
   on-stage performances 20
   own works, afterlife in 204–7
   personal iconography 58, 62
   sense of realness 145
   studies 7–8
BowieNet 147, 196–7, 203
   "Sailor" 147, 196
Bowie 83 promotional material 71
BowieWorld 110, 205, 205 n.1
"Boys Keep Swinging" (Bowie) 40
Brando, Marlon 24, 119
Brel, Jacques 175, 181
Brigadoon 134
Brighton, David 156, 158
Broackes, Victoria 9
Brooks, Louise 11
Brown, James 149
Buckley, David 4
Burns, Terry 172
Burretti, Freddie 21, 28, 55–6, 85, 148
Burroughs, William S. 92
   The Third Mind 92
   The Wild Boys 87

Cabaret 50, 79–80, 82, 85–9, 99, 101
   "Maybe This Time" 88
   "Tomorrow Belongs to Me" 89
   "Willkommen" 87
Cahiers du Cinéma 20–2
Canby, Vincent 121
Cann, Kevin 11
Capitol/EMI memo 113–14, 123, 141
Capote, Truman 23–4
Carlos, Wendy 96 n.62
Carmen 77
Carol 197 n.47
Carpenter, Alexander 128
Cavell, Stanley 26
"Changes" 90
Cherry, Ava 80, 91
Cher series (CBS) 79
Childers, Leee Black 28
Chion, Michel 3
cinephile, Bowie as 9–12, 21, 70, 118
Clark, Robin 91
Clement, Jemaine 176, 186–8
Clift, Montgomery 24
Coates, Norma 77
Council of Fashion Designers of America 148
Crowe, Cameron 144
cultural signs 22, 36, 39, 175, 185–6, 194
Curry, Ben 185

D'Adamo, Amadeo 170
Dalí, Salvador 163
David Bowie Archive 14, 16, 72–3, 77, 100, 100 n.74, 205
David Bowie Is app 73, 102, 204
David Bowie Is exhibition 16, 44, 61, 70, 73, 79, 100 n.74, 101–2, 104, 107, 161, 204
David Bowie (Space Oddity) 1, 7, 9, 31, 37
David Live (Bowie) 32, 84
"Day In Day Out" (Bowie) 61, 110
D'Cruz, Glenn 178
DeFries, Tony 24, 27, 119, 149, 171
Deneuve, Catherine 125, 127, 130
Denisoff, Serge 113, 124
Desogus, Paolo 30
Devereux, Eoin 58, 62, 69 n.55

Dexter, John 83
Diamond Dogs (Bowie) 4, 11, 14, 26, 32, 71–3, 77, 82–3, 96–7, 99–103, 110, 115, 158, 163, 168, 172, 208–9
   analyzing 103–6
   archival materials 75
   "Big Brother" 88–9
   Canada and the United States 72
   "Chant of the Ever-Circling Skeletal Family" 88
   as concept album 86
   features of 80–1
   film and video in 92–9
   "Future Legend" 87, 109
   Halloween Jack 87, 101, 109
   narrative structure 86–9
   "1984" 78–80, 88
   planning stages 84–6
   "Rebel Rebel" 90, 176, 188
   storyboards and narrative 106–9
   "Sweet Thing"/"Candidate" 32, 74, 80–1, 88, 109
   technical staging concerns 89–92
   "TheaTour" 14, 84, 98–9
   theatrical elements 75
   tour (1974) 73–4, 74 n.6, 204
   "The Year of the Diamond Dogs" 75–6, 84
Dickinson, Kay 57
Dietrich, Marlene 20, 119
Dillane, Aileen 58, 62, 69 n.55
Doggett, Peter 4
Dombal, Ryan 33
Donna and the Dynamos (group) 5
Dove, John 103–4
Doyle, Sean 116
Dyer, Richard 14, 22, 115, 138–40
   anomic types 140–1
   Stars 24–5, 118–20
Dylan, Bob 22, 55 n.26

Earthling (Bowie) 46, 64, 158
Ebert, Roger 124, 174
Eco, Umberto 29
   meaning-making and transmission 31
   unlimited semiosis 29–30
Eisner, Lotte 107

Elsaesser, Thomas 106
Elson, Steve 32
Eno, Brian 167, 175
Ernie Johnson (Bowie) 4, 204
Expressionist films 2, 11, 31, 44, 85, 104, 106–7
Extras (tv show) 176

Fahrenheit 451 190
Faithfull, Marianne 77
Farthingale, Hermione 39
Ferry, Bryan 180
Fisher, Jules 2, 9, 14, 73, 75, 79, 81–6, 89–92, 94–5, 98
   budget 96–7
   lighting musical works 90
   mood story 91
Fisher, Lucy 53
Five Years 1964–1968 205
Flashdance 124
Fletcher, Dexter, *Rocketman* 171
1980 Floor Show 14, 44, 72–3, 76–81, 102, 106
   "1984" 78–80
   cabaret-style performance 79
   "1984/Dodo" 78–9, 78 n.17, 81
   theatrical set 78
Footloose 124
Foxe, Cyrinda 101
Frampton, Owen 8
Frampton, Peter 8
Frayling, Christopher 28–9, 37
Freud, Sigmund, unheimlich concept 158, 158 n.25
Frith, Simon 22
A Funny Thing Happened on the Way to the Forum 88
Furstenberg, Diane von 161

Gaiman, Neil 172–3
   "The Return of the Thin White Duke" 173
Galt, Rosalind 122, 135, 141
Gamson, Joshua 115
Garbo, Greta 20
Garland, Judy 175, 203
Gavras, Romain 162
gender fluidity 183

Genesis (rock band) 74
  Lamb Lies Down on Broadway 94
George, Boy 192
gesamtkunstwerk 3–7, 23, 36, 84
"Get in David's Pants" (*CREEM*) 148
glam rock phenomenon/work 25, 76, 116, 170–1, 185, 189–90, 193–4, 199–201. *See also* Haynes, Todd, *Velvet Goldmine*
  persona 176
  semiotics 170, 176, 178–86, 198
  transgressive reinvention 177–8
  visual and musical signs 186
Glass Spider tour 76, 155
Goldblum, Jeff 121
Goodall, Howard 170
Goodwin, Andrew 47
The Gouster (Bowie) 76, 76 n.12
Graff, Todd, *Bandslam* 174
Grammys award ceremony 148
Grant Lee Buffalo (rock band), "The Whole Shebang" 189–90
Gross, Terry 7, 25–6
Grosz, George 80, 82
  Berlin 80
  Metropolis 108
  Twilight 80
groundbreaking approach 11, 28, 47, 75, 136
Guess, Jason 80
Gyn, Ben 101
Gysin, Brion, *The Third Mind* 92

Hadfield, David 8
Hall, Michael C. 6
Halliwell, Martin 86, 94
Harry Potter fandom 10
Hawking, Tom 68
Hawkins, Stan 57
Haynes, Todd, *Velvet Goldmine* 15, 24, 170, 173–7, 185–6, 201
  Arthur Stuart 177, 194–5, 198, 200
  "Ballad of Maxwell Demon" 189–91, 200
  Brian Slade 178, 189, 191–5, 200
  and *Conchords* "Bowie" 186
  Curt Wild 193, 197–8
  "Hot One" 191–2, 200
  newly composed songs 189–91
  online repository 197, 199
  public performances, personal reinvention 194–200
  real object 193
  "Venus in Furs" 198
  visual traces in 191–4
Hebdige, Dick 34, 179–80
Heckel, Erich 11
Heckerling, Amy 121
Hegarty, Paul 86, 94
Help! (the Beatles) 39
Hemmings, David, *Just a Gigolo* 123–4
Hendler, Glenn 79, 80 n.21, 89, 95
  Diamond Dogs 86–7
Henson, Jim 136
  The Dark Crystal 131
  Labyrinth (*see Labyrinth* (Henson))
Hepburn, Audrey 163
Hepburn, Katharine 119, 141
"*Heroes*" (Bowie) 11, 31, 119, 161–2
"Heroes" 54, 57
Hertzberg, Hendrik 94
Heydon, Stacy 96
Hilfiger, Tommy 148
Hitchcock, Alfred 21
Holland, Arnold 113, 141
Hollywood studio films 38, 47–8, 115
Holmes, Su 24
Holm-Hudson, Kevin 94
Hullabaloo (TV show) 77
Hunger City. *See Diamond Dogs* (Bowie)
Hunky Dory (Bowie) 4, 8, 23, 28, 189
  "Oh! You Pretty Things" 189–90
  "Quicksand" 203
Hutcheon, Linda 186

iconoclastic image 68, 144–5, 156, 158, 162, 164–5, 167–8, 175–6
Iman 122, 148, 175
Ingram, Susan 66
interobjective comparison material (IOCM) 30, 183
In the Court of the Crimson King 181
Isherwood, Christopher 26
Isley Brothers (musical group) 149

Jackson, Michael 146, 151–4, 167
  "Billie Jean" 153
  "The Concert" 152–3

Jagger, Mick 94, 97–8, 132
Jenkins, Henry 34, 196, 201
Jesus Christ Superstar 86
Jobriath, *Jobriath* 200
Joel, Billy, *Movin' Out* 5
John, Elton 181, 183
"John, I'm Only Dancing" (Bowie) 37, 48, 50–4, 57, 78
Johnson, Kathryn 74
Jones, David 27, 37, 69, 114, 172
Jones, Duncan 171–4, 202

Kardos, Leah 4, 33, 36, 47, 206
  Blackstar Theory 5
Keathley, Christian 10
Kemp, Lindsay 50–1, 58, 182
Kimberlite, "Different Colors Made of Tears" 198
King, Jimmy 70
The Kinks (rock band) 36, 182–3
  Village Green Preservation Society ("Do You Remember Walter?") 182
Kit Kat Club 87
Klein, Bethany 143
Klevan, Andrew 26
Kon-rads 8
Kracauer, Siegfried 104, 108
Kubrick, Stanley 9, 20–1, 44
  2001: A Space Odyssey 11, 40, 105
  A Clockwork Orange 2, 10–11, 96 n.62, 105
Kunzru, Hari 169

Labyrinth (Henson) 1, 15, 118, 123–4, 131–9, 141, 152, 163, 175
  "As the World Falls Down" 135–7, 162
  "Chilly Down" 135
  innovative forces 136
  Jareth the Goblin King 1, 114, 131–6, 138–9, 163, 175
  vs. "L'Invitation Au Voyage" 163–4
  "Magic Dance" 133–4, 136–7
  Sarah 131–6
  "Underground" 133, 137–8
La La La Human Steps (dance group) 96–7
Landis, *Into the Night* 120–1
Lane, Anthony 120–1, 140

Lang, Fritz, *Metropolis* 2, 11–12, 20, 82, 85, 96, 104–7, 209
Laroche, Pierre 21, 55–6
"The Laughing Gnome" (Bowie) 206
Lear, Amanda 77
Led Zeppelin (rock band) 36, 93
Leibetseder, Doris 181
Lennon, John 10
LeSueur, Lucille 118
Let's Dance (Bowie) 12, 117, 130, 132, 153, 188
  "China Girl" 151
  "Let's Dance" 131, 151, 153
  "Modern Love" 131–2, 143, 151–3, 188
Lewis, Jerry Lee 98
"Life on Mars?" (Bowie) 1, 14, 27–8, 37, 43, 45, 47, 51, 59–60, 63, 68–9, 107, 153, 157, 188, 191
  and Bowie's visual vocabulary 52–7
  intimacy, creation 55
  Vogue look 52
lingua franca 2, 29
lives and careers (Bowie) 3, 16, 27, 33–4, 40, 43, 45, 51, 65, 114, 123, 137–8, 169, 174, 205
  dramatis personae 170
  as experimenting 2
  goal 6
  and public life 172
  stages 14, 94, 151
Loder, Kurt 76
London's Marquee Club 77
"Look Back in Anger" (Bowie) 96
Lothian, Alexis 197
Louis Vuitton short ("L'Invitation au Voyage") 144–5, 155, 160, 161–7
  audience participation 162
  BETC Paris's ad, emotion and atmosphere 166
  vs. *Labyrinth* (Henson) 163–4
  Menswear soundscape 166
  Venetian Mix 165
Love, Joanna 146
Love You till Tuesday (film) 1, 13, 37–8, 55, 61, 187
  allusion, mime, and gesture 39–41
  camera and gaze 38–9
  "Let Me Sleep beside You" 38–40

"Love You till Tuesday" 38 n.43
"The Mask (A Mime)" 1, 41
"Rubber Band" 1, 23, 40
"Sell Me a Coat" 38, 40
"Space Oddity" 1, 37, 40, 58, 73–4, 157, 176, 187–8
"When I Live My Dream" 39
Low (Bowie) 33, 158
Lucas, George 136
Lugosi, Bela 127–9

Madison Square Garden show 64, 99
Madonna 146, 151, 153–4, 167, 207
MainMan 76, 82–5, 91, 102, 148
Major Tom (film) 102, 172
Major Tom ("Space Oddity") 40, 58–62, 157, 172, 206
Mallet, David 3, 59–60, 62
Manghani, Sunil 60
The Man Who Sold the World (Bowie) 32, 40, 158, 181
  "Black Country Rock" 184
Marshall, P. David 34
  constructive consumption 22
  creative consumption 34
  productive consumption 170
Martin, Steve 132
McDonald, Paul 150–1
Mckenzie, Bret 176, 187–8
McQueen, Alexander 149, 161
meaning-making process 10, 13, 31, 35, 45, 175, 197, 201, 208
Meier, Leslie M., promotional ubiquitous music 145
Melody Maker 76
Menon, Bhaskar 113
Mercury, Freddie 132
Meyers, Jonathan Rhys 193
Midnight Special ("1980 Floor Show") 14, 44, 77, 81
Miller, Troy, *Flight of the Conchords* 15, 170, 173–6, 201
  "Bowie" 170, 174–5, 186–7
  "Bowie's in Space" 176, 187–9
Monáe, Janelle 208–10
  Dirty Computer 75, 208
  Metropolis Suite 209
  "Tightrope" 209

The Monkees (rock band) 1
Monroe, Marilyn 119
"Moonage Daydream" (Bowie) 190
Moore, Allan F. 53 n.23
Moore, Suzanne 169
Moran, Joe 191
Moroder, Giorgio, "Cat People (Putting Out Fire)" 11–12, 152
Morrissey, *Autobiography* 192
Moss, Kate 28
moving image 1, 13, 15–16, 20, 28, 31, 36–7, 41, 45, 48, 65, 167, 178, 204, 207
  apparatus 52
  applications 41
  gesamtkunstwerk and 3–8
  importance of 7, 20
  pillars of 70
  self-invention 23
  varied and interconnected uses 29, 35
MTV 43, 45, 47, 57, 64, 66, 123, 125, 127, 133, 138, 151, 167
multimedia works 4, 6–7, 12–13, 22, 44, 51, 72, 75, 80, 93, 110, 114, 146, 208–9
Mulvey, Laura
  Hollywood film 48
  "Visual Pleasure and Narrative Cinema" 47–8, 48 n.10
The Muppet Movie 132
Murphy, James 69
Murphy, Peter 125–8
Muse, Arizona 162
museme, concept 70
musical eclecticism 180
musical signs 36, 176, 182, 185–6
musical valency 185 n.30
music hall style 182–3, 182 n.25
music videos 5, 9, 13, 43, 45–8, 68, 70, 78, 116, 144, 157–8. *See also specific music videos*
  audiovisual style 47
  development 45–7
  gaze and power 47
  hybrid audio-visual text 44
  late style 63–8
  medium 43, 45
  memory process 67

modus operandi 64
MTV golden age 66
recycling and rebirth 57–63
  in the 1970s 50–2
  storyboarding 44, 61
  stylistic permutations 47
  visual language 43
  visual lexicon 51
  for young audiences 184

Nathan Adler (*1.Outside*) 172
"Never Gonna Get Old" (Bowie) 156
Never Let Me Down (Bowie) 137, 143, 151–2
Newley, Anthony 20, 35–6, 116
Newton, Thomas Jerome 4, 6, 114, 116–17, 206
The New Yorker 22, 94, 120
The Next Day (Bowie) 6, 31–3, 33 n.33, 36, 63 n.44, 64–5, 68, 161, 163, 165–7
  "Dirty Boys" 32–3
  "I'd Rather Be High" 161–2, 165
  "Love Is Lost" 14, 33, 69–70
  "Where Are We Now?" 6, 14, 32, 45, 63–9, 63 n.44, 161
Nichols, Wanda 154–5
Nolan, Christopher, *The Prestige* 120–1
"No Plan" (Bowie) 206
Nothing Has Changed (Bowie) 158
Nyro, Laura 90

O'Connell, John, *Bowie's Bookshelf* 9
O'Leary, Chris 36, 137, 156, 181
Oliver Twist 87
Omicron 110
1.Outside (Bowie) 4, 46, 172, 175
Orwell, George 26, 102
  1984 76, 86–7, 89, 92, 95, 100, 102, 198, 203
  Two Minutes Hate 89
Oscars award ceremony 148
Ōshima, Nagisa, *Merry Christmas Mr. Lawrence* 12, 117–18, 124, 128, 135, 152
Oursler, Tony 63–7, 94

Pabst, Georg Wilhelm, *Pandora's Box* 11
Paglia, Camille 77
Paik, Nam June 94
Palmer, Landon 75, 117, 122–4, 208
Pegg, Nicolas 3, 196
Peirce, Charles Sanders 29, 184, 184 n.28, 185 n.30, 193 n.37
  infinite semiosis 29, 185
  types of signs 29
Pennebaker, D.A. 27, 51
Pepsi 167
  "Choice of a New Generation" campaign 143, 152, 154
  "Creation" advertisement 143, 145, 151–5, 158
  "We've Got the Taste" 155
Peraino, Judith 34
Perone, James 5
Perrins, Darryl 62, 67
Perrott, Lisa 9, 35, 45–6, 68, 206
personal identity 145, 172
persona/personae 6, 15, 26–7, 39, 58, 60, 68–9, 114, 123, 128, 139, 156, 164, 167, 178
  developing 22–8
  musical and filmic 117
  and productive consumption 33–7
  and public image 37
  self and 146
  Thin White Duke 19, 25–6, 69, 75–6, 114, 138, 172–3
  Ziggy Stardust 10, 12, 19, 25–7, 45, 51, 80, 85, 98, 114, 116–18, 136, 139, 186, 191
Pete, Olivia 206–7
Phillips, Grant Lee 190
photostat machine approach 175, 177
Pierrot in Turquoise (Or The Looking Glass Murders) 50, 58, 61
Pin Ups (Bowie) 34, 78
  "Sorrow" 77, 80
Pitt, Kenneth 1, 37–8
Plasketes, George 124
"Please Mr. Gravedigger" (Bowie) 23
Pop, Iggy 65
  The Idiot 11
Portnow, Neil 137
Powell, Sandy 191
Power, Martin J. 58, 62, 69 n.55, 85
Presley, Elvis 1, 40, 122–3
prosaic language 180

public image 7, 15, 25, 27, 37, 42, 45, 56, 61, 113, 116, 132, 145
public persona 1, 14–16, 19, 21, 23, 41, 117–18, 121, 139, 145–6, 148–50, 156, 197, 207

The Quartermass Experiment 203
Qvick, Sanna 134, 136

Rainbow Theater (London) 50, 78
Ramsay, Peter 172
Range, Gabriel, *Stardust* 171–3
Ravitz, Mark 2, 9, 14, 73, 79, 81–5, 95–6, 100–1
RCA 44, 71, 84, 103, 114, 117, 119, 162
Reality (Bowie) 168
　"Never Get Old" 156
Redmond, Sean 120, 140, 146–8
Reed, Lou, *Transformer* 193
Reynolds, Simon 166
Richard, Little 98
Richardson, John 47
The Rise and Fall of Ziggy Stardust and the Spiders from Mars (Bowie) 4, 19, 35, 72, 86, 88, 91, 96 n.62, 128, 176, 180–1, 184–5, 189–90, 201
　"Five Years" 191
　"It Ain't Easy" 184
　"Lady Stardust" 182–4, 187, 189
　"Star" 184
　"Starman" 36, 54, 182, 191–2
Rivers, Joan 132
Robertson, Robbie 55 n.26
Rock, Mick 27–8, 40, 50–7, 61, 70
Rock and Roll Hall of Fame Library and Archive 14
"Rock and Roll Suicide" (Bowie) 116
Rockwell, John 74, 99
Rodgers, Nile 151
Roeg, Nicolas 118
　The Man Who Fell to Earth 4, 12, 114, 116–18, 123, 125, 129, 152, 206
　Performance 117
The Rolling Stones (rock band) 1, 22, 75, 94–5, 97–8, 175, 181
　"Little Queenie" 95
Romanowski, William 113
Ronson, Mick 54, 55 n.26, 99, 191–2

Ronson, Suzi 21
Rotten, Johnny 181
Roxy Music (rock band) 175, 180

Sacher-Masoch, Leopold von, "*Venus in Furs*" 198
Sands, Brian 196
Sandvoss, Cornel 195
Sarandon, Susan 125, 130
Satellite of Love 197, 199
Saussure, Ferdinand de 29 n.23
Scary Monsters (and Super Creeps) (Bowie) 158
Schneider, Gunther 37
Schoenberg, Arnold 58
Schuftan, Eugene 104
Schwab, Coco 6, 70
Scott, Tony, *The Hunger* 12, 15, 118, 123–31, 136–7, 139, 141, 152
　aural and visual alignment 127
　John Blaylock 125–6, 129, 131
　opening scene 129
　shower scene 130
"Screamin' Lord Byron" (*Jazzin' for Blue Jean*) 153
screen roles 113, 117, 141
second-wave innovator, Bowie as 175
Sedgwick, Eve 181
self-creation 20, 22–3, 33–5, 41
semiotics 15, 22, 28–33, 42, 45, 62, 120, 151, 175–86, 198, 201, 210
Serious Moonlight tour 76, 130, 143, 151
Sexton, Jamie 118
Sgt. Pepper's Lonely Hearts Club Band 181
Shepard, Richard, *The Linguini Incident* 122
Shindig! (TV show) 77
Shudder to Think
　"Ballad of Maxwell Demon" 189–91
　"Hot One" 191–2, 200
Shuftan process 104
Sigma Sound Studios (Philadelphia) 76
Singer, Bryan, *Bohemian Rhapsody* 171, 173
Slick, Earl 32
Slimane, Hedi (Dior Homme) 149, 161
social capital 15
"Song of Norway" 63

The Song Remains the Same 93
sonic space 53 n.23
Sony Portapak 94
sound and vision 3, 15, 70, 72–3, 77, 79–80, 82, 84, 100, 127–8, 166, 186, 188, 192
soundbox 53 n.23, 54, 109
Sound + Vision tour 96–7, 116
star-audience relationship 157
star brand 150
star image 6, 13–15, 21–2, 24–6, 33, 114, 141, 144, 155, 157–60, 168, 174–5, 205
    acting roles *vs.* filmic and musical 140
    in advertising, fan relationships and 146–51
    creation and use 151
    in film 118–24
    Labyrinth and 131–9
    musical and filmic 123
    musical and visual reuse 15
    as negotiation 115
    as person-as-brand 150
    strategies 22
    transmedia 123
Station to Station (Bowie) 75, 96, 173
Steiner, George 25, 180
Stevenson, Nick 13
Stiller, Ben, *Zoolander* 120, 161, 176
Stilwell, Robynn 194
Sting 132
Stranger in a Strange Land 123
Strummer, Joe 181
Surrealist Ball (1972, Rothschilds) 163
Swinton, Tilda 28

T. Rex (rock band) 116, 175, 179, 182–3
Tagg, Philip 30, 70
Taylor, Timothy 160
Temple, Julien 14, 61, 153
    Absolute Beginners (see *Absolute Beginners* (Temple))
    Jazzin' for Blue Jean 153
Tesla, Nikola 120
Tevis, Walter 117
theatricality 74–5, 77, 83–4, 86, 93–4, 98–9, 116

Thomson, Malcolm J. 38
"Thursday's Child" (Bowie) 158
Tin Machine 122
    Tin Machine II 110
Tonight (Bowie) 137, 143, 151
    "Blue Jean" 153
Top Gun (TV show) 124
Top of the Pops (TV show) 54, 77, 191
Trevor 191
The Troggs 77
Turner, Steve 24, 27
Turner, Tina 143, 152–5

Ueno, Hannah 46
Un chien andalou 2, 96
Underwood, George 9, 58

Vadim, Roger 121
Vandross, Luther 91
van Hove, Ivo 6
Vanilla, Cherry 28
Varda the Message 198–9
VCR 94
Vernallis, Carol 46–7, 49, 61
    new media swirl 44–5
Victoria and Albert Museum 16, 161
video technology 94, 97
Viertel, Jack 88
Visconti, Tony 32, 65, 87, 166
visual arts 2, 7–12
visual encyclopedia 8, 45, 63
visual references 21, 157, 163, 176–7, 186, 200, 206
visual vocabulary 52–7
Vittel ad ("Never Get Old") 145, 155–60, 164
Vogue UK 162

Wagner, Richard
    "artwork of the future" 4
    total artwork 3
Waksman, Steve 95
Waldrep, Shelton 3, 23–4, 41, 68, 87, 95, 117, 179, 207
    The Aesthetics of Self-Invention 20
Walker, Michael 93
Wallace, Heidi 179

Walley 113
Walton, Aaron 155
Warhol, Andy 23–4, 44
　Pork 28
　singing 28–33
Watts, Michael 19, 25
Waugh, Evelyn 165
Wedren, Craig 190–1
Weird Science-style 152
Wenders, Wim 9
Whately, Francis
　Five Years 16, 205
　The Last Five Years 16, 100, 100 n.72
White, Rob 199
whole effect 83
The Who (rock band) 74, 93
　Tommy 93

Wiene, Robert, *The Cabinet of Dr. Caligari* 11, 96, 106–9
Wilde, Oscar 23–4, 84, 177
Willis, Ellen 24
　attractive packaging 22–3
Wolk, Douglas 205
Wright, Julie Lobalzo 115–17, 122, 135

Yamamoto, Kansai 21, 136, 148, 161
Yentob, Alan, *Cracked Actor* 81, 92, 116
Young Americans (Bowie) 76, 91

Zanetta, Tony 28
Ziggy Stardust 10, 12, 19, 25–7, 45, 51, 80, 85, 98, 114, 116–18, 136, 139, 186, 191

www.ingramcontent.com/pod-product-compliance
Lightning Source LLC
Chambersburg PA
CBHW050326020526
44117CB00031B/1817